A NEW KIND OF
CHRISTIANITY

A NEW KIND OF CHRISTIANITY

Ten questions that are transforming the faith

BRIAN D. MCLAREN

HODDER &
STOUGHTON

First published in Great Britain in 2010 by Hodder & Stoughton
An Hachette UK company

1

A CIP catalogue record for this title is
available from the British Library

ISBN 978 0 340 99548 8

Typeset in Sabon MT by Palimpsest Book Production Limited,
Grangemouth, Stirlingshire

Printed and bound by
CPI Mackays, Chatham ME5 8TD

Hodder & Stoughton policy is to use papers that are natural, renewable
and recyclable products and made from wood grown in sustainable forests.
The logging and manufacturing processes are expected to conform to the
environmental regulations of the country of origin.

Hodder & Stoughton Ltd
338 Euston Road
London NW1 3BH

www.hodderfaith.com

Contents

TEN: **THE WHAT-DO-WE-DO-NOW QUESTION**

CONCLUSION

NOTES

Preface

In hot, ramshackle urban slums in Latin America, in tree-shaded rural villages in Africa, in well-appointed conference centres, church basements and coffee shops in Asia, Europe and the Americas, I've had the opportunity to enter into conversation and friendship with an amazing array of Christian leaders from across the denominational spectrum: Roman Catholic, Eastern Orthodox, historic Protestant, evangelical and Pentecostal. They have convinced me of some bad news and some encouraging news. The bad news: *the Christian faith in all its forms is in trouble*. The good news: *the Christian faith in all its forms is pregnant with new possibilities*.

Some might recall the stories of Sarah and Elizabeth, older women in the Bible who confounded the biological clock and gave birth when everyone thought it was too late. Some people see the Christian faith that way – as an old woman, past her prime, closer to a nursing home than to nursing new life. But I see it differently. I believe that, in every new generation, the

Christian faith (like every faith) must in a sense be born again. That means Christian faith has the possibility of being forever young. (Imagine strains of the Bob Dylan classic playing here.) So from the womb of the Christian faith in all its wild diversity, I see a new generation of Christian disciples being formed and born, coming alive and coming of age, and they hold amazing promise, even as they face huge challenges (not the least of which are misunderstanding and criticism from some of their elders).

I know the Christian faith from the inside. I grew up in conservative evangelical churches. Then, having become a passionately committed disciple in my teen years through the Jesus movement in the early 1970s, I gained exposure to mainline Protestant and Catholic churches. I married a Catholic girl and together we opened our home to help form a fellowship group that morphed into a little house church that eventually grew into the community I served as pastor for twenty-four years. During those years I developed a deep interest in Church history, in Eastern Orthodoxy, in Celtic Christianity and in the Anabaptist tradition. Through work on the board of a mission agency and then as a conference speaker, I gained street-level experience with Latin American Pentecostalism, African indigenous churches, Asian Christianity, historic European Christianity and the wide range of faith expressions that thrive and struggle around the world, from tiny rural villages to mega-cities and in between.

I left the pastorate just over three years ago to write, network, be a pastor to pastors and speak about what I'm learning along the way. I still find myself processing my experience serving in a local church. I know I made a lot of mistakes as a pastor, and

I know I had a lot of limitations. I wish I had known at the beginning half of what I had learned by the end. I also know I cared a lot and worked hard and poured out my heart. I guess I feel about my tenure as a pastor the same way I feel about my experience as a father: I've given it my very best, but my kids – and my congregation – deserved much better, so I always feel like apologising.

Even though I am no longer a local church pastor, I love church life. I love churches. I love singing good songs, praying rich prayers, sharing in the mystery of the Eucharist and listening to sincere, passionate and thoughtful sermons. (As a listener, I've noticed I like them shorter than I did back when I was a preacher!) Of course, I've seen enough churches at close enough range for long enough that I'm not naïve about them, nor am I unaware of their serious problems and dysfunctions. But I believe in 'one, holy, catholic and apostolic Church', as the old creed says, and in the holy faith with which she is entrusted. And I believe that, like Sarah and Elizabeth, just when you think the old girl is over the hill, she might take a pregnancy test and surprise us all.

This book is divided into two main sections. After some introduction, Book 1 addresses five profound and critical questions that are being raised by followers of Christ around the world. These questions, I believe, have the potential to unlock us from a prison in which we have been held hostage for a long time. Once we unbolt long-held assumptions for long enough to raise these questions, new possibilities will open – hence the title for Book 1, 'Unlocking and Opening'.

In Book 2 we'll consider five more questions that are, perhaps, less profound or theologically radical, but are equally important because of their down-to-earth practicality and the intensity of debate they engender. Once we begin to emerge from the first section's constricting conventional paradigms, we will be able to explore these intense practical questions in fresh and highly constructive ways, hence the title to the second section, 'Emerging and Exploring'.

These ten questions are by no means the only important questions being raised. In fact, stopping with these ten questions would qualify as an adventure in missing the point. But my sense is that we can't get better answers to other urgent questions until we first unlock and open the first five, and then emerge and explore the second five. I'll identify some good candidates for the next round of questions in the Conclusion at the book's end. Between here and there, I hope you'll begin to feel the thrill of something trying to be born.

CHAPTER 1

Between Something Real and Something Wrong

A small town in England, just before nine in the morning. Beautiful countryside, partly cloudy, an occasional shower, chilly, a little windy. I'm here to speak about the challenges and opportunities Christians face at this moment in history – in our theology, in local church life, in our mission in the world. A mixed group of clergy and laypeople are taking their seats, and as I move around the room I meet Anglican priests, Baptist ministers, charismatic network leaders, some Roman Catholics, some who describe themselves as de-churched or church dropouts. There are mums, dads, grandparents, Bible college students, youth workers. The organisers are a little worried because some local Christian fundamentalists have written letters to the local paper and threatened to picket the event, protesting against the organisers because they invited a 'known heretic' to speak in their town. So far, no picketers.

Ninety minutes later, during the mid-morning coffee break, I look out of the window and see four concerned people rushing from car to car in the car park, hurriedly placing sheets of canary-yellow paper under the windscreen wipers. The leaflets warn participants about this 'controversial religious leader' who will speak. He is 'dangerous', they say, and 'unbiblical'. *Wow*, I say to myself, noticing how the yellow leaflets flutter in the breeze on each windscreen. *How did a mild-mannered guy like me get into so much trouble?*

Back inside the conference centre, the day rolls along splendidly – stimulating Q&A sessions at the end of each of my four lectures, conversations humming over lunch and during breaks. At the day's end a line forms, with people wanting to make personal contact, maybe have a book signed, maybe ask one more question or make a comment. A young evangelical pastor is first in line: 'I would have left the ministry and the Christian faith altogether if it weren't for your book *A New Kind of Christian*. Thanks for saving my faith.' A middle-aged pastor is next: 'This was the most refreshing day spiritually that I have ever had in my life. Thanks for coming.' Then an older woman says, 'My pastor warned us from the pulpit last Sunday not to come and hear you, but my kids love your books, so I came. Don't let anybody discourage you. You're saying what we need to hear.' A senior citizen in a white shirt and tie leans forward and says, 'I was told terrible things about you. I don't see what the fuss is about. This was lovely. Solid, common-sense stuff.'

A twenty-something fellow is next in line: 'I grew up as a missionary kid, but these last few years I've been an atheist some days and an agnostic others. Today, though, I feel as if I just may be able to believe again.' The man running the video equipment comes up: 'I've been ashamed to associate myself with the word *Christian* for a long time. But after this . . . today I felt

2

as if I could see what it's supposed to be about again.' A young Roman Catholic woman says, 'I tend to feel like a second-class citizen out on the margins of my church, but today I feel that there's a place for me in God's work.' The last person in line, a woman who had been married to a pastor who left her and then left the ministry, wipes her eyes and says with a shaky voice, 'You've put into words what I've always known was true but I was afraid to say.'

As my hosts escort me to their car, I see the canary-yellow flyer damp but still fluttering on their windscreen. I pull it out, glance at it, and the joy of the day gives way to a feeling of tension – a buzzing in my head, a churning in my heart, a heavy feeling in my limbs. Expansion inside the building, contraction outside. Hope in the conference centre, fear in the car park. Open hearts among participants, clenched teeth among our critics. Enthusiasm and encouragement in the greetings five minutes ago, suspicion and accusation on the canary-yellow flyer in my hand. Again, I wonder to myself, *How did I get into this swirl of controversy?*

I never planned to become a 'controversial religious leader'. As a boy I loved wild animals and wanted to be either a zoo keeper or a forest ranger. For a while I loved comic books and dreamed of a career as a comic book author – until I realised that my talent for drawing was mediocre at best. Like a lot of teenage guitar-players of my generation, I dreamed of making it as a professional songwriter and musician, but the life of a rock star or wandering folk singer never materialised. Even though I had grown up in a conservative evangelical family, and even after several powerful spiritual experiences in my youth, I never thought of becoming a missionary or pastor. (I do

3

remember imagining myself becoming a crusade evangelist like Billy Graham for a few days in my late teens, but that soon faded.) In secondary school I fell in love with literature, which eventually inspired me to become an English teacher, which I did, teaching at college level for about eight years.

Along the way, I had briefly considered going into the Episcopal ministry, and had joked with my then fiancée about what it would be like for her to tell her Catholic relatives she was marrying a Protestant priest. But on Friday afternoon of the weekend I was supposed to go on the 'discernment retreat' with the bishop to talk about entering theological college, I got cold feet. *I love God, and I love the idea of serving God and helping people spiritually*, I said to myself, *but I don't feel like a great fit for the religious bureaucracy and politics that are an inescapable part of the life of a religious professional. I think I can do more good for the spiritual cause outside the institutional Church than inside it.* So I became a teacher and felt very fulfilled living out my faith in the environment of a secular university.

While I was teaching and finishing my Master's degree, my wife and I started a little weekly dinner group – home-made soup and fresh-baked bread every Thursday night and good conversation about matters of faith and life. That dinner morphed into an ongoing fellowship group, complete with a Bible study, a few songs with a guitar accompaniment, some prayer and plenty of time at the end just to hang around and chat. Eventually, from that fellowship group, a little non-denominational church grew, of which I was one of the lay leaders. A few years later, our little leadership team began talking about the need for a full-time pastor. I was the natural one to take on the role:

I was comfortable teaching, I knew the people and, since I was already living on a modest teacher's income, it wouldn't be hard for the little congregation to match my salary, so I was a bargain.

I asked Grace what she thought about it. 'Well,' she said, raising four fingers, one at a time, 'you're already a full-time husband, a full-time father, a full-time college English instructor and a part-time volunteer church leader. I don't think that's sustainable. My guess is that you can continue any three out of those four long-term and survive.' Then she added, 'That means one thing has to go. You pick.' Thus came my call to ministry, at least as I remember it.

At around this time, I read a book that explained in statistics what I had seen every day at my secular university: the Church was losing touch with 'normal people'.[1] Her preachers had forgotten how to speak their language. Her pastors didn't understand their questions, doubts and concerns. Her leaders only knew, as the old cliché goes, how to preach to the choir, and they preoccupied themselves with institutional maintenance. About 40 per cent of Americans, the book explained, attend church regularly, and 60 per cent don't, but the former number is shrinking and the latter growing. When you talk to the people who walk down the aisle at a Billy Graham-style crusade to make a 'first-time Christian commitment', or who say something called 'the sinner's prayer' in response to an evangelistic invitation, or who join a new church, you discover that over 90 per cent of them are *already lifelong churchgoers*. That means that over 90 per cent of the so-called new converts come from the 40 per cent of the population who are already 'in the choir', and less than 10 per cent come from the 'unchurched majority'.

So we have a lot of Baptists becoming Pentecostals, and Catholics becoming Episcopalians, and so on ... but surprisingly few 'unchurched' or 'non-church' people getting connected with the Church.

That book connected with my own sense of calling. So when I became a full-time pastor, I didn't want to forget about the spiritual seekers who came from the 'non-church majority'. I wanted to be sure that everything we said and did was as accessible as possible to them so that they could discover the goodness inherent in the Christian good news. Unless the church wanted to become an isolated little enclave that could only talk to its own, we needed to welcome people in from the non-church majority – with all their questions, uncertainties, scepticism and honesty – which required first of all that we would listen to them without judgement and understand them without condemnation.

As time went on, we managed to create that kind of safe space in our little congregation, and many spiritual seekers came to us from the non-church majority. Since we lived near several universities and a number of scientific research facilities including NASA, many of these seekers were highly educated. And since we also lived in an economically diverse part of the Washington, DC suburbs, we had a lot of needy people too, and over time we developed a reputation as a church that 'accepted addicts' and welcomed broken people. I'd frequently hear people before or after services say things to each other like, 'I recognise you. We were in detox together. Remember?'

I used to say that our congregation was one of the few where you could sit with a PhD on one side of you and a GED on the other.[2] One thing that spiritual seekers – whether they're PhDs or GEDs – have in common is an aversion to religious . . . pretence (I resisted the temptation to use the more colourful word the seekers themselves would have used). So I had the pleasure of working with people who spoke straight and weren't afraid to tell me what they really thought.

Sometimes what they had to say was encouraging, even if the way they said it was unconventional, like the time a long-haired and tattooed recovering heroin addict said to me after church one Sunday, 'S***, man, that was a d*** good talk you gave today. I usually think preachers are full of s***, you know, 'cause they're so ***** and I can never understand a single **** word they say. But my friend from Narcotics Anonymous invited me to come, and h***, man, you kind of got through to me. I was getting like choked up or something in there. D***!' (Two life-long churchgoers overheard our conversation. They just stood there, wide-eyed and appalled. I knew they wanted me to rebuke the fellow for his language, but I just smiled and thanked him and told him I hoped he'd be back next week, eager for any encouragement I could get!)

Sometimes, the honest feedback of our spiritual seekers was not this positive. People would visit the church for a few weeks or months, listen intently, and then come to see me with their questions. Typically, they'd say something like this: 'I've been listening to your sermons for six months now, and I really like a lot of what you're saying. But some of your dogma is really sticking in my throat. I just can't swallow it all.' So they'd ask me some questions, and I would give them my best answers, but often, after they left, I felt hollow. If they 'bought' my answers, I was strangely disappointed. If they pushed back and told me my answers still made no sense to them, I would think, *Good for you, because some of them don't really make that much sense to me either.*

So week after week, satisfied or not, spiritual seekers left my office with the best answers I had to offer, and I was left with their best questions. And soon their questions became my own. Gradually, this reservoir of unanswered questions and unsatisfying answers overflowed into a kind of spiritual crisis that started me on a quest: a quest for honesty, for authenticity, and for a faith that made more sense to me and to others.[3] For several years it seemed that with every passing month my theology was unravelling a little more. I was afraid that soon there wouldn't be anything left at all – which is unsettling in any case, but especially when you make your living as a pastor. I remember taking long walks alone during this time, praying, thinking, wondering what would happen to me if better answers never came. I couldn't think of anyone with whom I could share my deep agony. It was a scary and tough time.

My disillusionment was intensified by what was happening in the Christian community in America during the 1980s and 90s. A large portion of both Protestant and Catholic leaders had aligned with a neo-conservative political ideology, trumpeting what they called 'conservative family values' but minimising biblical community values. They supported wars of choice, defended torture, opposed environmental protection and seemed to care more about protecting the rich from taxes than liberating the poor from poverty or the minorities from racism. They spoke against big government as if big was bad, yet it seemed that big military and big business were inherently good to them. They wanted to protect unborn human life inside the womb, but didn't seem to care about born human life inside slums or prisons or nations they considered enemies. They loved to paint gay people as a threat to marriage, seeming to miss the irony that heterosexual people were damaging marriage at a furious pace without any help from gay couples. They consistently relegated females to second-class status, often while covering up for their fellow males when they fell into scandal or committed criminal abuse. They interpreted the Bible to favour the government of Israel and to marginalise Palestinians, and even before 11 September 2001 I feared that through their influence Muslims were being cast as the new scapegoats, targets of a scary kind of religiously inspired bigotry.

Their stridency and selectivity in choosing issues and priorities at first annoyed, then depressed, and then angered me. They had created a powerful and wealthy stealth domination dedicated to mobilising fighters in their 'culture war'. I began referring to the new religious establishment they had created as *radio-orthodoxy* because its message spread through religious radio and TV. They had turned the way of Jesus, I felt, into the club of the Pharisees, and they didn't speak for me, even though their spokesmen dominated the dialogue night after night on TV. I also felt that the terms 'evangelical' and even 'Christian' had become like discredited brands through their energetic but misguided work.[4] I increasingly understood why more and more of my friends winced when the name 'Jesus' was mentioned in public: it wasn't due to a loss of respect for Jesus, but a loss of respect for those who most used his name. In spite of all this, few of my fellow pastors and leaders had the courage to speak out for fear of losing members or their contributions. For a while, I'm ashamed to say, I was among their silent number.

Morning after morning I woke up in the brutal tension

between *something real* and *something wrong* in Christian faith. The sense of *something real* kept me in ministry and in Christian faith; the sense of *something wrong* kept me looking for a way out. Somehow, by the grace of God, I held on to the *something real* for long enough to begin to figure out what the *something wrong* might be. And eventually I began to get some sense of what to do to disentangle the one from the other, to hold on to the *something real* and let the other go.

The process was slow, however – two steps forward and one back, it seemed. For about five years I felt I was standing in a deepening welter of theological fragments. My spirituality was intact – because I was learning that there is a kind of faith that runs deeper than mere beliefs – but my belief system was in shambles. Little by little, though, a new coherence began to emerge. That coherence was more a *new way of believing*, and less a rebuilt *system of beliefs* – and I felt compelled to try to share what I was learning and experiencing. So I began to write, and from that time of theological collapse and spiritual recovery my first book took shape, *The Church on the Other Side* (Zondervan, 1998).

'The other side' referred to what I called 'the postmodern transition'. On the past side of the transition, in the modern era, nearly all our Protestant denominations had been formed. They were institutional children of the era of Sir Isaac Newton, the conquistadors, colonialism, the Enlightenment, nationalism and capitalism. Each denomination made sense of Christianity within the lines and boxes of modernity. You might say they rewrote and rearranged the ancient 'data' of Christianity in a modern program, programming language, paradigm or framework.

But on the future side of the transition, the modern paradigm with its absolute scientific laws, consumerist individualism and rational certainty was giving way to a postmodern paradigm of pluralism, relativism, globalism and uncertainty – or at least a different kind of certainty, at its best more akin to humble confidence. Modern Protestantism in both its liberal and conservative forms was being lost in transition and lost in translation. Both forms of modernist Christianity seemed equally clueless in understanding the non-modern and postmodern people outside their stained-glass windows. Roman Catholicism found itself in a remarkably similar situation to Protestantism, having seized two opportunities to disembed from its medieval paradigm and reboot itself as a more modern religion, first through the Council of Trent and then in Vatican II. Just like their Protestant cousins, Catholics made this adjustment in a bipolar way, splitting themselves into left/liberal and right/conservative parties, both sides increasingly reacting to one another and losing touch with the changing world outside their religiously gated community.

This modern–postmodern transition, this colonial–postcolonial cultural shift, was a major obstacle in the path of my spiritually seeking friends, and it had become my own struggle. Meanwhile, unbeknown to me, it was also becoming a struggle shared by millions of lifelong Christians around the world, many of whom were drifting away from Church and faith. When I began writing that first book, I didn't know a single author or pastor who saw what I was seeing. But during the writing process I began to find a few (notably Sally Morgenthaler and Dr Leonard Sweet).[5] When the book was published, people started coming out of the woodwork, saying, 'I thought I was

the only one who had these questions. I'm not alone after all.'
I discovered that many new networks were forming to grapple
with the same kinds of questions I had felt so alone in asking
– groups like the Younger Leader Networks (which later became
Emergent Village, at emergentvillage.com), theooze.com (created
by spiritual entrepreneur Spencer Burke and friends), Center for
Action and Contemplation (cac.org), and the Gospel and Our
Culture Network (gocn.org) in the US, the Alternative Worship
networks in the UK (Jonny Baker offers a good round-up at
http://jonnybaker.blogs.com/jonnybaker/2009/06/lancaster-
linkage.html), Evangile et Culture (http://pagesperso-orange.fr/
endirect/evangile-et-culture.html) in France, and La Red del
Camino (www.lareddelcamino.net) in Latin America.[6]

In spite of our diverse backgrounds, we all agreed: *something
isn't working any more in the way we're doing Christianity.*
And although we didn't know exactly what to do about it, we
knew that we needed to keep talking and searching together –
through the internet, through conferences and retreats, through
books, through networks. So our quest for a new kind of
Christianity had begun.

Meanwhile, groups like the Lily Foundation and the Barna
Group were sponsoring street-level statistical research on church
life.[7] Study after study confirmed our shared intuition that something was seriously wrong and needed to be addressed. In mainline Protestant churches numerical decline had been well
documented since the 1960s. Not only were historic Protestant
denominations shrinking numerically, but the remaining
churchgoers were wrinkling. The average age rose as young
people dropped out after school or college. Episcopalians in the
US, for example, were losing the equivalent of a diocese per

year, and the average age had crept up to sixty-two – almost twice the average age (thirty-two) of the average American. The decline and ageing of Roman Catholic churchgoers was masked to a degree by immigration, but without immigrants the news was similarly alarming. 'Protestant churches say they have no young adults between the ages of eighteen and thirty-five,' one Catholic sociologist told me. 'The truth is, we Catholics have largely lost the generations between eighteen and fifty-five.'

Through the 1980s and 90s, conservative evangelicals could contrast their growth statistics with the decline of their 'liberal' Christian counterparts. They frequently suggested that their theological and socio-economic conservatism was the secret to their statistical success. But in the first decade of the new millennium, evangelicals too discovered that their trend-lines were turning south: they too were losing their younger generations.[8] And in almost all cases their growth rates, excluding immigrants, had either slowed, stopped or reversed. Youth workers began feeling the pain first, and soon so did faculty and staff at Christian colleges and universities, as did workers in para-church ministries and mission agencies, with church-planters and pastors and priests in local churches not far behind.[9] As time went on, administrators and leaders in denominations began seeing the writing on their office walls too.

I continued to write about the Church's struggles in the post-modern transition and two of my books, released in the early and mid-2000s, seemed to strike a special chord. *A New Kind of Christian* (Jossey-Bass, 2001) tried to define and describe the problem through a semi-fictional (and semi-autobiographical) story about a pastor whose faith was falling apart on him. It suggested that the Christian faith would need to disembed from the paradigm of modernity and experience something akin to a total makeover or rebirth in a postmodern context. *A Generous Orthodoxy* tried to be more constructive, describing what a post-liberal, post-conservative, post-sectarian and postmodern approach to Christian faith might look and feel like. Along with my other books, these two in particular were being discussed in reading groups, college classes, conferences and retreats. As a result, I began receiving speaking invitations from across denominations both in North America and around the world. Christian leaders in Europe, Asia, Latin America and Africa, I discovered, were experiencing similar kinds of struggles and many of them were far ahead of us in the US in realising that a defining moment had come, a moment of deep shift, a moment in which a new kind of Christianity needed to be born.

So I was certainly not alone in addressing this moment of crisis and opportunity. Many voices arose, like mine, from evangelical backgrounds, but parallel conversations were emerging among mainline Protestants and Roman Catholics, and Eastern Orthodox thinkers were cautiously joining conversations in a few places as well. Two recent books, in my opinion, have contributed to the dialogue in an especially helpful way. As the former religion editor for *Publisher's Weekly*, Phyllis Tickle was well placed to observe what was happening in the American religious landscape. Born Presbyterian and an active Episcopalian in her adult life, Phyllis proposed in *The Great Emergence* that every five hundred years or so the Christian faith holds a 'rummage sale', or jumble sale. It sorts through all that it has accumulated over recent centuries. What feels like extra baggage it sends to the recycling centre, and what feels like essential travel gear it preserves for the future, thus opening a new chapter in Christian history. This kind of sorting process had occurred with the Great Collapse of the Roman Empire (around 500 AD), the Great Schism (around 1000 AD) and the Great Reformation (around 1500 AD). And now, she proposed, we are in the Great Emergence.

A leading theologian at Harvard Divinity School, an influential author and an American Baptist, Harvey Cox made a similar assertion in *The Future of Faith*. Cox assessed history a little differently. He spoke of the first era of Christianity (from Jesus to about 300 AD) as the Age of Faith. That age had been characterised by diversity, energy, vitality, suffering, persecution, courage and rapid growth. But that era ended when the Roman Emperor Constantine converted (as the story goes) to Christianity and then converted Christianity to a troubling alliance with his Roman Empire. In that alliance, unity of belief became politically useful – and enforceable. So the Empire that had crucified Jesus now claimed to be the agent, patron and police force of a newly dominant Christian religion. As such, it demanded the full allegiance of all believers. In order to promote unity in the Church and in the Empire, the Emperor mandated that the bishops gather to develop creeds, thus enlisting the clergy to help enforce submission to the Emperor's regime. The Roman Empire could thus claim to be validated by the God of the Christians, not just the ancient Greco-Roman pantheon. Thus the Age of Belief was born.

The Age of Belief marked the Christianisation of the Empire and the imperialisation (or Greco-Romanisation) of Christianity. The fusion was problematic from the beginning, because in its first 250 years, the bishops of the Church participated in the identification and execution of about 25,000 people as heretics.

Do you see the irony of this – or perhaps *tragedy* or *atrocity* would be better words? The religion that was ostensibly founded by a non-violent man of peace had now embraced the very violence he rejected. The religion that grew in response to a man who was tortured and killed by the Roman Empire was now torturing and killing others in league with that Empire. Dynamic faith that moves mountains was out; static belief that burns or banishes heretics was in. Catalytic faith as an agent of social transformation was out; codified belief as a tool of social control was in. And that kind of belief has stayed 'in' ever since. As I ponder what this atrocity has meant in our world, I recall Woody Allen's statement that if Jesus could see what people have done in his name, he would 'never stop throwing up'.

For these reasons and more, Cox does not mourn the demise of the Age of Belief. He sees, emerging in its place, what he calls the Age of the Spirit, an approach to Christian faith that tries to preserve the treasures of previous eras and face and embrace the challenges of the twenty-first century. So something is happening. Something is afoot. A change is in the wind. Whether we call it the *Great Emergence* with Tickle or the *Age of the Spirit* with Cox, whether we call it *a Christianity worth believing* with Doug Pagitt or *the New Christians* with Tony Jones, whether we call it *Generative Christianity* with Church historian Diana Butler Bass or *Emerging Christianity* with Marcus Borg, or a *Generous Orthodoxy* with Hans Frei or *Integral Mission* with René Padilla or something else – whatever we call it, something is trying to be born among those of us who believe and follow Jesus Christ. That's what *a new kind of Christianity* in this book's title points towards.

That's what I'd like to help you understand in these pages. But there's more: I also hope to inspire you to join together with others to help create it, guided by God's creative Spirit.

Of course, as evidenced by those canary-yellow flyers flapping under windscreen wipers in that car park, not everyone agrees with Phyllis, Harvey, Doug, Tony, Diana, Marcus and the rest of us. Not everyone wants to join the quest for a new kind of Christianity. But that's OK. Their resistance, suspicion and opposition are actually a gift, and through their critique we on the quest will grow wiser and stronger. In this way, even they will contribute to what is trying to be born in, through and among us.

However, giving birth, as any mother will tell you, is no Sunday-school picnic. So before we go any further, we'd better get realistic about the obstacles we face.

CHAPTER 2

The Quest and the Questions

Imagine it's 1775. You are a young citizen in the Thirteen Colonies, listening to Thomas Paine or Thomas Jefferson dream aloud about a new nation – 'a government without a king', they say, 'of, by and for the people', they say. *Don't kings rule by divine right?* you wonder. *Isn't monarchy God's way, reflecting in human society the sacred hierarchy of heaven? Is some new democratic arrangement theologically permissible, not to mention politically possible?* How would you respond when either Tom invites you to join the movement?

Or imagine it's the early nineteenth century. You're voyaging with Alfred Russel Wallace between the islands of Indonesia, or you're on board the *Beagle* with Charles Darwin, exploring the Galapagos Islands. You're noticing patterns – patterns of variation among closely related species of bird, turtle, bat and other animals, and patterns of distribution of those species across islands and continents. Church dogma says that all species now alive disseminated from Mount Ararat in Turkey less than six thousand years ago, after Noah's flood. If that's true, you'd expect species to radiate out from that one centre, but the patterns you're observing don't support that dogma at all. You wonder: *Why don't the facts conform to the dogma? Should another explanation be sought?*

Or imagine it's 1905. You're in Bern, having coffee with an unknown would-be physicist named Albert Einstein who is working on an article with a strange equation in it. Is it possible to imagine with Albert that matter and energy are not absolute, and that one can be transformed into the other? Or imagine it's a few years later, and now the young scientist has proposed the relativity of time and space. Will you give such absurd ideas a second thought, or will you call it all nonsense, muttering about slippery slopes, pledging fealty to Sir Isaac Newton and his world of secure laws and simple formulas?

Or imagine it's the early 1960s, and you're watching Walter Cronkite on the *CBS Evening News* on your black-and-white TV. The scene cuts to Dr Martin Luther King, Jr, as he preaches about a beloved community replacing a segregated society. Or maybe it's 1991 and you're a white South African, and you're watching SATV, and Nelson Mandela, newly released from prison, is proclaiming a new vision for his apartheid-torn nation. Will you dare question conventional wisdom enough to consider signing up to Martin's or Nelson's wild new viewpoints and dangerous dreams, or maybe even join them in a march or boycott?

Or zip back to 1610, in Italy, and imagine you're standing in starlight among friends on Galileo's rooftop. You're taking turns gazing at Jupiter through his newfangled telescope – and there you see . . . amazing! . . . against the deep night, three, no, four luminous moons suspended as if by magic around the banded planet. Suddenly you feel yourself dizzy, as if you're falling out of one universe and into another. And not only dizzy, but afraid, because somehow you know that Church leaders would not be happy about your observations and the speculations they may lead to. After all, for over a thousand years, all Christians have known with absolute and objective certainty that the earth is fixed and immovable in the centre of the universe, with the moon, planets, sun and stars securely embedded in ten majestic crystalline spheres that rotate around the earth. This model, the invention of Claudius Ptolemy in the second century, has worked perfectly for a long time . . . well, almost perfectly. There has been one pesky problem.

If you look at heavenly bodies on consecutive nights, you'll notice that nearly all of them stay in formation, in the same relative positions, creating stable patterns that we call constellations. But a few heavenly bodies don't follow the pattern. These renegades move across the background constellations. That's why the ancient Greeks called them 'wanderers' (which is the origin of the word *planets*). Even though their motion was different from that of the starry background, at least it was consistent: they would wander from west to east, night after night, and the model of Ptolemy could even explain this movement. Usually, that is.

Sometimes, some planets would pause in their eastward course, dip, reverse course and move west for a while, and then loop back again to the east. How could this be? Why would every other heavenly body move in an orderly motion across the sky, but these dancers would step out of line and behave erratically? These are the questions that helped bring down a paradigm that had held sway for over a thousand years.

Ptolemy's model couldn't account for this phenomenon. That's why medieval scholars called anomalies like this one *appearances*. Since they *appeared to* violate the model, they had to be illusions. Now, in 1610, in Jupiter's moons you have seen additional contrary data with your own eyes, so you have a choice: to explain away the appearances, or to 'save' them, even though they are an embarrassment to an otherwise perfect system of explanation. To do the former would betray the data, and to do the latter would betray accepted dogma.

Paradigms and dogma can be defended and enforced with guns and prisons, bullets and bonfires, threats and humiliations, fatwas and excommunications. But paradigms and dogma remain profoundly vulnerable when anomalies are present. They can be undone by something as simple as a question ... a question about the divine right of kings, about the origin of species, about the relation between matter and energy, about the way races can and should relate to one another, about the motion of planets, and about standard operating procedures used by the Church.

That's what got a young trainee priest named Martin Luther into hot water. On 31 October 1517 he dared question the issuance of indulgences, a procedure by which Church officials transformed religious devotion into religious donations. The devoted, by making generous donations to the Church treasury, could negotiate the early release of loved ones from purgatory to heaven. This ultimate commercialisation of God's house and commodification of salvation deserved to be questioned, so he posted a document on the door of the Castle Church in Wittenberg, Germany (or so the story goes). It began like this:

Out of love for the truth and the desire to bring it to light, the following propositions will be discussed at Wittenberg, under the presidency of the Reverend Father Martin Luther, Master of Arts and of Sacred Theology ... Wherefore he requests that those who are unable to be present and debate orally with us, may do so by letter.

Imagine you're a fellow student, reading the invitation. Would you attend and get involved in the debate? Watch from a distance? Call the authorities and demand an inquisition? Hand out canary-yellow flyers?

Luther's invitation for discussion was followed by ninety-five provocative statements, or theses, to be debated. Those ninety-five theses successfully sparked a debate that further desta-bilised the uneasy status quo of the late Middle Ages, thus helping to tip the Christian community from its medieval state into a new modern state. That's what *statements* can do: create *debate* (and sometimes, sadly, *hate*) that move us into a new *state*. Now, nearly five hundred years later, Luther's ninety-five theses have completed their job. It's time for another tipping point; it's time, we might say, for a ninety-sixth thesis.

But the ninety-sixth thesis for today must be very different from the original ninety-five, because we already have more hate than we need, and a surplus of debate too, much of which is inversely proportional in intensity to the actual importance of its substance. At this moment in history, we need something more radical and transformative than a new state: we need a new *quest*. We need more than a new static location from which we proclaim, 'Here I stand!' Instead, we need a new dynamic *direction* into which we move together, proclaiming, 'Here we go!'[1] We need a deep shift, not merely from our current state to a new state, but from a steady state to a dynamic story. We need, not a new set of beliefs, but a new way of believing; not simply new answers to the same old questions, but a new set of questions instead.

Again: new *statements* (theses, propositions, answers) can inspire *debate* and bring us to a new *state*. But only new *questions* can inspire *new conversations* that can launch us on a new *quest*. So, in homage to Martin Luther, this new statement or ninety-sixth thesis is humbly offered, in fear and trembling, to my fellow Christians of all denominations around the world:

> It's time for a new quest, launched by new questions – a quest across denominations and around the world, a quest for new ways to believe and new ways to live and serve faithfully in the way of Jesus, a quest for a new kind of Christian faith.[2]

I'm certain that, to some people, the quest for a new kind of Christian faith will be of no interest at all. *The old kind is just fine, thank you very much*, they'll say. For them, this quest will have no more appeal than Luther's original theses had to those religious dignitaries assembled at the Diet of Worms (if you don't know what that is, don't worry: it's not what you think . . .). To them, Luther instigated not renewal or reform but betrayal – betrayal of the past and of the beloved institutions and belief systems so many had worked so hard to construct and defend. If our quest is a betrayal, it is only the most faithful kind of betrayal: a betrayal of the actualities of the past and present in order to seize the future possibilities towards which they reached.[3] If it is a critique of the past, it is only a critique of the worst moments, while simultaneously celebrating the best moments and the best aspirations – and moving forward thus instructed and inspired.

So what are the questions that open the way for a new kind of Christianity? There are many, but in thousands of personal conversations and in hundreds of Q&R (question and response) sessions with Christian leaders across denominations and around the world, I've noticed ten in particular that keep coming up. These ten, I believe, have a special power to stimulate conversations that we need to have. And these conversations, in turn, can become the context for new friendships among unlikely people. Taken together, those questions, conversations and friendships have the potential simultaneously to weaken old, rigid paradigms and to help us imagine new and better possibilities. I sense the wind of the Spirit of God in these questions, and in them I feel a powerful summons to faith, hope and love.

1. The narrative question: What is the Overarching Storyline of the Bible??

Many people read the Bible as a series of disconnected quotes and episodes – yielding maxims, rules, formulas, anecdotes, propositions and wise sayings. They have little or no sense of the larger story into which the statements fit and in which their meaning took shape. Others read the Bible within a narrative – but that framing narrative is actually foreign to the Bible, and many of us believe it is too small, too narrow and too flat to do justice to the richness of the text. As it shrinks the text, it shrinks us too, so we ask: Is there a discernible plotline to the biblical library, and, if so, what is it? What are the deep problems that the original Christian story was trying to solve? What's the big picture? Where did we come from, where are we going, and where are we now, according to the Bible and its stories and story?

2. The authority question: How should the Bible be understood?

In a time when religious extremists constantly use their sacred texts to justify violence, many of us feel a moral obligation to question the ways the Bible has been used in the past to defend the indefensible and promote the unacceptable. If we continue to use the Bible as we did in the past, we render ourselves likely to repeat past atrocities. So we ask: What is the Bible – and what is it for? If the Bible is God's revelation, why can't Christians finally agree on what it says? Why does it so often seem to be in conflict with science? Why has it been so easy for so many people to use the Bible to justify terrible atrocities?[4]

3. The God question: Is God violent?

Nearly all religions – and certainly all monotheistic religions – seem at times hell-bent on inspiring people to kill each other, making atheism sometimes seem to be a more ethical alternative to conventional violence-prone belief. So we ask: Why does God seem so violent and genocidal in many Bible passages? Does God play favourites? Does God choose some and reject others? Does God sanction elitism, prejudice, violence or even genocide? Is God incurably violent, and is faith capable of becoming a stronger force for peace and reconciliation instead of violence in the future?

4. The Jesus question: Who is Jesus and why is he important?

Jesus appears to be a victim of identity theft. The versions of Jesus presented by contemporary Christian institutions could hardly be more different from one another – or from the four portraits of Jesus we find in the Gospels. And while the versions of Jesus typically presented by churches seem to turn more and more people off and away, interest in and attraction to the Jesus of the Gospels seems to grow and grow. So we ask: What accounts for the differences in descriptions of Jesus? Which versions of Jesus are more trustworthy than others? How can we tell? Why does it matter?

5. The gospel question: What is the gospel?

Some people see the gospel as information on how individuals can avoid hell and go to heaven after death. Some see it as a message of liberation and transformation for select individuals in this life. Some see it as a message of liberation and transformation for all people and all creation. And so we ask: Who is right? Why is there such a divergence of opinion on such an essential matter? Why does Jesus' gospel of the kingdom of God seem to morph into another gospel – of justification by faith – in other parts of the New Testament? Are the gospels of Jesus and Paul (not to mention the other apostolic writers) different and opposed to one another?

6. The Church question: What do we do about the Church?

The questions we consider in these pages will have to be grappled with in local faith communities. As they inspire new insights and conclusions, those insights and conclusions will have to be lived out in local congregations. And so we ask: In the light of the new understanding opened up by the previous questions, what must change for the Church – the local church, the denomination, and the larger community of Christians? How are we to conceive of God's Spirit at work in the Church and in the world? How do we co-operate with God's work in, through, outside and in spite of the Church?

7. The sex question: Can we find a way to address sexuality without fighting about it?

Our acute anxieties about human sexuality may be related to our discomfort with our humanity in general, and in particular to our dissatisfaction with conventional Christian accounts of the human being in the light of new discoveries in neuro-biology, psycho-pharmacology, anthropology and related fields. In particular, the issue of homosexuality preoccupies, divides and obsesses many churches and denominations like no other issue. Not only do people disagree on the matter, but they are unwilling to tolerate disagreement among their fellow Christians – in spite of the fact that they tolerate diversity of opinion on many other issues – important ones like pacifism, nuclear war, genocide, environmental destruction, wealth and poverty, torture, and consumptive affluence. And so we ask: Why is this issue so hot right now? How do the previous questions open up new ways of thinking about homosexuality, gender identity and sexuality in general? Can we move beyond paralysing polarisation into constructive dialogue about the whole range of challenges we face regarding human sexuality?

8. The future question: Can we find a better way of viewing the future?

For better or for worse, eschatology (the theological discipline that thinks about the future and what lies beyond this life) sells millions of books, raises millions of pounds and influences the domestic and foreign policies of some of the world's most powerful and militarised nations (the US and Iran both come to mind). And so we ask: If eschatologies are self-fulfilling prophecies, what kind of eschatology will contribute to a more just and joyful future? How will a new kind of Christianity develop a new kind of eschatology?

9. The pluralism question: How should followers of Jesus relate to people of other religions?

We wake up each day in a world whose very future is threatened by inter-religious fear, hatred and violence. Many of us wonder if there is a way to have both a deep identity in Christ and an eirenic, charitable, neighbourly attitude towards people of other faiths. So we ask: Is Jesus the only way? The only way to what? How can a belief in the uniqueness and universality of Christ be held without implying the religious supremacy and exclusivity of the Christian religion?

10. The what-do-we-do-now question: How can we translate our quest into action?

It's one thing to consider these questions in the private forum of one's mind, but when we begin engaging others in conversation about these issues, there can be many unintended negative consequences – including division, disruption and distraction in our beloved congregations, denominations, families and circles of friends. So we ask: What happens next? How can we on this quest pursue truth and hope in a loving spirit when our quest is opposed or ignored by many of our fellow Christians? How can we learn from history to introduce needed new ideas without also introducing needless division? How does our search for a new kind of Christianity relate to a renewed kind of spirituality? What new questions open up for us once we begin grappling with these? How can the kind of reflection in which we have engaged be translated into reflective practice and action?

These ten questions are, to recall Dylan's epic line, 'blowing in the wind' around us. Even if we've never heard them articulated, they have been hovering just outside our conscious awareness. They trouble our conventional paradigms of faith just as the ten plagues of frogs, gnats, flies, hail, etc. plagued the Egyptians in the exodus story. When people tell us to be quiet and accept the conventional answers we've been given in the past, many of us groan like the ancient Hebrews being forced to produce bricks without straw. We cry out to God, 'Please set us free!' We cry out to preachers and theologians, 'Let us go! Let us find some space to think, to worship God, outside the bars and walls and fences in which we are constrained and imprisoned. We'll head out into the wilderness – risk hunger, thirst, exposure, death – but we can't sustain this constrained way of thinking, believing, and living much longer. We need to ask the questions that are simmering in our souls.'

So we set out on our quest, our exodus, driven out of familiar territory and drawn into unmapped *terra nova* by ten questions stirring in our hearts. In the coming chapters we'll consider each question and then some provisional, preliminary, incomplete, but promising responses that I've cobbled together or gleaned from others on the journey. *Responses*, please remember, are not *answers*: the latter seek to end conversation, while the former seek to stimulate more of it. The responses I offer are not intended as a smash in tennis, delivered forcefully with a lot of top spin, in an effort to win the game and create a loser. Rather, they are offered as a gentle serve or lob; their primary goal is to start the interplay, to get things rolling, to invite your reply. Remember: our goal is not statement/debate/division and hate/new state, but rather question/conversation/friendship/new quest.

In each of our ten responses, I will present a close reading of at least one biblical passage. Through those biblical passages, I will be seeking a passageway, a passage out of our conventional paradigm and a passage into new territory, new possibilities. In this way, we'll be making passages through passages.

So may our quest begin.

CHAPTER 3

A Prayer on the Beach

It's 1620, and we're in Delfshaven, Holland. A group of pilgrims are about to embark on a quest. They have already had a hard road. They have defied religious authorities in their native England to stay true to their conscience and to seek the truth. They have relocated to Holland, and now they are preparing to relocate again. In a few moments they will take their greatest risk ever, setting sail for the New World in the hope of establishing a new community there, a community in which they can live out their faith in honesty, openness and freedom.

Their pastor, John Robinson, hopes to join them at a later date. (He will die prematurely before that hope can be realised.) They spend the entire night before their departure in prayer. Then, just before they board a little ship called the *Mayflower*, their pastor stands to speak. Even though they will soon be separated by a broad ocean, he considers them his flock and so he speaks to them once more as their pastor.

'I charge you before God and his blessed angels,' he begins, 'that you follow me no further than you have seen me follow Christ. If God reveal anything to you by any other instrument of his, be as ready to receive it as you were to receive any truth from my ministry, for I am verily persuaded the Lord hath more truth and light yet to break forth from his holy word.

'The Lutherans cannot be drawn to go beyond what Luther saw. Whatever part of his will our God has revealed to Calvin, they (Lutherans) will rather die than embrace it; and the Calvinists, you see, stick fast where they were left by that great man of God, who yet saw not all things. This is a misery much to be lamented. For though they were precious shining lights in their time, yet God has not revealed his whole will to them. And were they now living, they would be as ready and willing to embrace further light, as they had received.'

This is the attitude of a man, and a community, on a quest. They know that they do not yet see 'all things'. There is 'further light' to be embraced and more of God's will to be revealed, so they must not 'stick fast' to their current understandings, but must 'go beyond'. For 'the Lord hath more truth and light yet to break forth from his holy word'. They pray together one last time, and the *Mayflower* sets sail for Massachusetts.

Today, imagine that we are standing on a beach, ready to embark on our own voyage. John Robinson's words echo through the years to us, and now we kneel in the sand and share together in a prayer like this:

Lord, we acknowledge that we have made a mess of what Jesus started.

We affirm that we are wrong and Jesus is right.

We choose not to defend what we have done and what we have become.

We understand that many good Christians will not want to participate in our quest, and we welcome their charitable critique.

We acknowledge that various dimensions of the various Christianities we have created up to this point deserve reassessment and, in many cases, repentance.

We choose to seek a better path into the future than the one we have been on.

We desire to be born again as disciples of Jesus Christ.

Now grant us wisdom and guide us in our quest, and create something new and beautiful in and among us for the good of all creation and to your glory, Living God.

Each line of this prayer can be the basis for a meditation to prepare us for the journey ahead, our quest for a new kind of Christian faith.

1. We acknowledge that we have made a mess of what Jesus started.

Who would like to claim that their denomination, their church, their version of Christian faith is anywhere close to fulfilling what Jesus intended? Who would like to claim that their institutions or movements alone capture the spirit and mission of Jesus? What televangelist can make this claim? What Pentecostal shop-front church, what headquarters in New York or Middle America or Canterbury or Rome or Lagos? Aren't all Christians of all denominations fully unified in this realisation that what we have become is not a continuing faithful embodiment of Jesus, but rather – too often – a Disneyesque simulacrum and sometimes a tired fossilisation, in some cases even a comic parody or tragic catastrophe or veritable travesty, when compared to the vibrant life and way of Jesus?

2. We affirm that we are wrong and Jesus is right.

Would anyone like to assert that both they and Jesus are equally right? True, many are quick to claim and proclaim their right-ness in relation to other Christians – Calvinists know they are right when compared with Arminians, Catholics compared with Protestants, Pentecostals compared with non-Pentecostals, evangelicals compared with liberals, and the Orthodox compared with the non-Orthodox, and vice versa. But who would be so purely arrogant or demonically naïve to claim to be right on a par with Jesus? That person, that group, should never stoop to associate with the kinds of disreputable failures, notorious sinners and unwashed seekers, lovers and doubters who would dare to dream of a new kind of Christianity.

3. We choose not to defend what we have done and what we have become.

Again, we are all quick to defend ourselves in relation to one another. In the tradition of Peter, we point at John and say, 'Hey, what about him?' But when we stand before the Word of God alive and embodied in Jesus – ringing and singing in his life and work, his teaching, his death, his resurrection, his abiding presence – which of us wishes to defend himself or herself, his views or her views, his denomination or her denomination?

4. We understand that many good Christians will not want to participate in our quest, and we welcome their charitable critique.

A search for a new kind of Christian faith can't be reduced to another list of propositions about which debates rage and over which debaters indulge in hostile polemics, seeking to forge arguments that urge converts to defect from 'the heretical them' and affiliate with 'the righteous us'. This quest must instead work more like a wedding proposal, an invitation. It must be about free conversation, not forced conversion. It must demand nothing of anybody, and it must make no threats and strike no bargains, because threats and bargains would invalidate the tender nature of the proposal. Rather, it must open up a 'we' into which all are invited but none are coerced, shamed, pressured or even obligated. It would accept 'No' as being as valid a response as 'Yes', though it may do so with a tear because it is a proposal of love.

5. We acknowledge that various dimensions of the various Christianities we have created up to this point deserve reassessment and, in many cases, repentance.

We are not reassessing for the purpose of vilifying our ancestors in the faith, or in order to contrast a dark, backward 'them' with an enlightened, progressive 'us', snarkily implying that they got it wrong all along and (insert trumpet fanfare here) we have finally got it right after all these years. Such a damnably arrogant or pathetically naïve thesis doesn't deserve our attention, much less commitment. No, we are reassessing as a humble act of ethical responsibility, so that we can avoid merely carrying on 'the traditions of humans' as the Pharisees once did. We are in fact following the example of our ancestors, who again and again from the margins did this very kind of collective self-examination and repenting.

We are not reassessing and repenting of 'Christianity' as a sacred abstraction representing the highest and best ideals of Christians everywhere. Instead, we are beginning to reassess and repent of the actual versions and formulations of the faith *we have created*. We are acknowledging that the Christianities we have created – or constructed – deserve to be re-examined and deconstructed, not so that we may slide into agnosticism or atheism or secular patriotic consumerism, but so that our religious traditions can be seen for what they are. They are not simply a pure, abstracted and ideal 'essence of Christianity', but rather they are evolving, embodied, situated versions of the faith – each of which is unfinished, imperfect and sometimes pretentious, and each of which is often beautiful and wonderful, renewable and serviceable too.

6. We choose to seek a better path into the future than the one we have been on.

We do not sense in the gospel of Jesus a once-upon-a-time newness. We do not experience the gospel as new only in contrast to something called 'the Old Testament', leaving the gospel over time to grow arthritic, hardened, stiff and crotchety. No: we sense in the gospel a perpetual fountain of youthful newness, an ongoing advent, a constant beginning, a continually generative genesis, always fermenting like new wine, a tide that rises, wave by wave. We do not conceive of our faith as a promise to our ancestors, a vow dutifully to carry on something that was theirs and we have inherited. No: it is more like God's promise uttered to us from the future, towards which we reach an outstretched and hopeful hand, just as our ancestors did. The gospel is for us a beckoning, a summons, always associated with transitive words like *leave, come, go, follow*. So, just as a new path opens up new territory in which cities can be built, the gospel is for us a movement, a pioneering adventure, leaving behind it a pathway along which institutions are constructed, renewed, replaced. But the movement is never contained or controlled by the institution any more than the wind is contained or controlled by the branches through which it blows; no city along the path should be taken as the journey's end.

7. We desire to be born again as disciples of Jesus Christ.

There has been much talk of 'born-again Christians' in recent years, but the truth is, most of us who identify ourselves as born-again Christians could stand to be born again *again*. In fact, we need to be born again *again and again*, not simply as lost people born into foundness, or damned people born into forgiveness, or the walking dead born into new life, or outsiders born into insider status, but as non-disciples (whether know-nothings or know-enoughs or know-it-alls, it doesn't matter) born into a lifelong experiential learning adventure of discipleship. We might say that *Christians* are people who have entered a certain sedentary membership or arrived at a status validated by some group or institution, while *disciples* are learners (and unlearners) who have started on a rigorous and unending journey or quest in relation to Jesus Christ. It's worth noting in this regard that the word *Christian* occurs in the New Testament exactly three times and the word *Christianity* exactly zero times. The word *disciple*, however, is found 263 times.

In no way are we who seek this new birth as disciples claiming a superior status. We have no interest in distinguishing ourselves as super-Christians, better than anybody else: if anything, we are surrendering our status as first- or even second-class Christians (and our critics constantly assist us in this regard). Some of us figuratively, and some perhaps literally, are voluntarily demoting ourselves below full Christian status, seeing ourselves as third-rate sub-Christians who have not yet arrived, people sojourning but still far from our home. We may have crossed a starting line, but we have not crossed a finishing line, so we are still in motion.

8. We pray that God will create something new and beautiful in and among us for the good of all creation and to the glory of the living God.

What we need is not simply a new way of thinking, although our quest leads deep into and through the mind. We also need a new way of being, a new inner ecology, a new spirituality that does more than make us opinionated or fastidious, but renders our souls an orchard of trees bearing good fruit, rooted in who we are before God and who we are becoming in God. We are seeking to be people of 'orthopathy', in whom the deep orientation or attitudes or feelings (pathos) of love, joy, peace, patience, kindness, goodness, faithfulness, gentleness and self-control are increasingly normative.

This inward transformation, of course, requires community – a social, communal, relational reality that perhaps could be captured by coining a term like 'ortho-affinity' – a good and right way of relating to one another in communities of faith and to our neighbours (including those who consider themselves our enemies) outside our faith communities.[1]

Our faith is vain and self-centred if it brings blessing only for us or to us. It also must result in blessing that flows through us to the world. Good thinking (orthodoxy), good being (orthopathy) and good relating (ortho-affinity) must interact with and express themselves through good work and practice (orthopraxy) in the world – the creation which God made, loves and will never abandon or betray.

We do not expect ourselves to be capable of completing this quest in our own strength, guided only by our own flickering lights, so we pray, expressing our dependence on the gracious and living Holy Spirit from whom we have received life and every good thing, in whom we live, move and have our being, and towards whom we move in our journey through life.

Rare moments come to us in our journey when the penny drops, the tumblers click, the pieces fall into place, the lights come on and our breath is taken away. The old paradigm falls away behind us like a port of departure and we are won over to new possibilities, caught up in a new way of seeing, looking towards a new and wide horizon. The Lord has more light and truth to break forth, we believe, and so we raise our sails to the wind of the Spirit. We are embarked on our quest launched by a prayer.

Book 1

Unlocking and Opening

You can't go on a quest for something new if you are locked in a closet, cell or concentration camp. But our captivity is often a comfortable one: padded chairs, nice music, entertaining shows with songs and talks designed — like all that happens within the dome of the classic movie *The Truman Show* — to keep us content inside. And maybe they're designed to keep us a little afraid of the world outside the dome too.

To make matters worse, the chains, bars and barbed wire that hold us are often invisible. The guards are often disguised in clerical robes or casual suits, and they hold advanced degrees and have mastered the techniques of friendly manipulation, always with a penetrating smile and a firm, heavy hand on the shoulder.

The gates that hold us where we are can be unlocked, however. The key is a question. When you ask it, you are free.

ONE

THE NARRATIVE QUESTION

CHAPTER 4

What is the Overarching Storyline of the Bible?

When I began to feel the tension between *something real* and *something wrong* in my faith, I started to dig through layers and layers of practice, piety and theology. After over a decade of searching, I had identified a lot in the *something real* category, but I still struggled to locate the heart of what didn't feel right. Gradually, though, I began to notice something that had been there all along, so obvious that I had missed it. To be a Christian – in the West at least, since the fifth or sixth century or so – has required us to believe that the Bible presents one very specific storyline, a storyline by which we assess all of history, all of human experience, all of our own experience. Most of us know the storyline implicitly, subconsciously, even though it has never been made explicit for us. We begin our quest for a new kind of Christian faith by questioning this storyline.

This unspoken storyline of the Bible that we were explicitly taught – or that we implicitly caught – could be shown in a diagram with six simple, elegant lines:

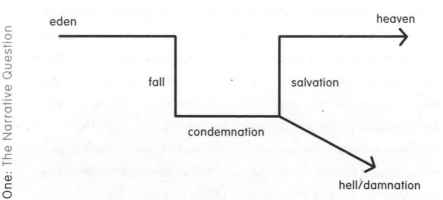

We start on the left with absolute perfection in the Garden of Eden. Then comes something called 'the fall into original sin' – 'the fall' and 'original sin' (like 'absolute perfection') being terms that are never found in the Bible, but are fundamental to Catholic and Protestant Christian faith as we know it. The bottom of the trough, in which we are now living, is a state we could call 'the fallen world', 'human history', or 'life on earth'. Next comes an ascending line, which we might call 'salvation', 'redemption', 'justification' or 'atonement' (depending on our tradition), leading us to the top line on the right, known as 'heaven' or 'eternity'.

Of course, for many people – perhaps the vast majority, according to some versions of this conventional storyline – the ending is not so happy. Instead, after everything they've suffered in this life, they face final damnation to hell, defined by most Western Christians as *eternal conscious torment*, supremely chilling words in spite of the fiery imagery they evoke. Few of us acknowledge that this master-narrative starts with one category of things, good and blessed, and then ends up with two categories of things, good and blessed on the top line and evil and tormented on the bottom. Might we dare to ask if this story can be reduced to a manufacturing process, producing a finished product of blessed souls on the top line, with a damned unfortunate by product on the bottom line? Could this be the story of a sorting and shipping process, the purpose of which is to deliver souls into their appropriate eternal bin? Can we dare to wonder, given an ending that has more evil and suffering than the beginning, if it would have been better for this story never to have begun?

In recent years, hundreds – probably thousands – of writers, pastors and thinkers have dared to tweak various elements or lines in this story, myself among them. We might question conventional theories of atonement, or the nature and popu-lation of hell, or whether concepts like *original sin* or *total depravity* need to be modified. In other words, we suggest that this line should be a little longer, that one a little shorter. But seldom do we question whether this shape is morally believable, and whether it can be found in the Bible itself. Did Abraham hold it, or Moses, or Jeremiah, or Jesus, Paul, or James? Is it ever explicitly taught in Scripture? Was it held in the first three centuries of Christian history? Does it help make sense of the Bible, revealing more than it conceals? Does it contribute to a higher vision of God, a deeper engagement with Christ, a more profound experience of the Holy Spirit? Does it motivate us to love God, neighbour, stranger and enemy more whole-heartedly?

It dawned on me only gradually that the answer to each of the above questions was 'No'. Up until that point, this narrative shape had been like my glasses, through which I saw everything but of which I was largely unconscious nearly all the time. That answer, 'No', appeared like a deep scratch on my glasses and it annoyed me no end. Increasing numbers of us share the feeling that our theological lens is scratched. That's why this quest begins not by tweaking details of the conventional six-line narrative, but by calling the entire narrative scheme into question. We do not for a second say, 'These six lines present the true shape of the biblical narrative, but we reject it.' Rather, we stare at this narrative, scratch our heads and, with a bewildered look, ask, 'How in the world, how in God's name, could anyone ever think this is the narrative of the Bible?'

One day a few years ago, during a Q&A session after a lecture, someone asked me a question that related to the shape of the biblical narrative. As I answered, it dawned on me that there are two ways to read the Bible, frontwards and backwards. Quite spontaneously, I invited seven people to come forward to help me illustrate my point. I stood them in a line, facing left, and then assigned each of them a name:

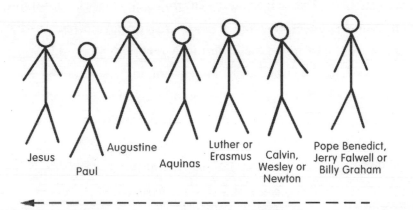

Then I said, 'When we look backwards to Jesus in this way, we aren't directly seeing Jesus. We're seeing Paul's view of Jesus, and then Augustine's view of Paul's view of Jesus, and then Aquinas' view of Augustine's view of Paul's view of Jesus,' and so on. Then I took Jesus and moved him to the right side of the room, faced him towards the right, and renamed the group like this:

For a minute or so, I didn't say anything, and gradually I think those present began to see what I had just seen. If we locate Jesus primarily in the light of the story that has unfolded since his time on earth, we will understand him in one way. But if we see him emerging from within a story that had been unfolding through his ancestors, and if we primarily locate him in that story, we might understand him in a very different way.

Once I had acknowledged (albeit roughly and crudely) these two very different ways of understanding Jesus, and once I had acknowledged that nobody in the Hebrew Scriptures ever talked about original sin, total depravity, 'the fall', or eternal conscious torment in hell, a suspicion began to grow in me about where the six-line narrative might possibly have come from. I was able to articulate it a few months later in a conversation with a friend, as I recounted my little exercise in setting up the backward and frontward lines of sight to see Jesus: 'What we call the biblical storyline isn't the shape of the story of Adam, Abraham and their Jewish descendants. It's the shape of the Greek philosophical narrative that Plato taught! That's the descent into Plato's cave of illusion and the ascent into philosophical enlightenment.' Some time after that, in another conversation with another friend, I realised that it was also the social and political narrative of the Roman Empire, and so I began calling it *the Greco-Roman narrative*.[1]

What we call Western civilisation is the project that grew from a marriage between the Greek philosophical tradition and the Roman political, economic and military empire.[2] Greek philosophy was energised by a seminal argument between Plato and Aristotle.[3] Plato was a complex genius from the fourth/fifth century BC whose work can be read in widely differing ways, but the interpretation of Plato by Plotinus (another complex genius, of the third century AD, known as a father of Neo-Platonism) eventually became dominant in the Greco-Roman tradition.

According to Plotinus, Plato taught that ultimate reality was non-material, eternal and unchanging. The material, temporal and changing objects of this world, in this view, are a shadow, an illusion, like an image projected on a screen or a shadow cast on the wall of a dark cave. The realities that projected the images or cast the shadows were abstractions, conceptions, ideals. (Plato called them *forms*, but that term often confuses contemporary readers. *Conceptual models* or *archetypes* or *essences* may serve as rough correlations, if not as synonyms.) So, behind the frail world of material chairs is a sturdy ideal called 'chairness', and behind fragile skin-and-bone women and men are robust immaterial realities called 'maleness', 'femaleness', 'personhood', 'soul' and so on. Ultimate reality, then, is non-material, and material things are shadows or manifestations of 'the Non-material and Unchanging Real'.[4]

Plato's student Aristotle tried looking at the world from the opposite perspective, as students often do.[5] 'No,' Aristotle might say, 'what is real is the changing material world of furniture for sitting, and *chair* is just an unchanging word or name we put on those objects. What is real is that flesh-and-blood man Joe over there and that smiling woman Sue over there and millions more like them. *Humanity* or *woman* or *man* are just words or names – mere puffs of air – concepts or constructs we impose on those specific, constantly changing physical beings.' So reality is a collection of material things and, as such, it is inherently changeable. Joe gets old, Sue gets pregnant, the chair gets broken, the dog gets sick and then better and then dies.

So you can see why Plato-via-Plotinus' followers would say, 'Ultimate reality is non-material Being,' and Aristotle's followers would say, 'We beg to differ. Ultimate reality is material Becoming,' to which Plato's followers would respond, 'We believe it is changeless, and change is an illusion,' to which Aristotle's followers would reply, 'Wrong again. It is constantly changing, and changelessness is simply an idea or mental construction, not a reality.' Plato would point upward and say, 'Can't you see? It is the higher transcendent ideal that is real. All this stuff down here is mere illusion or appearance.' Then Aristotle would point to the earth and say, 'Can't you see? There is no chairness around us, nor is there maleness nor femaleness nor dogness. But we are surrounded by chairs, men, women and dogs. These things are reality. Your higher transcendent ideals are less real than the material things that surround us.'[6] This argument animated the Greeks and later the Romans, who assimilated and adopted Greek culture, creating the Greco-Roman culture.

This Greek philosophical mindset affected the Roman mind in at least three profound and history-changing ways. First, the Greco-Roman mind was habitually dualistic, which means that an enlightened or philosophic mind would always see the world divided in two: the profane physical world of matter, stuff and change on the low side, and the sacred metaphysical world of ideals, ideas, spirit and changelessness on the high side. The categories of dualism might change (morphing into capitalist versus communist, or left versus right, or conservative versus liberal, for example), but the dualistic outlook itself remains consistent.

Second, this argument infused the Greco-Roman world with a peculiar energy and confidence – so strong that we might even call it *superiority* or *supremacy*. Through their Aristotelian resources, the Greco-Roman culture attended carefully to the physical world and achieved amazing feats of engineering: cities, temples, road systems, fleets, aqueducts and other advancements in which they could take great pride. Through their Platonic resources, the Greco-Romans pioneered what we might call the life of the mind. Their intellectual achievements armed them with an astonishing confidence that their enlightened or 'philosophic' human minds could uniquely grasp the absolute, transcendent, universal truth. As a result, the Greco-Roman mind became highly certain of its own superiority. *Others have their messy 'barbarian' viewpoints and superstitions*, the Greco-Roman mind might muse, *but we have the clean and clear perspective, the absolute, objective 'philosophic' truth.*[7] *They depend on their brute physical senses for knowledge*, they might add, *but we depend on pure reason.*

Third, this philosophical dualism and intellectual superiority fused in a corresponding social dualism and superiority. The Greco-Roman mind epitomised an us/them, in-group/out-group society, where 'we' are civilised and superior, and the rest of the world is barbarian and inferior. To the Greco-Roman mind, the story of the Roman Empire represents the real plotline of history, and every other culture has value only in what it contributes to Greco-Romanism.[8] To illustrate, imagine that each culture conceives of its own historical timeline, creating a messy tangle like this:[9]

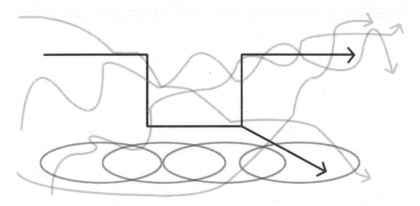

But then imagine that we render them all invisible and insignificant by focusing only on one timeline: our six-line Greco-Roman version, in bold. At that moment, we have effectively marginalised all other cultures to the level of an annoying sideshow – *in the way* of the only past, present and future that really matter, namely, *our own*.[10]

It's hard to overestimate the power of this social dualism. (It's also hard for those of us who inherited it to even see it, or imagine seeing without it.) The Greco-Roman dream was to create a high society of philosophical enlightenment and material prosperity, characterised by stasis and order, the *Pax Romana* (or Roman peace) being a social approximation of an ideal society in a Platonic sense.[11] In contrast, the barbarian nations were bumbling along on the lower level, their lives tragically excluded from the noble plane of Greco-Roman civilisation. Even within the Empire, it was only Roman citizens who really counted: the dualism between free citizens and slaves mirrored the dualism between Roman and barbarian.

The Jews, by the way, were barbarians in this scenario, as were the Christians until they managed to construct an identity first as a 'third race' (a concept articulated by early theologians like Aristides, Tertullian and others) and later as holders of the 'true philosophy' to which the Greeks had always aspired (especially in the writings of Clement).[12] The Jews themselves also had a binary social outlook, dividing the world between the circumcised Jewish *us* and the uncircumcised Gentile *them*, but their outlook was rarely imperial. Yes, they believed they were called by God to bless all nations and be respected by all nations, but they seldom if ever aspired to rule all nations in a Roman way. They (at their best) acknowledged the right of other nations to have their own languages and customs and even religions: they just didn't want to assimilate into or be assimilated by those other Gentile cultures.

Coming back to our narrative diagram, I believe the Christian religion in the West, as it habitually read the Bible backwards through the lenses of later Christians, largely lost track of the frontwards storyline of Adam, Abraham, Moses, etc., within which Jesus had emerged. It unwittingly traded its true heritage through Jesus from Judaism for an alien heritage drawn from Greek philosophy and Roman politics.[13] Through this profound and unconscious syncretism (or mixing of sources), biblical data was reframed by the Greco-Roman narrative, which could be rendered like this:

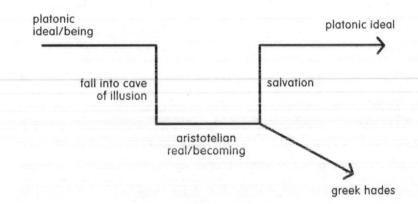

In this way, the Greco-Roman mind transforms the Garden of Eden from its original earthy stuff into a transcendent Platonic ideal. It is no longer a *good* Jewish garden; it is a *perfect* Platonic, Greco-Roman garden. In this perfect Platonic garden nothing ever changes, because in perfection the only change can be for the worse. This changelessness means that the Platonic Eden is a *state*, not a *story*: a state of perfect innocence. Framed this way, the fall into sin, it turns out, isn't simply a move from innocence to experience, or even obedience to disobedience. As Adam and Eve disobey the 'don't eat fruit from that tree' rule that maintains them in their state of innocent perfection, they plunge from state to story, from being into becoming, from Plato's world into Aristotle's world . . . and from the absolute light of day into the relative darkness of a cave, to conjure up Plato's most famous parable.[14]

So what Western theologians call 'The Fall' (often capitalised to show its transcendent importance) isn't simply a matter of human beings becoming less innocent or obedient, because *becoming* is the one thing that can't happen in a Platonic world. The fall utterly transforms all of creation from something at perfect Platonic stasis and rest to something in Aristotelian change and motion, from something changeless to something changeable, from something perfect/static/pristine to something imperfect/dynamic/decaying. The fall, conceived in this way, is an utterly radical change in being.

The new condition is no longer an ideal state in the Platonic sense. It is, rather, a deplorable shift in status. A philosopher might say it is an *ontological* fall, which is to say that the universe has failed to maintain perfection. It has dropped out of its pristine Platonic state. It has hurled itself down, down, down into the cave, into the dark, damp, changeable, shifty, non-absolute story of Aristotelian becoming.

Now the god of this Greco-Roman version of the biblical story bears a strange similarity in many ways to Zeus (Jupiter for the Romans), but we will name him *Theos*. The Greco-Roman god Theos, I suggest, is a far different deity from the Jewish *Elohim* of Genesis 1, or *Lord* (referring to the unspeakable name of the Creator) of Genesis 2 and 12, not to mention the *Abba* to whom Jesus prayed. As a good – no, make that *perfect* – Platonic god, Theos loves spirit, state and being and hates matter, story and becoming, since once again the latter involve change, and the only way to change or move from perfection is downward into decay. In fact, as soon as something drops out of the state of perfection, Theos is possessed by a pure and irresistible urge to destroy it.

So, having created a perfect world, now Theos is perfectly furious because it has been spoiled and is decaying. It has fallen from its high table of perfection and is shattered on the floor. It has dropped out of its alma mater, Ideal State Secondary School, and is hanging out smoking cigarettes on the street corner with Aristotle and his gang of tattooed thugs and crooks telling and participating in (swallow hard here) *stories*, unpredictable stories, unscripted stories, unsanitised stories, in which things happen, which is something that should never occur in the world of Theos.

What we call *history* is this tragic thrashing about in the Aristotelian real, where (shudder) things keep happening and (gulp) changing. Theos stands above, holding his thunderbolts ready to strike, ready to melt the whole damned thing down to primal lava, ready to set it all on fire to purge all that is imperfect so that only perfect purified being remains. Every person born into this creation begins in this deplorable fallen status, according to conventional Christian theology. Every time we use terms like *the fall* and *original sin*, I believe, many of us are unknowingly importing more or less of this package of Greco-Roman, non-Jewish and therefore non-biblical concepts, like smugglers bringing foreign currency into the biblical economy, or tourists introducing invasive species into the biblical ecosystem.[15]

In the Greco-Roman telling of the story, salvation (which in this version of the story is virtually equivalent to atonement, justification or redemption) means Theos finding a way to forgive this fallen, dropout, broken creation for its lapse from perfect holy being into pathetic, detestable becoming. Various theories explain how this forgiveness is brought about, but each involves lifting back into a perfect forgiven or justified state what has fallen into this festering cesspool of change and decay. On an unconscious level, being forgiven, being saved, being born again and being justified mean being rescued from the sad story of Aristotelian becoming and restored to the high, timeless plane of perfect Platonic being, so the creatures in question can be loved by Theos again.[16] When Theos liberates them from the fatally flawed and absolutely unsalvageable Aristotelian universe – of which their bodies are a part – their essence, the ideal Platonic abstraction of them called *soul* or *spirit*, will enjoy perfect peace, perfect rest, perfect status, perfect, unending and unchanging (of course) joy in heaven. As the old tombstones used to say, in heaven they will rest in peace. They will be delivered from this world of stories to an eternal state where they will be safe for ever, for nothing will ever happen again.[17]

What happens to those who are not saved, justified, atoned for, or otherwise redeemed? Theos can't permit or command their essence to be extinguished, because that essence is spirit rather than flesh and therefore incurably immortal. Nor can Theos permit the universe to continue for much longer, because the whole thing, after all, is fallen and now reeks of Aristotelian becoming, a.k.a. decay, and that rotting smell is inherently detestable to Theos, Greco-Roman Neo-Platonist that he is. Theos has no choice, really: this tainted universe and all it contains must be destroyed, which will leave the eternal essences of the unredeemed all undressed with no place to go. So they are banished to hell – the Greek Hades, intensified and decorated with plenty of borrowings from its Zoroastrian counterpart, and seasoned liberally with imagery misappropriated from Jesus' parables and sermons.[18] And what is hell? It must be a state, since no story can ever exist in a universe purged of change and becoming. That's why nobody can ever repent and leave it: there is a sign saying 'DESPAIR ALL WHO ENTER HERE: NO BECOMING ALLOWED' over its infernal, eternally locked gates.

What remains in the end? Theos, plus the perfected souls of the redeemed in heaven, plus everyone else suffering the absolute, 'perfect' torment of eternal, unquenchable, pure and unchanging hate from Theos, getting what they deserve for being part of the detestable fallen universe.

This is – more or less, and put baldly the 'good news' taught by much of the Western Christian religion (not all of it, thank God), the religion in which I was raised, in which I have done my life's work, of which I am a part today. True, it could be worse: there could be even fewer in heaven and even more in hell. True, it is seldom put this crudely. True, its defenders will quarrel with various details here, because their version, no doubt, tries to avoid being this starkly dismal. But even those who quarrel have to admit that this version, or something very close to it, keeps popping up in Church history – if not in their back yard, then in somebody else's. Much of the energy of Christian theology, I propose, seeks to save this story from being as barbarous and hideous as it wants to be because of the Greco-Roman lines of thinking that determine its shape.

So theologians and pastors – I know, because I have done this – sew a patch on here, cover up that bit over there with some duct tape, put a nice coat of cheerful paint on that section over there, play really uplifting music to distract from that bit under there, move the furniture so that part doesn't show, and so on. They can only be thanked for their hard labour in this regard, and congratulated for their noble effort, and encouraged to keep up the good work.

But more and more of us are defecting from the project of cosmetically enhancing this story and trying to rehabilitate the image of Theos. We want to try reading the Bible frontwards for a while, to let it be a Jewish story that, through Jesus, opens to include all humanity. We believe it is time to escort the Greco-Roman reframing of the biblical narrative firmly to the door and seek what master-songwriter Michael Kelly Blanchard called 'the other God' – the God of Abraham, Isaac and Jacob, not the god of the Greek philosophers and Roman potentates.[19] Or, perhaps better said, it is time for us to exit the Greco-Roman narrative – to walk quietly and courageously out of the door and leave its six straight lines behind, in search of the Jewish story in which Jesus would have found himself, and in search of the One Jesus called 'Our Father'.

CHAPTER 5

Setting the Stage for the Biblical Narrative

When I began losing faith in the six-line narrative, when I started trying to read the Bible frontwards rather than backwards, I began to feel an exhilarating sense of relief and hope: *Maybe I can believe and be excited about the biblical story again, but in a new way.* But it's not easy to undo many years of training, or to see the Bible with fresh eyes, and the process took several years – and it is still ongoing, actually. Fortunately for me as a Christian, I could consult Jewish friends and authors to rediscover a frontwards reading. And I could learn from Christian scholars who were engaged in a similar project, although each with his or her own emphasis – Protestants like Walter Brueggemann, N. T. Wright, Marcus Borg, Ched Myers, William Herzog, Rita Brock and James Cone, and Catholics like Dominic Crossan, Leonardo Boff, Jon Sobrino, Gustavo Gutierrez, Richard Rohr, Joan Chittister and others.

So I went back and tried to adjust my sightline, not backwards through Calvin, Luther, Aquinas and Augustine to Jesus, but forwards through Abraham, Moses, David and the prophets to Jesus. In particular, I immersed myself in the first two books of the Bible, Genesis and Exodus, and the writings of the prophets, especially Isaiah.[1]

As I allowed Genesis, Exodus and Isaiah – rather than Plato, Aristotle and Caesar – to set the stage for the biblical narrative, what emerged dazzled me: a beautiful, powerful, gritty story that resonates with, gives meaning to, and continues to unfold in the life and teaching of Jesus. And this story invites our participation as well, not as pawns on squares on a cosmic chessboard, but as creative protagonists and junior partners with God in the story of creation.

This story begins with something better than the perfect realm of Plato: the good world of Genesis. Jewish *goodness*, it turns out, is far better than Greco-Roman *perfection*.[2] As we've seen, perfection in the Greco-Roman sense of the word is inherently stale and sterile, since nothing in it can change except for the worse. But Genesis does not begin with stasis and sterility. From the first 'Let there be . . .' it glows, whirls, swirls, vibrates, pulses and dances with change and fertility. It seems far closer to the Aristotelian world of becoming than to the Platonic plane of being. And Elohim, unlike Theos, doesn't pronounce this world perfect (or imperfect), but rather *good* – *very good*, in fact. (Even the idea of *very* applied to *good* suggests a world marked not by absolute perfection, but by relative goodness.)

For starters, this very good world has a beginning, which suggests a change from before the beginning. And this beginning is not complete: it unfolds in stages, with the first stage being a formless, uninhabited expanse. Into this expanse, light shines and sun and moon take shape. Seas are created and divided from land. Gradually, plant life emerges, then animal life, then human life. None of it is perfect in the Greco-Roman sense.[3] Instead, all of it is good and wonderful, constantly evolving into something even better and more wonderful.[4]

If it were perfect – in the Greco-Roman sense – the earth would have come into being fully populated, fully 'developed'.[5] But this creation has plenty of room for reproduction and development. A perfect world would have come into being complete with names, but each creature remains nameless until Adam names it. All that we call human culture also waits to be created in this good world – music, science, art, architecture, agriculture, engineering, even theology. These things will be created not by God, but by humans who, as image-bearers of the Creator, are themselves creative.[6]

Although this evolving creation-in-process would be appalling to Theos, it is delightful to Elohim, because Elohim, unlike Theos, loves stories and seems to have little taste for states. And Elohim's story is not a 'safe', predictable story, but rather a story with unpredictability and danger written into its first chapters. There, even chaos, barrenness and darkness have a place, first in the *tohu bohu* (formless and void) of Genesis 1:2, then in a limited but real presence in the seas, and finally in the tempting presence of a tree of knowledge of good and evil, the tree itself being part of the goodness of the primal garden.

We have been so thoroughly trained – can I say *brainwashed?* – to read Genesis through Greco-Roman bifocals and, as a result, Theos is so deeply embedded and enthroned in our minds that it is agonisingly difficult for us to recapture the wild, dynamic, story-unleashing goodness of Elohim, a goodness that differs so starkly, so radically, from the domesticated, static, controlled perfection of Theos. The difference multiplies as we come to the passage traditionally defined as 'the fall'.

It is patently obvious to me that these stories aren't intended to be taken literally, although it wasn't always so obvious, and I know it won't be so now for some of my readers. It is also powerfully clear to me that these non-literal stories are still to be taken seriously and mined for their rich meaning, because they distil time-tested, multilayered wisdom – through deep mythic language – about how our world came to be what it has become. They're intended, as all sacred creation narratives are, to situate and orientate us in a story so we will know how to live. But, again, that story does not happen at the bottom of our six-line diagram. It is not a tragic story of a fall from Platonic perfection, because the biblical story does not unfold in Theos's world at all. Instead, we must remember again, it is the story of Elohim in Elohim's world.[7]

In this world, there is not one isolated moment of ontological shift from state to story: it's all story from beginning to end, and likely before and after as well.[8] God doesn't respond to a loss of perfect status with a furious promise of eternal condemnation, damnation and destruction. God doesn't pronounce the perfect state ruined and the planet destined for geocide. The experiment is not a failure. All of these conventional conclusions flow from the Greco-Roman assumptions and biases with which the story has been read and taught for centuries. Take away those Theos-ological assumptions, and the story unfolds very differently.

Elohim's story, it seems to me, unfolds as a kind of compassionate coming-of-age story. Imagine that a father has a daughter whom he loves with all his heart. When she comes of age, Dad gives her a beautiful sports car. Dad tells her to drive safely and stay in her lane, but soon she crashes into a tree and writes off her vehicle. Dad gives her a stern lecture and, a few months later, replaces the sports car with a modest economy car, more of a starter car, you might say. Then she takes her new economy vehicle off-road and gets stuck in a muddy field. Dad pulls her out and requires her to take a refresher driving course before she can drive again. She finishes the course and then, a few weeks later, she speeds around a corner, recklessly loses control and drives herself into a river, and the economy car is ruined. At this point, Dad decides she isn't ready for a car and gives her a bicycle instead. Then she crashes her bike into a tower and breaks her arm. Dad again comes to the rescue and rushes her to the hospital.[9] In each case, what does the father do in response to his daughter's foolishness? Disown her? Lock her in a dungeon? Condemn her to eternal conscious torment? Not even close![10]

The protagonist of Genesis patiently bears with a rebellious and foolish humanity again and again. Consider how the Genesis story actually goes.

Scene 1. God tells Adam and Eve that they are free (this is a primary condition of their existence, 2:16), with one exception. If they eat of one specific tree, on the day they eat, they will die. Notice: the text does not say they will be condemned to hell, 'spiritually separated from God', pronounced 'fallen' or 'condemned', or tainted with something called 'original sin' that will be passed on to their children. There is only one consequence indicated by the text: they will die – not spiritually die, not relationally die, not ontologically die, but simply die; and not die *eventually*, but die *on the day* they eat. (Few commentators seem to take this seemingly significant detail of the text into account.)

Scene 2. What do they do? They abuse their freedom and eat of the one forbidden tree. And what does God do? Does he inflict immediate capital punishment on that very day as promised? No. God not only doesn't kill them, but he makes clothes for them, mercifully shielding them from their shame at being naked in one another's presence. God does let them suffer consequences for their behaviour, but not lethal ones. God pushes them out of the nest, the garden in which they have lived. Now they must go from being hunter-gatherers in a beautiful garden to being agriculturalists who must struggle with thorns and thistles to produce food by the sweat of their brow, entering into the harsh realities of marital and family struggle in a tougher world, out of the garden, east of Eden. Having tasted of the tree of the knowledge of good and evil, they will no longer have access to the tree of life, meaning they will someday return to the dust from which they were originally created.

That's the first crash, and the biblical text never even hints that it entails an 'ontological fall' from Platonic being and transcendent state down into Aristotelian becoming and debased story. Rather, it is the first stage of *ascent* as human beings progress from the life of hunter-gatherers to the life of agriculturalists and beyond. Their journey could be pictured like this:

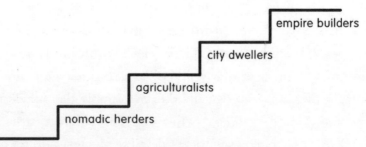

empire builders

city dwellers

agriculturalists

nomadic herders

hunter/gatherers

But the ascent is ironic, because with each gain, humans also *descend into loss*. They descend (or *fall* – there's nothing wrong with the word itself, just with the unrecognised baggage that may come with it) from the primal innocence of being naked without shame in one another's presence. They lose their fearlessness in relation to God. They cross a developmental threshold, leaving behind an original garden that can never be re-entered. Their departure is truly ambivalent, because although it is the result of the disobeying of one command (don't eat from the forbidden tree), it results in obedience to a former command which never could have been obeyed from within the garden (be fruitful, multiply, fill and subdue the earth). This is a classic coming-of-age story, filled with ambivalence – a childhood lost, an adulthood gained. So the human journey could equally be seen as a tragic descent into evil, in increasing complexity and severity:

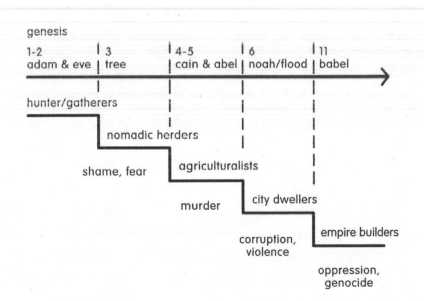

Each step of socio-economic and technological ascent thus makes possible new depths of moral evil and social injustice. (The story can yield insights for an individual reading as well as a social reading, with the garden of childhood giving way to the gains and losses of adolescence, adulthood and old age.)

Scene 3. As the story continues east of Eden, the ex-hunter-gatherers have two boys, the younger (more 'primitive'?) Abel a nomadic herder and the older (more 'advanced'?) Cain a settled farmer. If the first crash episode tells us about the losses associated with ascent to an agricultural life, this episode tells us of the struggle between two forms of life outside the garden. We have moved from garden to field, a landscape tilled and planted by Cain. Abel's simpler life, it seems, is more acceptable to God, perhaps because nomadic life is not as morally compromised as settled farm life, with its fenced-in privately owned lands, accumulating possessions, violent seizure and defence, and related moral entanglements. So Cain's face grows dark in anger. What does God do to avert yet more evil in the world? This time, God doesn't threaten Cain with immediate capital punishment, as was done with Cain's parents; this time God sternly warns Cain that sin is crouching at the door and Cain must master his angry impulses.

Scene 4. What does Cain do? Just as his parents violated God's command, Cain ignores God's counsel, gives way to seething anger, and invites Abel into the field. The tilled landscape now becomes a crime scene. The very land that Cain has tilled now cries out with Abel's blood. What does God do in response? Again, God doesn't kill Cain, nor does God condemn him to eternal conscious torment in hell, nor does God tell him to make penance. Instead, God ejects Cain from his farm, just as Cain's parents had been ejected from their garden. Cain will have to be a restless wanderer – perhaps regressing to the state of a nomadic herder like Abel, or perhaps to the state of a hunter-gatherer like his parents once were.

Cain sees this as a cruel and unusual consequence: 'This punishment is more than I can bear,' he says. Landless and wandering, Cain fears he will be vulnerable to murder, just as his brother Abel had been. So what does God do? Just as God mercifully provided the disobedient and ashamed Adam and Eve with clothing to cover their nakedness, God protects Cain from being murdered by other landholders on whose property he might trespass. Now, representing humanity doubly expelled from the garden and the farm, the murderer Cain builds a city (4:18). The ironic ascent continues in the aftermath of the second crash.

Scene 5. Humanity, now distanced from both garden and farm, congregates in cities. Cities multiply and the habitual inclinations of the human mind and heart deteriorate all the more, becoming 'only evil all the time'. On the mean streets of human cities, human lives have collided in another moral crash. So God looks at what urbanised humanity has become – 'corrupt . . . and full of violence' – and God's heart is 'filled with pain'. God regrets the whole project and decides to wipe out everything.[11] But then God notices Noah. The pattern we have seen repeats itself again here. God refuses to let evil go unchallenged (you shall die that day, you will be a restless wanderer, I will destroy everything), but then God acts with surprising mercy (God lets the first couple live, God protects Cain from being treated as he treated his brother, God protects Noah and company).

What happens after Noah's long cruise? God seems to

recommence creation afresh, repeating the 'be fruitful and multiply . . . fill the earth' command as at the original creation. And God 'repents' of destroying the earth (as he had done with Adam and Eve in refraining from inflicting the promised capital punishment, and then with Cain in protecting him from the full consequences of his fratricide), and then vows to be faithful to humanity even though 'every inclination of his heart is evil from childhood'.

Scenes 6 and following. These patterns repeat themselves as Noah's family leaves the Ark. Noah drives drunk and creates another crash in which his sons are injured. God remains faithful. Then Noah's descendants decide to build a massive tower – using the newest brick-and-mortar technology – evocative of the next step in our ironic ascent from hunter-gatherers to nomadic herders to settled farmers to city dwellers to empire builders. And there's another crash, as their empire rises in prideful confidence and then collapses in misunderstanding and conflict, its various tribes divided through different languages. Again, God remains faithful.

Finally, after eleven chapters, this repeated pattern of human stupidity and divine fidelity opens into something new. God calls Abraham and Sarah and imbues them with a new identity: the father and mother of a nation who will be blessed in order to bring blessing to all nations. It is absolutely essential to notice what God is doing: not damning and rejecting all nations and exempting one from damnation, not hating all nations and loving one, not privileging one superior nation to conquer and rule all others, but blessing all nations through one, choosing one to bring benefit to all. This is not the Greco-Roman story!

Genesis ends with the story of Abraham's great-grandson Joseph, and Joseph's life plays out this calling of Abraham. Joseph's brothers show that they – like Adam and Eve, like Cain, like the city dwellers before the flood, like the builders of Babel – have developed a taste for the fruit of the tree of the knowledge of good and evil.[12] Like Cain before them, they want to kill their brother Joseph, but end up selling him into slavery instead. In spite of their evil intent, and in spite of a host of other characters who similarly betray and fail Joseph, God proves faithful. God eventually 'blesses' Joseph with a position of power in Egypt, where Joseph ultimately becomes a blessing first to the Egyptians and then to the very brothers who had betrayed him, forgoing revenge and saving their lives.[13]

God is faithful to Joseph, and through Joseph, God is gracious to Egypt, and through Joseph, God is even gracious to Joseph's wicked Cain-like brothers. Joseph is blessed, not to the exclusion of anyone, but for the blessing of everyone. Blessing triumphs. Goodness triumphs. God triumphs. And in the end, God provides something better than 'the knowledge of good and evil' offered by the serpent: just as God had brought light from darkness and order from chaos and life from barrenness, God now creates a good outcome from the evil intentions of Joseph's brothers. Through Joseph's willingness to forgive and forgo revenge, God overcomes evil with good.[14]

If Genesis sets the stage for the biblical narrative, this much is unmistakably clear: God's unfolding drama is not a narrative shaped by the six Greco-Roman lines of perfection, fall, condemnation, redemption, heavenly perfection and eternal perdition. It has a different storyline entirely. It's a story about the downside of 'progress' – a story of human foolishness and God's faithfulness, the human turn towards rebellion and God's turn towards reconciliation, the human intention towards evil and God's intention to overcome evil with good. It begins with God creating a good world, continues with human beings creating evil, and concludes with God creating good outcomes that overcome human evil. We might say it is the story of goodness being created and re-created: God creates a good world which humans damage and savage, but though humans have evil intent, God still creates good and God's good prevails. Good has the first word, and good has the last.

Not only does the shape of this Genesis narrative have little or nothing in common with the six-line Greco-Roman narrative, but the character named God in this story has little or nothing in common with the Greek Theos. The difference only intensifies as we consider the two remaining primary narratives of the Bible.

CHAPTER 6

The Biblical Narrative in Three Dimensions

Throughout my quest for a new kind of Christianity, I've had what seems to me (some won't agree!) an accidental advantage working for me: I wasn't formally trained in theology. Now I love theology, and I read it constantly and with great pleasure (unlike many of my college-trained friends, who seem to have exceeded their saturation point while they were students). My background was in the liberal arts, and especially in the study of English language and literature. My training taught me to read for scenes and plots, not doctrines; for protagonists and antagonists, not absolute and objective truths; for character development and conflict resolution, not raw material to be processed into a system of beliefs; for resonances and common patterns among many texts and traditions, not merely for uniqueness or superiority of one text or tradition; for multiple layers of interpretation, not merely one sanctioned one. When I was at university, the practice of 'deconstruction' was in its ascendancy, providing me with yet another advantage as I have pursued this quest. Deconstruction is not destruction (as many erroneously assume), but rather careful and loving attention to the construction of ideas, beliefs, systems, values and cultures.

When you approach the Bible literarily, aided by these kinds of advantages, the Genesis narrative sets the stage for what follows. As we've seen, it's the story of a good creation, marred by expanding human evil, countered by divine faithfulness, leading to profound reconciliation and healing. This narrative serves as a kind of fractal for the story as a whole and for its many parts. But Genesis is, in many ways, not the main story of the Hebrew Scriptures. It is more like a prequel to the prime or paradigmatic narrative: *Episode 1* in relation to *Star Wars*, if you will, or *The Hobbit* in relation to *Lord of the Rings*. That prime narrative comes to us in the book of Exodus. If Genesis is a story of sacred creation and reconciliation, Exodus is a story of sacred liberation and formation.

Exodus begins in pain. A new king has come to power in Egypt, and he has forgotten the good relationship Joseph had forged with his predecessor many generations earlier. Meanwhile, the Jewish people have proved very fertile. Their population explosion frightens the new king: the Jews might, if a war were to break out, side with Egypt's enemies. So Pharaoh decides to crack down and reduce the Jews to slavery, using them to build Egyptian storage cities so they will increase Egypt's security rather than threaten it. The Egyptians, we are told (Exod. 1:8–14), made the lives of the Jewish people 'bitter with harsh labour in brick and mortar and with all kinds of work in the fields; in all their harsh labour the Egyptians used them ruthlessly'.

Anyone who has been orientated to the biblical story in the

book of Genesis immediately hears bells ringing: harsh labour . . . brick and mortar . . . the fields. In Genesis, hunter-gatherers (Adam and Eve) were ejected from their original garden. In their life as agriculturalists 'east of Eden', they would work *the fields* with *harsh labour*. Then, when agriculturalists (like Cain) were driven from farm life to city life because of their violence, they eventually began building an empire (called Babel) of *brick and mortar* – exactly the kind of empire that in Genesis filled God's heart with pain because it was 'filled with evil continually'.

So, here again, human beings are toiling in the fields, lugging bricks and mortar, increasingly oppressed by an increasingly paranoid Egyptian despot. But the oppressed workers continue to 'be fruitful and multiply' in spite of their oppression, so Pharaoh resorts to genocide, mandating first that the Jewish midwives kill all newborn boys, and then mandating all Jews to throw their newborn sons into the Nile. This dark command is nothing less than a repudiation of Genesis – a command to kill rather than give life, to destroy rather than save. It is a command that must be defied – and it is, first by Jewish midwives (who form the first primitive trade union and practise organised resistance to oppression and exploitation), and then by a single Jewish mother and her daughter. They conspire to place the baby in a small boat, reminiscent of the Ark. And so the future of the story of God and Abraham's descendants floats in a fragile ark of reeds, hangs in the breath of a fragile little baby, drifts on the perilous waters of the Nile.

Here again, just as in Genesis, God does not abandon humanity in its tragic story of injustice and oppression. Instead, God gets involved, siding with the oppressed, the vulnerable, the downtrodden, working as their ally for their liberation. First,

God calls Moses – that little baby who once floated on the Nile, now grown into a man in the prime of life – to be his mouth-piece. Moses tells the tyrant Pharaoh to let God's people go, but Pharaoh refuses. God responds with a firm but gentle consequence: a plague on the Nile River, which is the lifeblood of the civilisation. Ironically, perhaps through a red tide, the lifeblood Nile turns red like blood. The despot still doesn't relent, but hardens his heart. Then the Nile produces a plague of frogs, which are followed by gnats, flies, diseases and other unpleasantries. Each time, Pharaoh is invited to repent and liberate the captives, but each time, he hardens his heart. It's as if the land itself – or the universe itself – is turning against an unjust regime. Finally, when a plague takes the firstborn sons of the Egyptians so they experience exactly the grief they had been inflicting on their slaves, Pharaoh says, 'OK. You can go.'

Predictably, however, the tyrant then has liberator's remorse and leads his army in pursuit of the refugees to re-enslave them. His plan fails and his whole army is destroyed in the Red Sea. The people are liberated at last. We're skipping over a hundred fascinating – and at times troubling – details in this telling of the exodus, but the basic shape of the story is clear: God sides with the oppressed, and God confronts oppressors with intensifying negative consequences until they change their ways, and in the end the oppressors are humbled and the oppressed are liberated.

The story is striking in many ways. God is amazingly patient with Pharaoh (just as God had been with Cain, for example, in Genesis). God refuses to force compliance, but also refuses to tolerate injustice passively, persistently bringing the oppressor to repentance, temporary as that repentance proves to be.

Through it all, God never works directly, only indirectly – through Moses, through Aaron, through frogs, gnats, weather, diseases and other natural phenomena. The so-called supernatural, in this way, seems remarkably natural.[1]

The liberation from Pharaoh, however, takes up only the first half of Exodus – and in spite of the fact that Pharaoh is clearly the bad guy in the first half, the newly liberated people are hardly the good guys in the second half. Their grumbling and ingratitude in the second half seem to try God's patience almost as much as Pharaoh's hard-heartedness did in the first half. If the first half of Exodus is about liberation from external oppression, the second half (including the wilderness episodes recounted in the book of Numbers) is about liberation from internal oppression, the domination of human beings by fear, greed, impatience, ingratitude, and so on.

Another word for internal liberation is *formation*: through law and ritual and trial, God forms character and faith and dignity in a people who have been debased by generations of slavery. If Pharaoh's heart can be softened by only *ten demands* ('Let my people go!') followed by ten intensifying consequences of disobedience, the newly liberated slaves' hearts can be strengthened only by *ten commands* and by many episodes of trial and testing. Exodus thus exposes evil in both its social/systemic and its personal/individual dimensions – striking a balance that human beings still struggle to understand.

If the first narrative situates us in God's good, evolving world which has been marred and scarred by human evil, the second narrative situates us in humanity's oppressive, resistant world in which God is active as liberator – freeing us from external and internal oppression and forming us as the people of God. If the first narrative presents God as creator and faithful reconciler, the second presents God as liberator from external and internal oppression. But the Exodus narrative ends in motion, as it were, with 'To Be Continued . . .' on the last frame. The former slaves, now liberated, are on a journey, en route, in transit. Where will their journey lead? The third narrative gives the answer.

If Genesis is the prequel to Exodus, the third narrative is its sequel: the sacred dream of the peaceable kingdom. Its primal form brims with fertile images of a promised land flowing with milk and honey – a powerful vision for freed slaves travelling through barren wasteland (or later, for nostalgic refugees dreaming of home). It burns brightly, but briefly, in the glory of the reign of King David. But the dream, once it moves from imagination to experience, degenerates and leaves the dreamers unfulfilled.[2] Even so, the dream refuses to die, even as the descendants of Abraham live for many generations under a long list of failed regimes. Their nation is torn by civil war, sickened by corruption, threatened by a succession of powerful enemies and eventually conquered. Its brightest and best are carried away as exiles to Babylon. Even then, under the intense pressures of dislocation and assimilation, the dream doesn't die, but grows even more fervent.

In fact, during the exile, the dream of a peaceable kingdom becomes even more radical and all-encompassing. It now finds expression less in the language of *land or space* and more in terms of *a day or a time*. It morphs from a promised land to a promised time, the Day of the Lord, when oppressors will be overthrown, when corruption and infidelity will be replaced by virtue and integrity, and when the blessing, justice and *shalom* of God flow like a river and fill the earth as waters fill the oceans. The following rich collage of images, taken from Isaiah,

Joel, Hosea and Micah, deserves to be savoured slowly with
imagination fully engaged.[3]

> They will beat their swords into ploughshares
> and their spears into pruning hooks.
> Nation will not take up sword against nation,
> nor will they train for war any more.
> *(Isa. 2:4)*

> The wolf will live with the lamb,
> the leopard will lie down with the goat,
> the calf and the lion and the yearling together;
> and a little child will lead them.
> The cow will feed with the bear,
> their young will lie down together,
> and the lion will eat straw like the ox.
> Infants will play near the hole of the cobra;
> young children will put their hands into the viper's nest.
> They will neither harm nor destroy
> on all my holy mountain,
> for the earth will be filled with the knowledge of the LORD
> as the waters cover the sea.
> *(Isa. 11:6–9)*

> 'See, I will create
> new heavens and a new earth.
> The former things will not be remembered,
> nor will they come to mind.
> . . . I will rejoice over Jerusalem
> and take delight in my people;

the sound of weeping and of crying
will be heard in it no more.
Never again will there be in it
infants who live but a few days,
or older people who do not live out their years;
those who die at a hundred
will be thought mere youths;
those who fail to reach a hundred
will be considered accursed.
They will build houses and dwell in them;
they will plant vineyards and eat their fruit.
No longer will they build houses and others live in them,
or plant and others eat.
For as the days of a tree,
so will be the days of my people;
my chosen ones will long enjoy
the work of their hands.
They will not labour in vain,
nor will they bear children doomed to misfortune;
for they will be a people blessed by the LORD,
they and their descendants with them.
Before they call I will answer;
while they are still speaking I will hear.
The wolf and the lamb will feed together,
and the lion will eat straw like the ox,
but dust will be the serpent's food.
They will neither harm nor destroy
on all my holy mountain,'
says the LORD.
(Isa. 65:17–25)

Many nations will come and say,

'Come, let us go up to the mountain of the LORD,

to the house of the God of Jacob.

He will teach us his ways,

so that we may walk in his paths.'

The law will go out from Zion,

the word of the LORD from Jerusalem.

He will judge between many peoples

and will settle disputes for strong nations far and wide.

They will beat their swords into ploughshares

and their spears into pruning hooks.

Nation will not take up sword against nation,

nor will they train for war any more.

Everyone will sit under their own vine

and under their own fig-tree,

and no one will make them afraid,

for the LORD Almighty has spoken.

(Mic. 4:2–4)

Never again will my people be shamed . . .

I will pour out my Spirit on all people.

Your sons and daughters will prophesy,

your old men will dream dreams,

your young men will see visions.

Even on my servants, both men and women,

I will pour out my Spirit in those days.

(Joel 2:27–9)

In that day I will make a covenant for them

with the beasts of the field, the birds in the sky

and the creatures that move along the ground.

Bow and sword and battle

I will abolish from the land,

so that all may lie down in safety.

I will betroth you to me for ever;

I will betroth you in righteousness and justice,

in love and compassion.

(Hos. 2:18–19)

Many of us modern Christians, having been trained to read the Bible within the six-line Greco-Roman narrative, 'know' what to do with these passages. We push them into the distant future, beyond history as we know it, applying them (a) to heaven, or (b) to a literalist 'millennial' period, or (c) to a little bit of both. But what if we were to receive these images in a different way?

If we are people who live in the Genesis narrative of creation and reconciliation and the Exodus narrative of liberation and formation, what if we were to receive these images as a vision of the kind of future towards which God is inviting us in history? What if we saw them less as an eternal destination beyond history and more as a guiding star within it, less as a literal description and prediction and more as a promise and hope, less as a doctrine to be debated and more as an unquenchable dream that inspires us to unceasing constructive action? What if we saw them as a good future unfolding in time, not a perfect state beyond time?

If we take the third narrative in this way, we are immediately freed from arguments about a deterministic future (a subject to which we will return in our eighth question), because the future in this approach is waiting to be created, not fatalistically predetermined. God hasn't already pre-recorded history so that it waits like digital information on a disk, already 'made' but only being 'played' in real time. No, by taking this new approach, the narrative of the peaceable kingdom becomes the desired future towards which the people of God orientate themselves, the constellation they set course and sail by, the dream, goal, vision or imagination that they pursue. In this view, history and life are not pre-recorded: life is 'live'. History isn't a 'show' – not even a 'reality show'. History is unscripted, unrehearsed reality, happening now – really happening. (You might want to pinch yourself before reading on, and ask yourself if you really believe the previous sentence.)

As this approach relieves us of literalistic interpretations, it frees us to let the poetry work as poetry is supposed to. Swords into ploughshares: today that would mean dreaming about tanks being melted down into playground jungle gyms and machine-guns being recast as swing sets. Lions lying down with lambs: today that would mean Christians, Jews and Muslims throwing a picnic together, or left- and right-wingers forming a band and singing in harmony, or nuclear weapons engineers being redeployed to develop green energy. Children playing with cobras, centenarians seeming to be in the prime of life: that wouldn't suggest snake-handling in heaven or the need for bigger retirement funds, but rather a time of deep safety for vulnerable people, without gaps in the health-care system, so all can live a full life from childhood to senior citizenship. Everyone with a vine and fig tree: that wouldn't necessarily mean a literal return to an agricultural economy for everyone, but it would suggest full employment for all families everywhere, all having some secure place in a healthy, sustainable, regenerative economy. Men and women prophesying, the knowledge of the Lord covering the earth as water covers the ocean basin: that would mean a deep kind of universal and egalitarian spirituality, and so on.

There are foretastes of the dream coming true, of course, even though the dream itself always beckons and is never fully grasped. As we mentioned earlier, King David represents a move towards the peaceable kingdom. But even he, a man of war, disappoints in the end. Solomon's kingdom has a certain opulence and power, but in the end he tragically adopts the same totalitarian practices as Pharaoh's regime. Nehemiah and Ezra lead in a kind of echo-exodus, but even their return to the promised land, for all its joy, is fraught with partiality, ambiguity and disappointment. The temple is rebuilt, but its very existence evokes even greater dreams: that the Spirit of God would one day fill not just a temple, but the whole earth; that God's glory would not just be localised in one temple and one holy city, but that someday temples would be unnecessary because people in every city would walk in the light of the Lord, 24/7; that God would dwell not just within the stones of the temple, but within the hearts of all people. Ezekiel, among many others, tries to articulate this dream:

> I will give them an undivided heart and put a new spirit in them; I will remove from them their heart of stone and give them a heart of flesh. Then they will follow my decrees and be careful to keep my laws. They will be my people, and I will be their God.
> *(Ezek. 11:19–20)*

> I will sprinkle clean water on you, and you will be clean; I will cleanse you from all your impurities and from all your idols. I will give you a new heart and put a new spirit in you; I will

remove from you your heart of stone and give you a heart of flesh. And I will put my Spirit in you and move you to follow my decrees and be careful to keep my laws.
(*Ezek. 36:25–7*)

When God says, 'They will be my people, and I will be their God,' he proposes a relationship of mutual belonging and unity, like king and kingdom, husband and wife, parent and children, head and body. In mutual, unifying relationships, each refers to the other as 'my' – my king/my people, my beloved/my beloved, my mother or father/my child, my head/my body. So, if we were looking for some kind of shorthand for this narrative of a time of fulfilment, safety, joy and *shalom*, we would refer to the peaceable (or peace-making) kingdom of God, the marriage of God and creation, the family of God, or the embodiment of God. We shouldn't be surprised that these are exactly the images explored by the prophets and, later, by Jesus and the apostles.

If the Genesis story sets the stage by giving us a sacred vision of the past, and if the Exodus story situates us in the sacred present on a pilgrimage towards external and internal liberation, then the story of the peace-making kingdom ignites our faith with a sacred vision of the future, a vision of hope, a vision of love. It represents a new creation and a new exodus – a new promised land that isn't one patch of ground, but which encompasses the whole earth.[4] It acknowledges that, whatever we have become or ruined, there is hope for a better tomorrow; whatever we have achieved or destroyed, new possibilities await us; no matter how far we have come or backslidden, there are new and more glorious adventures ahead. And, the prophets aver, this is not just a human pipe dream, wishful thinking, whistling in the dark: this hope is the very word of the Lord, the firm promise of the living God.

The wild, passionate, creative, liberating, hope-inspiring God whose image emerges in these three sacred narratives is not the dread cosmic dictator of the six-line Greco-Roman framework. No, that deity, we must conclude, is an idol, a damnable idol. Yes, that idol is popular, perhaps even predominant, and defended by many a well-meaning but misguided scholar and fire-breathing preacher. But, in the end, you cannot serve two masters, Theos and Elohim, the god of the philosophers and Caesars and the God of Abraham, Isaac and Jacob, the god of profit proclaimed by the empire and the God of justice proclaimed by the prophets.

You can try for centuries to hybridise them and compromise them, but, like oil and water, they eventually separate and prove incompatible. They refuse to alloy. They produce irreconcilable narratives and create different worlds. It's time to abandon the long experimental project of recasting the Bible in an alien narrative and reframing God in an alien story. It's time to stop holding God's people captive in that alien construction. God liberated his people from the economic and political concentration camp of the Egyptians and the Babylonians; perhaps now it's time to be liberated from the conceptual tyranny of the Greco-Romans as well. Perhaps the word of the Lord can be heard again, crying from the wilderness, *Let my people go!* – or perhaps, *My people, let's go! Let's leave the narrow six-line narrative of the Greco-Roman Empire and inhabit the spacious three-dimensional world of God the creator, liberator and reconciler.*

Does anyone dare say 'Amen'?

TWO

THE AUTHORITY QUESTION

CHAPTER 7

How Should the Bible Be Understood?

I love the Bible. This love goes back to childhood for me, to warm memories of when my parents would read me Bible stories, either directly from a big, black, leather-bound, red-letter King James Version, or from a children's illustrated story Bible. (David held special appeal to boys like me because of that cool sling-shot he had.) In my teenage years, I began to read the Bible for myself and found treasure buried on every page. (David became even more interesting at that stage, for other reasons.) I began keeping a journal, recording my responses to what I was reading, and followed several different schemes for reading through the Bible every year or so. I even memorised long passages, a practice I still cherish.

In my twenties, I planned to be a college English professor because I loved literature. When I ended up switching careers and becoming a pastor instead, in a sense I got the chance to focus on the collection of literature I loved most of all, and I've never tired of the Bible through all these years. The more

I've asked of it, the more it has yielded to me. So, yes, I love the Bible. I'm in awe of it. At this very moment.

However, my quest for a new kind of Christianity has required me to ask some hard questions about the Bible I love. There will be no new kind of Christian faith without a new approach to the Bible, because we've got ourselves into a mess with the Bible.

First, we are in a scientific mess. Fundamentalism – whether in its Catholic, Protestant, Anglican, Pentecostal or Orthodox forms (for it exists in all streams of Christian faith) – again and again paints itself into a corner by requiring that the Bible be treated as a divinely dictated science textbook providing us with true information in all areas of life, including when and how the earth was created, what the shape of the earth is, what rotates around what in space, and so on.

This approach has set up Christians on the wrong side of truth again and again – from Galileo's time, to Darwin's, to our own. For example, I remember in my younger years hearing preachers passionately decry psychology and psychiatry: the only relevant categories in the Bible were disobedience and demon possession, so there was no place for counselling or lithium or Prozac. As a pastor, I heard stories of suicides committed by young Christians whose churches would not allow them to get psychiatric help, including one from the former president of a Bible college whose sister was one of the casualties. She had been counselled by her pastor to pray and fast as the only 'biblical cure' for depression, and had been forbidden to seek professional help. That pastor, it turned out, had been trained at the college led by the woman's brother. Similarly destructive patterns of Bible abuse are being repeated even now, with many pious people denying our environmental crisis by quoting Bible verses and mocking science. Just as they were the last to acknowledge the rotation and revolution of the earth around the sun, so they'll be the last to acquiesce to what science is telling us about our growing ecological crisis.

Second, we are in trouble in relation to ethics. The Bible, when taken as an ethical rulebook, offers us no clear categories for many of our most significant and vexing socio-ethical quandaries. We find no explicit mention, for example, of abortion, capitalism, communism, socialism, schizophrenia, bipolar disorder, obsessive-compulsive disorder, autism, systemic racism, affirmative action, human rights, nationalism, sexual orientation, pornography, global climate change, imprisonment, extinction of species, energy efficiency, environmental sustainability, genetic engineering, space travel, and so on – not to mention nuclear weapons, biological warfare and just war theory.

If we must steer our ship – personally and socially – by forcibly bringing biblical passages to bear on these issues in a simple 'thou shalt not' way, we will find ourselves stuck precisely where we are stuck now: largely paralysed in solving major, life-and-death-of-the-planet issues, and largely obsessed with smaller hot-button feuds that end up being litmus tests for political affiliation and little more. Not only that, but we can look back over history to see how various groups pulled verses from the Bible to justify unjustifiable ethical positions, and we don't want to repeat those performances. I remember in my own childhood hearing white people use the Bible to justify segregation and forbid inter-racial dating or marriage. In the 1980s, I heard Christian reconstructionists use the Bible in much the same way that Islamic fundamentalists might use the Quran – to advocate the death penalty for homosexuality and rebellion towards parents. As I mentioned earlier, I was devastated recently to read that white evangelical Christians are the most fervent advocates of government-sanctioned torture, and that frequent church-going is a statistical indicator of support for torture. Quoting Bible verses to buttress 'ethical' positions clearly protects nobody from being a moral buffoon or clod.

Third, we are in deep trouble relating to peace. As much as we love the Bible, many of us are afraid that the Bible is becoming a box-cutter or suitcase bomb in the hands of too many preachers, pastors, priests and others. When careless preachers use the Bible as a club or sword to dominate or wound, they discredit the Bible in a way that no sceptic can. I was appalled during the build-up to the Iraq war in 2002 to hear radio preachers pull out a Bible verse about God 'crushing Satan' under 'our feet' to justify a pre-emptive war. In 2005, I appeared on a radio talk show with a popular radio host who used similar 'Bible-based logic' to argue that the US should pre-emptively declare war on Iran.

Last year I talked with Rwandan Tutsis who told me that some of their preachers used to claim that they were descendants of the sexual union between King Solomon and the Ethiopian Queen of Sheba. To these preachers, this possession of 'Jewish blood' justified their being in a position of dominance over the Hutu majority . . . which in turn helped set the stage for the horrible outcomes there. You could probably turn on a Christian radio broadcast today and hear a preacher deny human rights to Palestinians on similar 'biblical' grounds. It's an old and tired game: quoting sacred texts to strengthen an us-versus-them mentality that, in today's world, could too easily lead to a last-tango, nuclear-biochemical kamikaze-crusade-jihad.[1] In case after case in the past, there is a kind of Bible-quoting intoxication under the influence of which we religious people lose the ability to distinguish between what God says and what *we say God says*. No wonder, in my travels around the world, that I am asked questions about the relation between the Bible and violence (and, linked to that, about how Christians should relate to people of other faiths) more than any other single question.

This triplet of troubles presents us with corresponding moral obligations, I believe. We must find new approaches to our sacred texts – approaches that sanely, critically and fairly engage with honest scientific inquiry, approaches that help us derive constructive and relevant guidance in dealing with pressing personal and social problems, and approaches that lead us in the sweet pathway of peace-making rather than the broad, deep rut of mutually assured destruction.

These obligations became more obvious than ever to me a few years ago when I prepared some lectures on how to read the Bible. I decided to go back into American history and investigate how the Bible was used by the defenders of slavery in contrast to the promoters of abolition. What I found was deeply disturbing.

Slavery, of course, has a long history. One might say that, in its earliest form, it represented a step up from genocide and abandonment. Instead of being exterminated, the vanquished males were allowed to survive as slaves of the victors, or instead of being slaughtered or abandoned to starve to death, destitute women and children were allowed to survive as slaves of the rich. But from there, slavery extended into a far-reaching global industry, culminating in the Euro-American trade in African slaves that lasted for about 450 years and stole the freedom and future of 11.5 million Africans.[2] Nearly everyone alive today experiences benefits or losses or both in the aftermath of this (in)human tragedy.

When I began my research, I quickly discovered how hard it is to find pro-slavery literature today. As Eric McKitrick said, 'Nothing is more susceptible to oblivion than an argument, however ingenious, that has been discredited by events; and such is the case with the body of writing which was produced in the antebellum South in defense of Negro slavery.'[3] Several authors, however, have summarised that literature, notably William S. Jenkins in *Pro-Slavery Thought in the Old South* (Peter Smith Publishers, Inc., 1935, 1959) and Larry E. Tise in *Proslavery: A History of the Defense of Slavery in America, 1701–1840* (UGA Press, 1987).

Tise studied the writings of 275 pre-Civil War pro-slavery writers in America. They came from all parts of the country (not just the South) and from all denominations – notably Presbyterian (almost 30 per cent), Episcopalian (20 per cent) and Baptist (17 per cent). Their lines of argument closely resembled similar arguments posed by pro-slavery British and Caribbean writers from 1770 to 1830. In addition to popular speech-makers and tract-writers, there were highly educated pro-slavery advocates like Thomas Cobb, the lawyer who wrote the Confederate Constitution and the Georgia Constitution and helped found the University of Georgia School of Law. In addition to writing an important pro-slavery text, he painted these words in large letters on his house, showing his passion for the subject: 'RESISTANCE TO ABOLITION IS OBEDIENCE TO GOD'. He died in 1862 as a general in the Confederate Army at the

Battle of Fredericksburg, defending slavery with his last breath.

There were also many pro-slavery novels, counterparts to the abolitionists' famous *Uncle Tom's Cabin*. The last example of pro-slavery fiction was published in Georgia in 1864, as General Sherman was launching his scorched-earth campaign across that same state. It provides a kind of evolutionary 'high point' (and last gasp) in the development of the pro-slavery argument. The novel came from the pen of Ebenezer Willis Warren, a 44-year-old Protestant pastor from Macon, Georgia. It was entitled *Nellie Norton: or, Southern Slavery and the Bible: A Scriptural Refutation of the Principal Arguments Upon Which the Abolitionists Rely: A Vindication of Southern Slavery From the Old and New Testaments*.[4] The title suggests what becomes all too apparent when reading pro-slavery literature: to the defenders of slavery, the Bible was unquestionably on their side. Wouldn't it make sense for us to try to understand how so many Bible-reading, Bible-believing, Bible-quoting and Bible-preaching people could be so horribly wrong for so terribly long?

As the story opens in 1859, Nellie Norton, a beautiful young New Englander, naïvely believes slavery is cruel. Then she travels with her mother south to Savannah to visit relatives who own a plantation with slaves. She becomes convinced, after long arguments, that:

- slave-owners are *victims* of 'malignant abuse' and 'wicked and malicious slander' by ignorant, arrogant Northerners;
- 'the world is wrong [on the issue of human slavery], and the South must set it right';
- 'the world is in error, and is dependent upon the South for the truth';

- 'the welfare of the negro is best promoted when he is under the restraints of slavery';
- 'slavery is the normal condition of the negro'.

As the novel ends in 1860, Nellie falls in love with a wonderful slave-owner and turns her home into a hospital for wounded Confederate soldiers. One can trace five lines of argument through the novel. First, there is the classic and ever-popular *ad hominem* argument, asserting that abolitionists are despicable people. According to positive characters in the novel, abolitionists are 'ruthless' and 'fanatical', taking positions 'which embody the worst forms of infidelity ever known to the world'. They are sounding 'the funeral knell of a pure Christianity'.[5] One character asserts, 'I tell you, [abolitionists are] an offense against God, the Bible, religion, the peace of the Christian world, and against common sense, and the more enlightened experience of the age.'

Second is the argument from tradition, asserting, as one character does, that slavery is woven into the fabric of creation and society: 'The truth is, the world never has, and never can exist without slavery in some form . . . Where is the country or the period of history wherein slavery did not exist in some shape or other? . . . Slavery has always existed, and will continue so long as there is a disparity in the intellect or energy of men.'

Third, characters in *Nellie Norton* argue that the South is a kind of paradise, and slavery is an Edenic way of life:

- 'The slaves have many rights. The right of life and limb, the right to be fed and clothed, to be nursed when sick, and cared for in old age when they become helplessly infirm. They are rightfully entitled to protection from ill treatment.'

- Slave children are 'fat and saucy, jolly and lively' and they constantly enjoy 'cheerful songs and merry laughter'.
- Adult slaves are 'happy Ethiopians' with 'bright countenance[s] . . . smiling face[s], and ivory teeth' who 'are fed bountifully, clothed well, nursed when indisposed, and afforded [a] suitable diet'. They 'talk, and laugh, and sing, and pat, and dance', and are constantly 'singing, dancing, laughing, chattering'.
- Slave-masters are 'highly cultivated . . . men of superior general intelligence, refined, polite, [and] genteel . . . I know of no case where the master lives on his plantation with his slaves but what they are treated with justice and moderation'.

Fourth, side by side with these effusive celebrations of the joys of slavery come darker arguments, based on a doctrine of 'negro inferiority'. Repeatedly in *Nellie Norton*, blacks are said to be 'exceptions to the common brotherhood' of man, and are 'sensual and stupid, lazy, improvident, and vicious . . . an ignorant, degraded, indolent people . . . [who could] never . . . be equal with the white man'. What's more, one character asserts that the inferiority of 'negroes' was 'designed by their creator'.

But all four of these lines of argument come to rest on a fifth, the argument that the Bible defends and legitimises slavery. Consider this catalogue of quotes from various protagonists in the novel:

- 'The Bible is a pro-slavery Bible, and God is a pro-slavery God.'
- 'The North must give up the Bible and religion, or adopt our views of slavery.'

- 'Slavery is right, and its enforcement is according to the Scripture.'
- 'Slavery is taught in the Bible, and instituted in Heaven.'
- 'God has ordained slavery.'
- 'Slavery was made perpetual by the positive enactment of heaven.'
- 'There cannot be found . . . in the Bible a single injunction to slaveholders to liberate those held by them in bondage.'
- '[To speak against slavery] is to abominate the law of God, and the sentiments inculcated by his holy prophets and apostles.'
- '[A slave] cannot sunder bonds which bind him to his earthly master, without breaking those which unite him morally to his Redeemer.'

A number of Old Testament passages are quoted as definitive by pro-slavers in *Nellie Norton*: Exodus 21:2–6 (relating to the slavery of poverty-stricken Hebrews), Deuteronomy 15:16–17 (also relating to the slavery of poverty-stricken Hebrews), Genesis 9:26–7 (relating to the curse of Canaan, used to legitimise racism). But the key text was Leviticus 25:44–6 (relating to the buying, keeping and inheriting of slaves):

> Both thy bondmen, and thy bondmaids, which thou shalt have, shall be of the heathen that are round about you; of them shall ye buy bondmen and bondmaids. Moreover of the children of the strangers that do sojourn among you, of them shall ye buy, and of their families that are with you, which they begat in your land; and they shall be your possession. And ye shall take them as an inheritance for your children after you, to inherit them for a possession; they shall be your bondmen for ever.

The King James Version's placement and punctuation of the non-restrictive clause 'which thou shalt have' seemed to render slavery nothing short of a command. It's no wonder, in the light of these verses from the Bible, that a character would say to the young Nellie, 'There is nothing, not one word, in the Old Testament to condemn, but very much to establish, enforce, and regulate slavery'. But it's not only the Old Testament to which pro-slavers go to defend the practice. The New Testament and even the Golden Rule supported slavery in their minds. In fact, they saw in slavery a form of Christian neighbourliness because it put slaves in better conditions than they had experienced in Africa, and exposed them to soul-saving Christian influences as well, a theme known as 'the Ennoblement of the Heathen', which was also used to justify inhumane treatment of the Native peoples.

So characters in the novel joyfully cite the three New Testament passages that exhort slaves to be obedient to their masters: Ephesians 6:5–8; Titus 2:9–10, and Colossians 3:22–4. No wonder a character in the novel concludes: '[I]n the catalogue of sins denounced by the Savior and His Apostles, slavery is not once mentioned . . . not one word is said by the prophets, apostles, or the holy Redeemer against slavery . . . the Apostles admitted slaveholders and their slaves to church membership, without requiring a dissolution of the relation.'[6]

As I re-read these lines of reasoning, a sick feeling gnaws at my stomach. This way of using the Bible is indistinguishable from the way I hear the Bible used today on Christian radio and the way I see it used today in blog discussions. I've seen this way of using the Bible employed in countless sermons and books all my life. Protestants, Pentecostals, Catholics and Orthodox could all be found proving points by referring to Scripture in exactly the way the pro-slavers did. In fact, I have used the Bible myself in exactly this way in more sermons than I want to remember.

Of course, nobody defends slavery today. (Almost nobody. You'd be surprised to read what some do defend in e-mails I've received.) In McKitrick's words, the whole argument ended up in 'oblivion' because it was 'discredited by events'. We not only stopped defending it, we repented of it, so that now a pro-slavery advocate would be excommunicated from the very denominations whose leading pastors once defended slavery in the name of a 'pro-slavery God', quoting a 'pro-slavery Bible'.

We've gone through a similar process in regard to anti-Semitism, segregation and apartheid. Many of us have also gone through a similar process regarding the status of women in the Church, and some of us regarding the status of gay, lesbian and transgendered people. We are also going through a similar process regarding stewardship of the environment, religious supremacy and (I hope) the sanctioning of war.

But very few Christians today, in my experience anyway, have given a second thought to – much less repented of – *this habitual, conventional way of reading and interpreting the Bible* that allowed slavery, anti-Semitism, apartheid, chauvinism, environmental plundering, prejudice towards gay people and other injustices to be legitimised and defended for so long. Yes, we stopped using the Bible to defend certain things once they were 'discredited by events', but we still use the Bible *in the same way* to defend any number of other things that have not yet been fully discredited, but soon may be. By and large, few of us have become self-critical regarding our assumptions about the Bible and our ways of using it that flow from those assumptions – often leading to 'discredited' results. That self-critical turn is at the heart of the second passage in our quest. Our quest for a new kind of Christianity requires a new, more mature and responsible approach to the Bible.

We pursue this new approach to the Bible not out of a capitulation to 'moral relativism' (as some critics will no doubt accuse), but because of a passion for goodness and justice. Our goal is not to lower our moral standards, but rather to raise them by facing and repenting of habits of the mind and heart that harmed human beings and dishonoured God in the past. We have no desire to descend down a slippery slope into moral compromise, but rather we want to admit that we slid down that slope long ago, Bibles in hand, and we need to climb out of the ditch before we are complicit in more atrocities. Repentance means more than being sorry: it means being different.

CHAPTER 8

From Legal Constitution to Cultural Library

As I look back on my own experience with the Bible, I figure I've heard or given over two thousand 'live' sermons on the Bible, not counting radio and TV sermons I've taken in. I've also read thousands of theological books and engaged in thousands of theological conversations. How would I describe the way we typically use the Bible – especially in conservative settings like my own heritage? In short, *we read and use the Bible as a legal constitution*.[1] It shouldn't surprise us that people raised in a constitutional era would tend to read the Bible in a constitutional way. Lawyers in the courtroom quote articles, sections, paragraphs and subparagraphs to win their case, and we do the same with testaments, books, chapters and verses.[2]

Like lawyers, we look for precedents in past cases of interpretation, sometimes favouring older interpretations as precedents, sometimes asserting that newer ones have rendered the old ones obsolete. We seek to distinguish 'spirit' from 'letter' and argue the 'framers' intent', seldom questioning whether the passage under review was actually intended by the original authors and editors to be a universal, eternally binding law. As a result, we turn our Bible colleges and denominational bodies into versions of a Supreme Court.[3] At every turn, we approach the biblical text as if it were an annotated code instead of what it actually is: a portable library of poems, prophecies, histories, fables, parables, letters, sagely sayings, quarrels, and so on.

Read as a constitution, the Bible has passages that can be and have been used to justify, if not just about anything, an awful lot of wildly different things. For example, let's say we approach the Bible with this question: How should we treat our enemies? Matthew 5:44 tells us to love them. Romans 12 tells us to do good to them and never seek revenge against them. 1 Peter 3 tells us to suffer at their hands and set an example for them. Psalm 137:9 says we should joyfully dash their infants against a stone. Psalm 139:19 says we should hate them. Deuteronomy 7 says we should destroy them utterly and show them no mercy. If we want to call down fire on them, we can refer to 1 Kings 18:38, but before we do so, we'd better check Luke 9:51–6, which condemns that kind of thinking. Similarly, we could find verse precedents in the Bible to justify polygamy and celibacy as equal or better alternatives to monogamy (Gen. 4:19; Exod. 21:10; Deut. 25:5–10; Titus 1:6; 1 Cor. 7:1, 29), not to mention a wide array of rules governing dietary, sanitary, clothing, personal grooming and agricultural matters.

To deal with these tensions, Christian scholars have suggested any number of interpretive techniques. For example, some say 'first mention' is primary. Others say that last mention trumps first mention. Some say the Old Testament is valid unless the New Testament overturns it. Others say no, it's a *new* Testament so it doesn't depend on the old, but replaces it. Some say the Bible permits whatever it doesn't forbid, and others say it forbids whatever it doesn't permit. Some say we should 'interpret Scripture with Scripture', but they never quite make it clear which Scripture trumps the other: does Psalm 139:19 trump Matthew 5:44, or vice versa? Some say the more general trumps the more specific, and others say the specific eclipses the general. How do we decide?

When we're in a quandary, some say (maybe not this bluntly, and maybe not in public) that we should interpret a text the way our denominational founders, current leaders, radio/TV preachers or leading college professors ask us to. Others say no, you've got to go back to the sixteenth-century Reformers and their interpretations. Yet others say no, we need to go back further, to St Thomas, or St Augustine, or the Patristic period. Still others say no, we go straight back to the Bible itself₁ – it's *sola scriptura* to the rescue – and never let human traditions and opinions get in the way of your own private interpretation. And still others say – well, they don't say this, but this is what they do – you should interpret the Bible pragmatically, meaning in the way that won't get you fired, or in the way that will keep converts and 'love gifts' and 'amens' flowing in.

One other feature of our current use of the Bible deserves to be mentioned – and questioned. Whom does our current approach favour or empower? Clearly, the constitutional approach to the Bible provides authority and employment for people who learn to read it and use it with a lawyerly approach. Their approach to the Bible bolsters their authority in the communities to which they belong. That doesn't make the approach wrong, but it does suggest that 'insiders' who depend on the constitutional system for their salary and social status will be unlikely to question it, and equally likely to defend it passionately. They are far from disinterested 'objective scholars' in this matter.

When I began to realise the degree to which we use the Bible as lawyers use a constitution, I knew we were in trouble. At least good constitutions can be amended. At least lawyers, for all their reputed hubris, don't claim to speak for God, and, even if they did, there would be other lawyers with divine pretensions in the courtroom with an obligation to challenge their position. In contrast, in many religious settings, there are no checks and balances, and challenging an authority figure's interpretation can lead to excommunication.

Beyond that, however, no writer in the Bible ever understood himself to be writing a constitution that would be read by people hundreds or thousands of years in the future, and thousands of miles away. No, they were writing for their own times, to address specific problems and questions of their day. And beyond that, for all of the Old Testament writers whose works occur in the Bible, when they wrote, there was no Bible! Jesus himself wrote nothing – on paper, that is: according to a disputed passage in John 8, he did write in the dust one day with his finger, an evocative action, by the way, that may have had more symbolic significance than first meets the eye.[4] The Gospels that tell his life were written decades later, and the whole collection of ancient documents that comprise the Christian Bible today were only gathered in their current form centuries after that.

So, whatever the Bible is, it simply is not a constitution. I would like to propose that it is something far more interesting and important: it's the library of a culture and community – the culture and community of people who trace their history back to Abraham, Isaac and Jacob. Think, for example, of a public library today. People sort through all the possible books that could be included, and select some hundreds or thousands to make available to the local public. A medical library selects books of special interest to people who belong to the medical profession; a Shakespeare library selects books of interest to members of the literary guild; a presidential library selects books of interest to historians of a particular president. The biblical library, similarly, is a carefully selected group of ancient documents of paramount importance for people who want to understand and belong to the community of people who seek for God, and in particular, the God of Abraham, Moses, David, the prophets and Jesus.

But here's the problem: the expectations we bring to a constitution and a library couldn't be more different. For starters, a constitution is neat, and we assume it has internal consistency. A culture is messy and full of internal tension, and those characteristics would be reflected in a good library. In fact, some have defined a culture as a group of people who argue about the same things over many generations (as, we have seen, top-down deductive Platonists and bottom-up inductive Aristotelians have done in Greco-Roman history). That may sound like a depressingly contentious definition, but, on second thoughts, a culture's arguments signal a deeper unity: we think certain questions are so important that we keep struggling with them over many generations.[5]

For example, in my own country, the USA, we've been united by a set of perennial political and economic arguments: What are the rights of the nation in relation to the rights of the state and the individual? What are the rights of the majority in relation to the rights of minorities? Is the nation (or the family, or the religion) the fundamental reality, and we are all human embodiments or expressions of the nation, or is the individual the fundamental reality, and the nation is primarily a service agency to uphold individual rights? Are the poor more dependent on the well-being of the rich, or the rich more dependent on the well-being of the poor? When we get lazy or squelch dissent and stop debating these issues, we seem to get into trouble; when we keep the arguments alive, we seem to stay healthier.

Other cultures have been united by different arguments about different questions. For example, some cultures have argued for generations about the relative rights of the dead and the living. Are the living obligated to submit to the wisdom (or folly) of their ancestors? In the future, cultures may argue more (I hope) about the rights of the living versus the not-yet-living: what obligations do we today have to our unborn descendants seven or one hundred generations into the future?

A culture, then, is a group of people who say different things about the same things. They propose a variety of answers to the same basic questions. To be part of the culture means you agree that your culture's shared questions are vitally important, whatever answers you prefer or propose. Seen in this way, the Bible would be expected to contain the very opposite of the internal consistency we require in a constitution; we would expect to find vigorous internal debate around key questions that were precious to the theological culture in which it was produced.

So we judge internal tension and debate as flaws or failures in the components of a constitution, but we see them as a sign of vitality and vigour in the literature of a culture.[6] Now at this point, somebody is waving his hand at the back of the room, just about ready to explode: 'Yes, but the Bible is inspired! What about inspiration?' And I would reply, 'Imagine an inspired constitution. What would it look like? How would we respond to it? Now imagine an inspired cultural library. What would it look like? How would we respond to it?' In my reply, I'd be trying to show how constitutional assumptions sneak into the definition of the word 'inspired', so to say 'the Bible is inspired' comes to mean 'the Bible is an inspired constitution'. The same thing happens with a word like 'authoritative'. An authoritative library is very different from an authoritative constitution. An authoritative library preserves key arguments; an authoritative constitution preserves enforceable agreements.

As a follower of Jesus and a devoted student of the Bible for many decades, I certainly believe that in a unique and powerful way God breathes life into the Bible, and through it into the community of faith and its members, and into my soul. And I certainly believe that the biblical library has a unique role in the life of the community of faith, resourcing, challenging and guiding that community in ways that no other texts can. It is uniquely profitable to teach, reprove, correct, train and equip us for love and good works, as the apostle Paul says. It provides a kind of encouragement that is central and unique to the community of Christian faith.

I freely acknowledge that Plato and Aristotle, Marcus Aurelius and Einstein, Mohammed and the Buddha all say interesting, brilliant and inspiring things, and I can learn a lot from reading their words, as I can from Clement, Gregory, Benedict, Francis, Teresa, Simons, Luther, Calvin, Wesley, Bediako, Borg, Wright, Brueggemann, Crossan and thousands of other gifted writers and speakers – even though they disagree with one another on many points. But to say that God inspired the Bible is to say that, for the community of people who seek to be part of the tradition of Abraham and Sarah, Isaac and Rebecca, Jacob, Moses, Ruth, David, Amos, John, Mary and Jesus, the Bible has a unique and unparalleled role that none of these other voices can claim.[7] *But that still doesn't mean it serves as a constitution!*

We have plenty of scholarship that grows from the assumption that the Bible is a divinely inspired constitution. And we have plenty of scholarship that reads the Bible as a collection of human literature and nothing more, devoid of inspiration altogether. I'm advocating a third approach. I'm recommending that we read the Bible as an inspired library. This inspired library preserves, presents and inspires an ongoing vigorous conversation with and about God, a living and vital civil argument into which we are all invited and through which God is revealed.[8]

This explains why my Brazilian friend Claudio Oliver says *the Bible is a book that isn't meant to be read.* (It might be wise to puzzle over the previous sentence for a moment before moving on.) By this he means that the Bible is supposed to be *heard*. It's not the solitary scholar with furrowed brow sequestered in a library, bent over a book, whose approach best resonates with the Bible as library: rather, it's a community gathering, listening to the Bible being read, then responding and interacting with it and with one another. After all, it's only the last several generations who have lived in a world where Bibles were mass produced and literacy was the norm instead of the exception.

I must add that this constitution metaphor has its weaknesses (especially for people who live in non-constitutionally based countries), but at least it allows us to grapple with important issues without resorting to a lot of complex terminology from the fields of epistemology, hermeneutics, intellectual history and Church history.[9] A number of other analogies could be developed to describe our problem, including one involving appropriate ways of seeing.

If you're a microbiologist looking at a bacterium, you'll see best through a microscope. If you're a crime scene investigator looking for fibres, you'll more likely use a magnifying glass, and if you're an astronomer trying to observe the Large Magellanic Cloud, a telescope will help most. If you're a birdwatcher trying to get a sighting of the ivory-billed woodpecker, you'll need binoculars (or, if the bird you're seeking is already extinct, sadly, a vivid imagination). If you're looking at a photograph in a magazine, the naked eye at arm's length will be about right.

But imagine you're looking at an Impressionist painting, say Georges Seurat's 'Bridge at Courbevoie' (1867) or Paul Signac's 'Clipper' (1887). They are examples of pointillism: the painter uses small, discrete dots of paint that the viewer's eye and brain must combine, creating both a higher degree of viewer involvement and a unique kind of shimmering, vibrant effect. To take them in for their desired effect, you need to stand back several feet, often looking across the room in a gallery. If you use a microscope, magnifying glass or the naked eye at arm's distance, you will be seeing the paint, but not really the *painting*.

This, of course, raises the question: What are the appropriate tools and distances to employ when we want to appreciate and understand the Bible? What would happen if we have habitually studied at arm's distance what should really be enjoyed from across the room, or if we have used a microscope when binoculars would have been more appropriate because of our historical and cultural distance from the people who produced the texts? It's not just what's on the canvas that counts, you see: there's more going on in the eye of the beholder than we often realise, not to mention the mind and eye of the painter. For us to be naïve about 'the eye of the beholder' regarding the Bible means that yesterday's atrocities could be repeated in the future. Slavery, anti-Semitism, colonialism, genocide, chauvinism, homophobia, environmental plunder, Inquisition, witch-burning, apartheid . . . aren't those worth taking care to avoid, for God's sake?

At this point, I need to speak directly to those for whom the Bible is a constitution and can be nothing but a constitution: *I am not pressuring you to change your view right now.* Yes, I would be happy if you would do so, but I understand that many people simply cannot in good conscience change their view, for reasons of intellectual conviction and formation, psychological integrity, job security or social loyalty to a constitutional congregation or denomination. My plea to you would be to be careful in the way you use the Bible as a constitution, because I'm sure you will want to avoid the disasters we've been considering. In addition, I hope you will understand that just as you cannot in good conscience cease to see the Bible as a constitution, many of us can no longer continue to do so in good conscience; that's why we are on a quest to find other ways to cherish, understand and follow the Bible.[10]

Even for those of us on this quest, breaking out of centuries-old habits won't be easy: first, because it is hard for a mind well trained in one way of seeing to learn a new way, and, second, because the religious thought police stand ready to raid places in which theological conversation strays from the familiar constitutional way of reading the Bible. After all, this approach to the Bible is institutionalised in many of our theological colleges; constitutional reading is the main skill many teach. In addition, the constitutional approach is implicit in many, if not most, of our historic denominational and congregational doctrinal statements, and it's modelled 24/7 in religious broadcasting to boot. No wonder those of us who want and need to change our approach may need to form twelve-step groups to deprogramme our thinking.

For all its difficulty, however, I anticipate that our quest for a new approach to the Bible will become more attractive the more we practise it. As we transcend the wrangle and tangle of theo-legal suits and countersuits, and as we politely notify the thought police that we don't fear them any more, we will humbly and joyfully add our voices to the age-old conversation with and about God, a vigorous and vibrant conversation rooted in and inspired by the fascinating array of voices in the Scriptures.

CHAPTER 9

Revelation through Conversation

I was speaking somewhere the other day and the MC introduced me by quoting a bunch of (to me) pretty outrageous things written about me on the internet – 'son of Lucifer', 'heretic', 'dim-witted', 'ignorant', 'arrogant', 'deceiver' – the same sorts of things said about abolitionists in the era of *Nellie Norton*, come to think of it. Everyone laughed, and I guess I chuckled too in an embarrassed sort of way, but I was struck again by how angry people get when their conventional constitutional readings of the Bible are challenged. This is serious business, and I suppose I should be grateful that it's only harsh words being bandied about. A few centuries ago, we on this quest for a new kind of Christian faith might have been facing decapitation, burning at the stake, hanging, imprisonment, the rack, flailing or (cringe) disembowelment. (It's amazing what people have cooked up to do to others in the name of God.)[1]

The book of Job provides an excellent case study on approaching the Bible in a post-constitutional way. People who study Job notice that it has three distinct sections: a brief introduction in prose, a long middle section in poetry, and a short conclusion in prose. The introduction recounts a chat between Satan and God. Satan is a figure who has never appeared in the Bible up until this moment. (If you ask, 'What about the serpent in Genesis?' I'd have to point out that the serpent is never called Satan there. He's just a talking serpent.) Satan was apparently a character from Zoroastrian religion who was borrowed from Babylonian culture and maintained in Judaism by some 'liberal' Jews we know as the Pharisees. (The more conservative Jews, the Sadducees, never accepted Satan as a legitimate Jewish belief.)[2]

The Satan story in Job is pretty strange to our ears, and it creates a truckload of theological 'problems' that we don't need to go into here. (These problems are most problematic for people who want Job to be a constitutional document that explains God's official position on why suffering and evil exist in the world. They're less problematic for those who expect Job to be an inspired expression of human beings struggling and arguing over the realities of suffering and evil.) By the end of the introduction, Satan has, with God's permission, destroyed Job's so-called life – killed his children, destroyed his farm, covered his body with festering sores and, in an act of savage mercy, left him only his wife whose raging despair just makes things worse.

The middle of Job consists of a lot of long speeches. Job utters some of them, in which he basically says, 'Why is this happening to me? What have I done to deserve this? I've been a good person. This is unacceptable. God is supposed to be fair, and what I'm experiencing isn't fair.' Three of Job's friends – Eliphaz the Temanite, Bildad the Shuhite and Zophar the

Naamathite, later joined by the 'angry young man' Elihu the Buzite – make the other speeches, where they say, in various ways, 'Job, stop talking like an idiot. You must have done something wrong. Good things happen to good people, and bad things to bad people, so God would never have let this happen to you if you didn't deserve it in some way. So stop whining and admit that you're getting what you deserve, and, in so doing, honour God.'

All of their speeches are highly poetic and, to contemporary ears, long-winded, and one more thing: *pious*. Whether it's Eliphaz, Bildad, Zophar or Elihu speaking, they say exactly the kinds of pious things we'd expect – what we might call conventional religious wisdom or predictable platitudes. Job sounds like the doubter and heretic; they sound like they've got good grades at Bible college and studied Deuteronomy and Proverbs in great detail.

Then comes the surprising conclusion to the book, where God finally intervenes and makes a long speech, which consists of a dazzling blizzard of questions – not propositions, not theses, not answers or explanations, but questions. And then what does God say? Does he say, 'Bildad, Eliphaz, Elihu and Zophar were right, Job. You should have listened to them'? No, God says the opposite: 'Job has spoken what is right about me, and Eliphaz and company have been a pack of pious windbags speaking nonsense.' And then God says, 'You guys had better ask Job to pray for you, so I won't treat you as a bunch of fools deserve to be treated.'

Now note what God doesn't do: he doesn't go back and explain the deal struck with Satan in the first chapter. If that explanation is supposed to help us, the readers of the story, why wasn't it offered to the poor protagonist of the story? Perhaps, for the author, or authors of Job, that whole explanation for Job's suffering is thus dismissed right along with the pious platitudes of Job's so-called friends. Perhaps?

All this raises a fascinating question. God has just told us that a large proportion of what is uttered in the book of Job is false and foolish. Yet we are taught that the book of Job, being part of the Bible, is the Word of God and is inspired by God. Does that mean that God inspired the introduction and conclusion, but not the middle section where the pious windbags speak? Or does it mean that God inspired the pious windbags' false statements? Or that God was pretending to inspire that part, but was crossing the divine fingers behind the divine back, so as to come out later on to say, 'I was only kidding in that part'?

Obviously, there isn't an easy way out of this problem in the constitutional approach to the Bible where God's message is supposed to be found in the plain words of the biblical text. We need a way, a passage, out of this whole method of reading the Bible, and I think the book of Job gives it to us here.

If we ask, 'Where does revelation occur?' we can't answer, 'Independently in every verse of the book of Job'. If we say that, then God is revealing nonsense half the time and later contradicts what had been revealed earlier. No. We might say, however, that revelation occurs not in the *words and statements of individuals*, but in *the conversation among individuals and God*. It doesn't simply occur in the black symbols on white paper, but it also occurs in the white space between letters and words and sentences – in the unspoken interactions, tensions and resolutions among the voices in the text. Revelation doesn't simply reside in this or that particular verse of Job like cereal in a box, waiting to be opened and poured out into a bowl. Instead it emerges through the whole story of Job, through the conversation that unfolds among these many voices, like meaning in a novel or perhaps even the punchline in a joke: it creeps up on you, sneaks its way into your thought process and then, when least expected, it surprises you. In the words of Emily Dickinson, it comes in 'slant', not direct, and 'dazzles gradually'.[3]

In this way, even the falsity of Job's friends' statements plays a part in the true revelation that comes through the book, as does the story of God's deal with the devil in the beginning and its conspicuous omission at the end. The meaning of the revelation that we carry away after reading the text takes shape in relation to the long-winded and false arguments that we find in its long middle section. Revelation thus happens through the course of the conversation, in the tension of the argument, through the interplay of statement and counterstatement. To snatch a verse from Job 10 or 14 or 23 would work fine if it were a constitution, but if it's this kind of story and conversation, verse-snatching mocks reverent reading.

Now here's where things get interesting: if God says Eliphaz, Bildad, Zophar or Elihu spoke nonsense, yet they were quoting or paraphrasing statements in Deuteronomy, which in turn claims to be quoting God, does that mean Deuteronomy is nonsense too? Which God is to be believed? Is it the God speaking in Deuteronomy, who says, 'Do good, and good will always happen to you; do evil, and evil will always happen to you'? Or is it the God that says the simple moral formulas of Deuteronomy are nonsense when echoed by Eliphaz, Bildad, Zophar or Elihu? I can only conclude that neither Deuteronomy nor Job speak nonsense, but, rather, we speak nonsense when we practise verse-snatching from Deuteronomy or the middle of Job, or anywhere else. Why? Because revelation doesn't simply happen in statements: it happens in conversations and arguments that take place within and among communities of people who share the same essential questions across generations. Revelation accumulates in the relationships and interactions and interplay between statements.

In this light, the biblical text doesn't give us cement blocks and mortar with which to construct a building of certainty from the ground up. It gives us a bunch of hammers and chisels in the form of stories and questions. With these tools we chip away at human constructions, and revelation is like the breeze or shaft of light that streams through the cracks. The Word or self-revealing of God, in this light, isn't a collection of points, lessons, morals, doctrines or beliefs that God dictates or otherwise encodes: it is an event, a turning point, a breaking open, a discovery, a transforming, humbling and ennobling encounter that occurs to readers when they engage with the text in faith – the text with all its tensions and unresolved issues intact.

To say that the Word (or message, or meaning, or revelation) of God is in the biblical text, then, does not mean that you can extract verses or statements from the text at will and call them 'God's words'. It means that if we enter the text together and feel the flow of its arguments, get stuck in its points of tension and struggle with its unfolding plot in all its twists and turns, God's revelation can happen to us. We can reach the point that Job and company did at the end of the book, where, after a lot of conflicted human talk and a conspicuously long divine silence, we finally hear God's voice.

Or not. Because if anything is clear in the aftermath of the Reformation, it has to be this: we human beings can interpret the Bible to say and mean an awful lot of different things. We can very easily confuse 'the Bible says' with 'I say the Bible says', which we can then equate with 'God says'. (A friend of mine says that the average religious leader begins by humbly speaking with God, then he speaks humbly of God, then he speaks proudly for God, and finally he speaks arrogantly as if he were God.) Ever since the leaders of the Reformation claimed *sola scriptura* – Scripture alone is enough! – we've had an avalanche of evidence that reasonably bright, sincere and well-meaning people can find just about anything in the Bible, not to mention the less bright, sincere or well-meaning.

So we have to turn back to *sola scriptura* and ask, 'Enough for what purpose?' Enough to provide quotes to create consti-tutions that legitimise the authority of those who extract the quotes and create the constitutions? Yes, enough to create hundreds of constitutions and legitimise thousands of authority figures! Enough to justify splits in denominations and some-times bitter competition among systematic theologies? Yes, enough to justify thousands of splits and to inspire centuries of bitter competition! Enough to keep preachers, theologians and writers in business for centuries? Yes, and I'm one of them – and so are my loyal critics!

Clearly, however, these outcomes aren't the point. They're not what the Bible is for.

Does the Bible alone provide enough clarity to resolve all questions as a good constitution should? No. We have no reason to believe it was ever meant to do that, as much as we've tried to force it to do so. From all sides it becomes clear that the Bible, if it is truly inspired by God, wasn't meant to end conversation and give the final word on controversies. If this were its purpose, it has failed miserably. (This fact must be faced.) But if instead it was inspired and intended to stimulate conversation, to keep people thinking and talking and arguing and seeking, across continents and centuries, it has succeeded and is succeeding in a truly remarkable way.[4]

That success shines in the last section of the book of Job. What does God do when he finally breaks silence and begins to speak? Does he explain the situation to Job and his friends? Does he definitively answer the question of human suffering and evil? Does he give them a precise description of the encounter with Satan that we readers are given in the introduction, and declare that the problem of evil's existence is now solved? As we've already seen, no, no, and no. God never does that. Instead, he responds with a hurricane of questions. What about this? God asks. What about that? How is snow formed? Do you understand that? How about this – how did the crocodile get his thick skin? Do you know? If it were today, God might be asking, 'How does DNA carry traits? How are instincts passed on in animals? How does consciousness arise in the human body and brain, and what is consciousness? What is dark matter? Why did the big bang happen? Why does the speed of light appear to be absolute? Is cold fusion possible? How do you programme a TV remote control?'

What is God revealing in all these questions? Certainly not answers! No, if we experience the Word or self-revealing of God in these questions, it doesn't come as an explanation, a statement, a solution. It comes as a sense of wonder, humility, rebuke and smallness in the face of the unknown. What if that is the truest and best kind of revelation there can ever be for creatures such as us?

So, in Job we have several voices: Satan's, Job's, his wife's, Eliphaz's, Bildad's, Zophar's, Elihu's and God's (or a character named God, a subject to which we will return shortly). And in the Hebrew Scriptures as a whole, we have so many voices, and voices of different kinds – priests, who differ from prophets, who differ from sages, who differ from poets, who differ from chroniclers or storytellers, and so on. Similarly, in the Christian Scriptures we have several Gospels: Matthew's, Mark's, Luke's, John's. And we have many other voices as well – Paul, John, Peter, James, Jude, Luke. Could Job be a fractal of the whole Bible: many voices, arguing, debating, stating and counterstating, asking and answering?

As we listen and enter into the conversation ourselves, could it be that God's Word, God's speaking, God's self-revealing happens to us, sneaks up and surprises and ambushes us, trans-forms us and disarms us – rather than arming us with 'truths' to use like weapons to savage other human beings? Could it be that God's Word intends not to give us easy answers and short cuts to confidence and authority, but rather, as I suggested above, to render us, again and again, into a posture of wonder, humility, rebuke and smallness in the face of the unknown?

The 'us' in the previous sentence raises another question. Do we have a voice in the biblical drama? In other words, does the Bible tell us to shut up and listen because everything is settled? Or does it invite us to be part of the conversation? Job itself may provide the answer. When Eliphaz, Bildad, Zophar or Elihu quote Deuteronomy to Job, that doesn't end the conver-sation. Job doesn't sit back and say, 'Thanks, I needed that.

Deuteronomy says it; I believe it; that settles it.' No, he says, 'Are you kidding? I can't buy that!' And then it is sceptical Job who gets God's commendation at the end, not Job's pious friends.

So perhaps, when God says Job has spoken rightly, God isn't saying, 'Eliphaz et al. have given false information about me, but Job has given true information.' Maybe God is saying, 'It is not right for fallible, limited creatures to speak of me the way Elihu et al. have. But Job, in your questioning and wrestling with me, in your refusal to give up faith on the one hand or to shut up and listen on the other, in your active engagement in the conversation, in your refusal to acquiesce to unsatisfying answers, you have spoken rightly of me – as a true and honest human being should. That's what I'm looking for. That's what it's about.'[5]

Reading the Bible this way is far inferior to the way many of us learned – inferior, that is, if we're expecting the Bible to be a constitution. But if you're expecting it to be a cultural library, the record of a vibrant conversation and a stimulus to ongoing conversation, it is . . . beautiful, I'd say.[6]

One more question needs to be asked. We've mentioned the many human voices in the text, but what about God's voice that we encounter in the introduction, striking rather strange bargains with Satan, and at the end, flinging out questions as a machine-gun spits out shells?[7] Can we trust God's voice to be God's voice? Or is even 'God' a character in the story too, not the actual God necessarily, but the imagined God, the author's best sense of God, the fictional character playing God for the sake of this dramatic work of art? This is a powerful and perhaps terrifying question.

We might answer, 'If the Bible says "God said it", then God

said it and that settles it.' But wouldn't that answer imply, 'Shut up and listen'? Wouldn't that shut down any conversation? Why include these other voices, if only one voice counts?

We might say, 'It's all just talk. "God" is just a fictional character, a poorly camouflaged projection of human anxiety, aggression and desire. The only voices are imaginary voices. There is no God, there is no Word, there is no revealing, just human words upon words upon words.' But wouldn't that answer also neutralise the conversation? What good is it? Why does it matter?

But we might say, 'God is indeed a character in the text, a representation, not the real God. But the same is true of "Job" and "Satan" and "Eliphaz" and "Bildad".' The real Job (if there was one; my sense is that the Job story is a kind of archetypal theological opera and has no intention of portraying what we would call a historical event) is represented in the text by a word, a name ... that's not the real Job. The whole text, in this sense, is a representation or construction, but not *just* a construction, any more than wedding vows or a court summons or a love poem are *just* words. To say the text is inspired is to say that people can encounter God – the real God – in a story full of characters named Job, Eliphaz, Bildad, Satan, and even one called *God*. Through stories like this, gathered in a library like this – not articles and amendments gathered in a constitution – God can self-reveal, so that the Word of God, the speaking and self-revealing of God, can burn like fire in the branches, twigs and leaves of the text.[8]

All this takes on an even more amazing feel if we take seriously our belief in God's Spirit. The Holy Spirit we see hovering over the primal creation in Genesis, evoking glorious possibilities of order and life from the swirling chaos and darkness, is the same Spirit running like a current among the characters Job, Eliphaz, Bildad, Zophar, Elihu and God. And, we might add, this is the same Spirit evoking the text from the chaos of human writers in a vigorous culture. And this is the same Spirit hovering over us now, running like a current among us today, at this moment, evoking understanding as we seek to understand, to know, to learn, drawing us like an orchestral conductor into the holy conversation and symphony of the sacred Scriptures. And this is the same Spirit by whom Jesus is conceived, filled and empowered, as we will consider in more detail in an upcoming question.

In this light, then, the Bible truly is enough – meaning that it provides enough of a cultural library for us to begin to encounter the living God. If we only had the middle of Job, we wouldn't encounter God as we do when we have the beginning and the end. If we only had the end, we wouldn't encounter the meaning inherent in the beginning and middle. We wouldn't have enough. But when we have them together, in all their sizzling, strained, sparking, squirming tension – Job's agonising cries, his friends' pious and sorry attempts at comfort and correction, and God's final assault with questions – we have enough.

Again, if we want the Bible to be a constitution, it isn't enough. It isn't at all. Nor is it enough as a roadmap for successful living, a set of blueprints for building a life or institution or nation, or an 'owner's manual' with handy information guaranteed to make your life successful, all at your fingertips, as easy as one-two-three. But as the portable library of an ongoing conversation about and with the living God, and as an entrée into that conversation so that we actually encounter and experience the living God – for that, the Bible is more than enough.

This approach, if you haven't realised it yet, defies both conservative and liberal categories. On the one hand, the conservative constitutional view claims to put us 'under' Scripture's authority, yet I'm sure I'm not the only one who has noticed that some of the most pompous and defensive people anywhere are found among those who stand and shout, 'The Bible says!' Nor am I the only one to notice that before the Bible can serve as a constitution, it must be interpreted as one, which renders amazing authority to those interpreters. The Bible they want to put us 'under' tends to be the Bible-as-*they*-have-interpreted-it, which unsurprisingly means we are actually under their authority as they stand over us with Bible in hand. On the other hand, the liberal view reacts strongly against all this conservative sleight-of-hand and largely resists using the language of authority at all when they speak of the Bible. The liberal view ends up bequeathing a great deal of authority to liberal scholars, just as the conservative view does to scholars of its tribe.

Perhaps the approach I'm recommending is no better in this regard. But here's what I hope: that this approach will not try to put us *under* the text like conservatives tend to do, nor will it lift us *over* it like liberals often seem to do, but that it instead will try to put us *in* the text – in the conversation, in the story, in the current and flow, in the predicament, in the Spirit, in the community of people who keep bumping into the living God ... loving God, betraying God, losing God and being found again by God. In this way, by placing us *in* the text, I hope this approach can help us enter and abide *in* the presence and love and reverence of the living God all the days of our lives, and *in* God's mission as humble, wholehearted servants day by day and moment by moment. Even now.

THREE

THE GOD QUESTION

CHAPTER 10

Is God Violent?

It would be nice if I could blame all our problems on the Greco-Roman captivity of the biblical narrative, or on a constitutional reading of the Bible, but it's never that simple. True, when I began breaking faith with Theos and returning to the God of Abraham, Isaac, Jacob and Jesus, a boatload of problems drifted away. And more problems disappeared for me when I allowed the Bible to be a portable library rather than a timeless constitution. But I have to admit that there are problems in the Bible-as-library too. Real problems. Big problems. In previous chapters, we saw God as the good Creator in Genesis, as the compassionate liberator in Exodus, and as the reconciling king, lover and Father of all people in the prophets. But as a serious reader of the Bible, I'm still a little uneasy, because I know about some of the other images of God that are also found in the Bible — violent images, cruel images, unChristlike images.

Now, before I address my uneasiness about those images, I need to say again that nowhere in the Hebrew Scriptures do

I find anything as horrible as Theos. Yes, I find a character named God who sends a flood that destroys all humanity except for Noah's family, but that's almost trivial compared to a deity who tortures the greater part of humanity for ever in infinite *eternal conscious torment* – three words that need to be read slowly and thoughtfully to feel their full import.[1] Yes, I find a character named God who directs a band of nomadic former slaves to fight and claim from more powerful nations a piece of land for themselves, but never does this God direct them to expand their borders, brutally conquer and occupy weaker nations and create a global totalitarian regime through slavery and genocide as Theos-Zeus-Jupiter likes to do. Yes, I find a character named God who does a good bit of smiting, but those who are smitten are simply smitten and buried, and that's it – they are not shamed and tortured for a while by the 'godly' before death and then shamed and tortured by God after death, for ever and ever, without end. Now, I am in no way interested in excusing or defending divine smiting, genocidal conquest or global quasi-geocidal flooding; I'm just saying that even if these are the crimes of Elohim/Adonai/Jehovah, they are far less serious crimes than those of Theos.

Many, perhaps most, perhaps all, of the disturbing deeds of God in the Bible look very different in the light of our responses to the first two questions in our quest. In my own experience as a lover and reader of the Bible, as I am freed from the literalistic and dualistic straitjacket in which the Greco-Roman and constitutional approaches constrained me, I feel I can breathe a little more freely and I begin to notice things that had been there all along, but I had been trained to ignore. Most notably, I begin to see how our ancestors' images and understandings of God continually changed, evolved and matured over the centuries. God, it seemed, kept initiating this evolution.

For example, in Exodus 6:3, God tells Moses that the mysterious divine name rendered in English as 'the LORD' had been intentionally withheld from Abraham, Isaac and Jacob. They had received only a preliminary revelation under the name God Almighty (El Shaddai), but now God takes Moses deeper into the knowledge of God's identity. Similarly, in Hosea (2:16), the Lord says that a time is coming when Israel will no longer refer to her Creator as 'my Master', but instead will pray to 'my Husband'. The more dominating understanding of God will fade and give way to a more intimate one. Jesus similarly tells his disciples that the time for thinking of themselves simply as his servants is passing, and the time for understanding themselves as his friends has come. He goes on to explain that, after his departure, the Spirit will continue to guide them into new, as yet unrevealed truth as they are able to bear it (John 15:1ff.; 16:12ff.). Paul similarly describes the people of God graduating from a childhood in which they had the law as a tutor (Gal. 3:23) to an age when they walk free in the Spirit.

The more I get comfortable with this evolving understanding of God across biblical history, the more I find myself able to love and enjoy the Bible – and love and enjoy God as well. I think you will have the same experience. If we could sit down and experiment with this approach over several months together, we'd begin to notice at least five specific lines of evolution in the biblical writers' understanding of God.[2]

First, we'd trace a gradual maturing among biblical writers in their understanding of *God's uniqueness*. Some early biblical passages present an image of one God – *our* God – who is supreme among many.[3] But over time faithful people come to see that only one God, in fact, is real and alive, and all the others are fragments, illusions, impostors, superstitions or deceptions. The Creator is not only unique among gods; the Creator is uniquely God.

Second, we would notice an important shift in understanding *God's ethics*. In many passages of Scripture, the one living God is primarily concerned about religious and ceremonial fidelity – rituals, sacrifices, vestments, holidays, dietary and cleanliness codes. This image is naturally promoted by the priests, who are passionately committed to maintaining purity in worship and devotion and seek technical perfection in the fulfilment of religious regulations. But, over time, the voices of the prophets are also heard in the land. They depict God as passionately committed to social justice – to showing practical concern for the poor and forgotten and to addressing the systemic flaws which plunge and imprison people in poverty and oppression. In fact, many of these prophets minimise the importance of priestly ceremonial devotion in view of the priority of social justice to the heart of God.[4]

Third, we could follow a pattern of growth in the understanding of God's *universality*. In some passages, the living God seems very tribal: God favours 'us', but disfavours everyone else. But, as time goes on, it becomes unquestionably clear that God created all people and loves all people. Chosenness, it becomes clear, does not give one people privileges over others as God's favourites, but rather responsibilities on behalf of others as God's servants and as channels of blessing. They are chosen not to the exclusion of all others whom God disfavours, but for the benefit of all others whom God loves.

Fourth, we could trace a maturing understanding of God's *agency*. In some passages, God's interventions have a magical and interventionist quality, as if God were generally outside and uninvolved in the universe until certain moments when God decides to step in and get involved. In other passages, we find two differing responses to this view. In one response (see Ecclesiastes, for example), God is largely distant or absent and the world is mystifying and chaotic. In another response (Matthew seems to lean in this direction), God is hyper-present, to the point of engineering and controlling everything or nearly everything, like a cosmic chess-master moving pieces from square to square, or like a live-in mother-in-law who hovers judgementally over her daughter-in-law's every move.

But all of these views seem to be taken up into a more mature view, highly nuanced and delicately balanced. We learn to discern that, yes, God is indeed at work in or along, with or through, or even in spite of events. In this way, God is not simply outside, distant and uninvolved. But that doesn't imply the opposite: God can't be rendered indistinguishable from the events themselves, nor is God deterministically controlling the universe as a machine or puppet. Rather, God's work and wisdom are gently but firmly present in the dynamic and unfolding processes of creation and history themselves. Even when some human beings do great evil, God is present to guide and empower other people to do even greater good. In this way, Paul can truly say, 'In all things, God works for the good . . .' (Rom. 8:28 9), echoing Joseph's realisation that God's good intentions had, through Joseph, bent even the evil intentions of his brothers towards unexpectedly good ends (Gen. 50:20).

Finally, if we were studying the Bible together over a period of time, we could trace the maturation process among biblical writers regarding God's *character*. In some passages, God appears violent, retaliatory, given to favouritism and careless of human life. But, over time, the image of God that predominates is gentle rather than cruel, compassionate rather than violent, fair to all rather than biased towards some, forgiving rather than retaliatory. In this more mature view, God is not capricious, bloodthirsty, hateful or prone to fits of vengeful rage. Rather, God loves justice, kindness, reconciliation and peace; grace gets the final word.

People who are part of what is often called fundamentalism today, whether Christians, Muslims or Jews, often find it difficult to acknowledge this kind of progression in understanding across the centuries. If anything, they feel obliged to defend and give priority to the early, raw, more primal, less tested and developed views of God, minimising or marginalising what I am calling the more mature and nuanced understandings. So the God of the fundamentalists is a competitive warrior – always jealous of rivals and determined to drive them into defeat and disgrace. And the God of the fundamentalists is superficially exacting – demanding technical perfection in regard to ceremonial and legal matters while minimising deeper concerns about social justice, especially when outsiders and outcasts are concerned. Similarly, the fundamentalist God is exclusive, faithfully loving one in-group and rejecting – perhaps even hating – all others. The fundamentalist God is also deterministic – controlling rather than interacting, a mover of events but never moved by them. And, finally, though the fundamentalist God may be patient for a while, he (fundamentalist versions of God tend to be very male) is ultimately violent, eventually destined to explode with unquenchable rage, condemnation, punishment, torture and vengeance if you push him too far.

The individual fundamentalist often doesn't want God to be this way. She may become profoundly uneasy, especially if she feels herself being conformed to the image of the God she worships.[5] Her emotional intelligence may actually recoil from this view of God, as she tells herself, 'God may act this way, but I must not.' Meanwhile, her analytic intelligence tells her that she must hold to this view because of the way she has answered our first and second questions about the six-line narrative and the Bible as religious constitution. She may try to minimise the uglier dimensions of the fundamentalist image of God and emphasise the more mature views, but if she goes too far she will be labelled *liberal* or *heretic* by the gatekeepers of her community. The fear of being labelled, ostracised and rejected by her beloved faith community (not to mention the fear of being blacklisted by the angry God in whom she partly believes) will force her to either capitulate or keep silent about her reservations for another day. And even if she manages to convince a small circle of friends to stretch into the evolutionary pattern found in the Bible – of moving from less to more mature views of God – periodic inquisitions will sweep through, seeking to reassert what gatekeepers defend as the more pure and rigorous understanding. Month after month my e-mail inbox fills with specific stories that illustrate this general pattern.

I hope you can see what I'm saying here, and what I'm not saying. I'm *not* saying that the Bible is free of passages that depict God as competitive, superficially exacting, exclusive, deterministic and violent. But neither am I saying that those passages are the last word on the character of God. I am *not* saying that the Bible reveals a process of evolution within God's actual character, as if God used to be rather adolescent, but has taken a turn for the better and is growing up nicely over the last few centuries. I *am* saying that human beings can't do better than their very best at any given moment to communicate about God as they understand God, and that Scripture faithfully reveals the evolution of our ancestors' best attempts to communicate their successive best understandings of God. As human capacity grows to conceive of a higher and wiser view of God, each new vision is faithfully preserved in Scripture like fossils in layers of sediment. If we read the Bible as a cultural library rather than as a constitution, and if we don't impose a Greco-Roman plot-line on the biblical narrative, we are free to learn from that evolutionary process – and, we might even add, to participate in it.[6]

An analogy may be helpful in seeing what this idea of progressive understanding means. Consider the Bible as a collection of maths textbooks. There's the elementary book, the second-stage book, and so on, all the way up to secondary-school/college textbooks that deal with geometry, algebra, trigonometry, maybe even calculus. Imagine opening the second-stage text and reading this sentence about subtraction: *You cannot subtract a larger number from a smaller number*. Then you open a more advanced textbook and see a chapter entitled *Negative Numbers*. The first sentence reads, *This chapter will teach you how to subtract larger numbers from smaller numbers*. How do we reconcile the statements? Were the authors of the second-stage book lying? Or were the authors of the advanced textbook relativists, doubting the absolute truth of an earlier text?

It's not that simple. The author of the second-stage book told the truth that was appropriate for the target audience. If young schoolchildren had to learn the subtraction of both positive and negative numbers, they would be overwhelmed. So experts in maths education have determined an order of operations, a set of skills that need to be mastered in a sensible order. Addition before subtraction, subtraction before multiplication, multiplication before division, positive numbers before negative numbers, solving for single variables before solving for multiple variables, and so on.

What if something similar must happen in the theological education of the human race? What if people who live in the 'primary-school' world of polytheism need to learn about one God as superior to others before they can handle the idea of one God as uniquely real? What if, in order to understand God's concern for social justice properly, they must first have a concept of God being pleased or displeased, and that concept can only be developed through the visceral reflexes of cleanliness and revulsion, which are in turn reinforced through ceremonial rules and taboos? What if the best way to create global solidarity is by first creating tribal solidarity, and then gradually teaching tribes to extend their tribal solidarity to 'the other'? What if, then, God must first be seen as the God of our tribe, and then as the God of all tribes?[7] What if we need to learn to find God in the face of our brother before we can find God in the face of the other, the stranger, even the enemy? And what if, until we find God in both our brother and the other, we can't truly say that we know God maturely?[8]

What if God's agency in the world is mysterious and complex, reflecting God's desire to have a world that is truly free yet truly relational? And what if, in order to get to that high-level theological calculus, we must first teach people to imagine a simply chaotic universe, and then to imagine its opposite – a simply determined and controlled universe? What if we must then transcend both of those simple paradigms in order to imagine an interactive, relational universe that has elements of both?

And what if, in order to understand the character of God that lies behind, beneath, above and within the agency of God, we must similarly pass through some stages where our understanding is imbalanced and incomplete? What if, for example, to view God as passionately committed to justice and goodness, we must first pass through a stage where we see God's passion for justice being expressed in the violent defeat of injustice? Or, to say the same thing slightly differently, what if the only way to get to a mature view of God as non-violently yet passionately committed to justice is to pass through an immature stage where God appears to be both passionately and violently committed to justice?[9] Don't we, as children, go through similar stages in coming to understand our parents?

Now, if you've followed me through this line of reasoning, you're probably aware already of what I need to say next: we cannot, we must not, assume that we have arrived. In other words, if we can look back and see the process unfolding in the past – in the Bible, in theological history – then we have no reason to believe that the process has stopped unfolding now, even at this very moment as I write, as you read. We have every reason to believe that even now we are in a stage of understanding that is a step up from where we used to be, but a step below where we could venture next. To be a member of a faith community, in this understanding, is not to be a lucky member of the group that has finally arrived: it is to be in a cohort that is learning together. It is to be a part of a group of first-years, or sixth-formers, or college students, or, better yet, a whole school that includes all levels, growing and learning together.

That means that some faith communities are good for some of us, even though they would not challenge others of us because we have already learned the lessons they are ready to teach. Other faith communities are over our head: they're doing calculus while we're still struggling with binomials. And that realisation, of course, has implications not only for how we deal with other denominations, but for how we deal with other religions as well, a subject to which we will return in our ninth question.

In the light of this unfolding understanding of biblical revelation, when we ask why God appears so violent in some passages of the Bible, we can suggest this hypothesis: if the human beings who produced those passages were violent in their own development, they would naturally see God through the lens of their experience. The fact that those disturbing descriptions are found in the Bible doesn't mean that we are stuck with them, any more than we are stuck with the idea that *you cannot subtract a larger number from a smaller number* just because that statement still exists in our school textbook. Remember, the Bible is not a constitution; it is like the library of maths textbooks that shows the history of the development of mathematical reasoning among human beings.

I've found that a second analogy sometimes helps people understand – although not necessarily agree with! – what I'm trying to say. Imagine we go through a time machine to the year 3013. (You might imagine that the machine will be invented in

3012 and so some of our descendants have decided to use the new machine to come back in time, take us to see what their world is like, and learn from us what our world is like.)

When we arrive, we find that people in the future are deeply spiritual. They have continued to grow in the knowledge and ways of the Lord over these many centuries. And they have grown socially as well as spiritually. Three huge social differences strike us immediately. First, they no longer fight wars. All conflicts are resolved through peaceful negotiation. Second, they no longer eat meat. They live more ecologically sustainable lives as vegetarians. And, third, they long ago outgrew the use of fossil fuels, having seen their catastrophic effects on human society and the global climate.

We are invited to be on a talk show where viewers call in to ask questions about the past. (I know, any culture that made these three advances would probably have moved beyond TV and talk shows long ago, but we're just being playful here.) The first caller asks, 'Is it true that some of you claim to be believers in God and still believe in war? Is it true that some of you even pray that God will bless your nation's war efforts? And is it true that only a minority of people who claim to be followers of Jesus are opposed to war?' We stumble through an answer, feeling a bit defensive: 'Yes, we hold to something called Just War Theory, and of course we pray for victory in war, because we know God is on the side of justice, and our cause is just. And, yes, a small, idealistic minority of followers of Christ opposes war, but most of us consider them impractical and unrealistic.'

The talk show host looks a little shocked, and then brings in the second caller, who asks, 'How can you possibly kill your fellow creatures for food? Don't you know that all creatures are made by God, and that therefore all life is sacred? Aren't you pro-life? And aren't you aware that the planet can only sustain a limited number of meat-eaters, but that it can provide sustenance for far more vegetarians? How can you be so selfish?' Again, we do our best to respond, but the question is based on assumptions that we don't share. After explaining to the best of our ability, we add, 'Besides, there's nothing better than freshly baked chicken wings or a thick steak hot off the grill!'

Now the talk show host has turned a bit grey, as if he might be about to vomit. We wonder if he will call for a commercial break, not realising that although our descendants still have TV talk shows, they no longer have commercials. He brings on the third caller, who says, 'I've heard that in the olden days, people who claimed to be devout believers actually used fossil fuels. They felt their personal comfort, convenience and transportation needs justified toxifying the planet and throwing the climate into imbalance, which as we all know resulted in billions of deaths and millions of extinctions. That isn't true, is it? It was only careless, amoral people who drove internal combustion cars and used dirty energy, right? Believers in God would never have participated in anything so destructive, right?'

What would we say? How would we feel? Does this little imaginative exercise – this role reversal – help us look at violence, patriarchy, religious supremacy and other disturbing characteristics of some biblical passages in a new light?

CHAPTER 11

From a Violent Tribal God to a Christlike God

Some readers were no doubt uncomfortable in the previous chapter when I suggested that less mature images of God can be found in the Bible along with more mature images. To say so grinds painfully against their constitutional view of the Bible, and it exposes the degree to which their vision of God is cast in the image of the Greek Theos and Roman Caesar. But it might help these readers if I add that even those less mature images must have been improvements over the even less mature images they were replacing.

For example, for me, today, the Noah story, in which God wipes out all living things except one boatload of refugees, has become profoundly disturbing. True, I learned it as a cute children's bedtime tale complete with cuddly pairs of furry animals. In line with the old maxim, 'What you focus on determines what you miss', I was trained to read it as a story of divine saving, so I missed the small detail of divine mass destruction on a planetary scale. In recent years, though, I began thinking about how some might use the story as a 'constitutional precedent': if God single-handedly practised 'ethnic cleansing' once, and if God cannot do evil, then there is apparently a time and place when genocide is justified. And that means that maybe we (or our enemies?) could be justified in playing the genocide card again at some point in the future – another sobering reason to take this quest for a new kind of Christianity seriously, in spite of the risks and opposition. The possibility of using the Bible to justify using the genocide card is chilling, especially when one recalls that this is not a hypothetical question. This very thing has happened again and again in the past, from Genesis 7 to Deuteronomy 7, to American colonisation, to the Holocaust, to the Rwandan genocide, to Darfur. In comparison to a global flood that destroys all life except for a tiny remnant on one lifeboat, a few nuclear bombs are, after all (I shudder to write this), minor disturbances.

In this light, a god who mandates an intentional supernatural disaster leading to unparalleled genocide is hardly worthy of belief, much less worship. How can you ask your children – or non-church colleagues and neighbours – to honour a deity so uncreative, over-reactive and utterly capricious regarding life? To make matters worse, the global holocaust strategy didn't even work: soon the 'good guy' Noah gets drunk, and soon after that his sons are up to no good, and soon after that we're right back to antediluvian violence and crime levels. Genocide, it turns out, doesn't really solve anything in Genesis, even if a character named 'God' does it. (Could that be a worthy moral lesson to draw from the text?)

It's useful to compare the Noah story to the earlier story it seeks to adapt and improve upon, the Utnapishtim story (from

Tablet 11 of the Epic of Gilgamesh, discovered in the mid-1800s, probably dating back in oral tradition to the second millennium BC and recorded in clay in the mid-seventh century BC). The Gilgamesh flood story pits one merciful deity against all the other more capricious ones, while the biblical story shows us one God whose character integrates concerns for justice and mercy. In the Gilgamesh flood story, genocide (we might even say geocide) is mandated in part because human beings are too noisy, keeping the gods from getting a good night's sleep, while in the biblical story, it is humanity's inhumanity and injustice that evoke catastrophic consequences.[1] In the Gilgamesh story, the gods get frightened by the flood, as if they've unleashed something that even they can't control. What's more, they need Utnapishtim to make animal sacrifices when the flood is over because they are hungry – all their normal food sources having been destroyed by the flood they caused. In the biblical story, God is neither frightened nor dependent on sacrificed meat to survive.

Now remember, in making this contrast, I'm not trying to defend the view of God in the Noah story as morally acceptable, ethically satisfying and theologically mature. Nor am I trying to make Gilgamesh look bad to make the Bible look good. Instead, I'm simply recommending that we compare the Noah story with its predecessors as well as its descendants. I'm recommending that we notice the theological progress the story demonstrates, instead of simply condemning it for not having progressed more. I'm acknowledging that, yes, the portrait of God found in the Noah story is far less satisfying in many ways than a portrait that will emerge later in the biblical library. Yet we can celebrate it for being a step up from the portraits it was correcting and seeking to replace, keeping in mind that the Gilgamesh epic itself no doubt provided a more satisfying explanation for some facets of human experience than the earlier myths it sought to augment or replace.

In this way of reading the Bible as an ongoing conversation about the character of God, we not only look to the antecedents of the Noah story, we also consider its descendants. So now consider another story about water and drowning and death and saving. Ponder the image of baby Moses floating on the crocodile-infested Nile River, protected by ... what? An *ark*, an ark of reeds. Could this be, among other things, an ironic commentary on the Noah story, a part of the ongoing and maturing conversation about the character of God? Could this story suggest that God should no longer be identified with a mighty potentate who, in his insecurity, drowns helpless children, but, rather, we should see God identifying with a tiny, fragile child who has been condemned to drowning? Obviously, this kind of reading has no place in a constitutional approach, but outside that framework, it seems to have real theological power.

This power will shine even more brightly when we come to the story of Jesus who seems, in episode after episode, to turn old stories on their heads. I've described elsewhere, for example, his healing encounter with a Canaanite woman in Matthew 15, after which Jesus feeds four thousand Gentiles just as he had previously fed five thousand fellow Jews. The two stories seem perfectly poised to overturn the original encounter between Jews and Canaanites in Deuteronomy 7. Now, under Jesus' leadership in contrast to Joshua's, instead of 'no mercy', we are to 'show mercy'. Now, following Jesus, instead of mercilessly destroying 'the other', we compassionately heal, feed and serve the other.

Now, with Jesus, instead of rejecting the other as a 'Gentile dog', we allow ourselves to listen and be 'converted' by the other, seeing her humanity and her great faith.[2]

This approach helps us see the biblical library as the record of a series of trade-ups, people courageously letting go of their state-of-the-art understanding of God when an even better understanding begins to emerge. This evolutionary approach also helps us understand one reason for the absolute refusal among the Jewish people to tolerate idols: idols freeze one's understanding of God in stone, as it were. This approach also warns us about the danger of another kind of idolatry to which we today are more susceptible. While few people today are tempted to freeze our understanding of God in graven images, we may too quickly freeze our understanding in printed images, rigid conceptual idols not chiselled in wood or stone but printed on paper in books, housed not in temples but in theological colleges and denominational headquarters, worshipped not through ancient ceremonies and rituals but through contemporary sermons and songs. In this way, the constitutional approach to the Bible, it turns out, too easily camouflages a subtle but vigorous and popular form of conceptual idolatry.[3]

This idea of trading up our images of God will still be scary to many. What's to keep us from trading down? What's to keep us from throwing out good things and keeping bad things? The concern is an important one, but it is not sufficient – especially in view of the ethical abuses of the Bible we considered earlier – to cause us to abort our quest. In fact, if we set our course as any ancient mariner would, by making use of three guiding stars, I believe we can move forward with proper confidence.

First, we must align ourselves with the trajectory set for us by the Scriptures read in a narrative (rather than constitutional) way. Consider this diagram, where each letter represents a biblical story, arranged in more or less chronological order. Let the horizontal axis represent progress in time, and let the vertical axis represent increasing maturity in the vision or understanding of God . . .

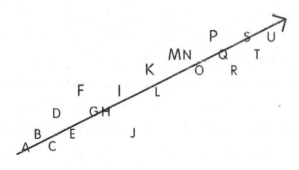

It's pretty clear, isn't it, that we can trace a certain narrative trajectory or plotline (depicted in the arrow) among these data points?[4]

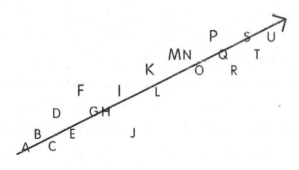

Now imagine that we are trying to choose between three different views of God, in relation to the biblical narrative. Each of the three numbers stands for a theology (or view of God) articulated by a faith community at a point in history.

3

2   P   S   U

MN   Q   T

K   O   R

F   I   L

D   GH

B   E   J   **1**

A   C

Even though View 1 has close affinities with stories J and L in the biblical narrative, and even though View 2 has close affinities with stories M and P, wouldn't it be clear that only View 3 can be seen as consistent with the whole narrative, even though it is distant from the earlier stories in many ways?

Of course this diagram simplifies a somewhat complex and nuanced interpretive process, but I think it also makes clear that this evolutionary view of our understanding of God does not leave us cast adrift in an 'anything goes' theological sea. We have even more clarity when we add a second feature to our diagram. X, Y and Z stand for a vision of the future given by the prophets, indicating the direction in which the story is intended to continue unfolding.

...Z

...Y

...X

P   S   U

MN   Q   T

K   O   R

F   I   L

D   GH

B   E   J

A   C

When we seek to orientate ourselves with these visions of the desired future, together with a sense of the trajectory of the past, we have an even clearer sense of the kind of story we are in, and a clearer feel for the kind of God who would be the protagonist in such a story. And, finally, we can add this:

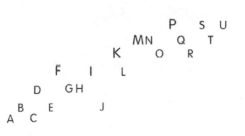

If the sun can represent Jesus, for us as Christians the ultimate Word of God, now we have not only a rich sense of the biblical narrative in the past, and not only a sense of a desired future, but also a profound sense of the character of God whose light shines through the whole story, from beginning to end, alpha to omega. In this way, God's character is never revealed fully at any single point in the story, nor can it be contained simply through any list of propositions or adjectives derived from the stories of the past. Instead, we can discern God's character in a mature way only from the vantage point of the end of the story, seen in the light of the story of Jesus.

The Quaker scholar Elton Trueblood approached the Bible in this way. One of Trueblood's students told me that he often heard his mentor say something like this: 'The historic Christian doctrine of the divinity of Christ does not simply mean that Jesus is like God. It is far more radical than that. It means that God is like Jesus.' In other words, the doctrines of the incarnation and deity of Christ are meant to tell us that we cannot start with a predetermined, set-in-stone idea of God derived from the rest of the Bible, and then extend that to Jesus. Jesus is not intended merely to fit into those predetermined categories; he is intended instead to explode them, transform them, alter them for ever and bring us to a new evolutionary level in our understanding of God. An old definition of God does not define Jesus: the experience of God in Jesus requires a brand-new definition or understanding of God.

Trueblood's insight, in my opinion, is the best single reason to be identified as a believer in Jesus, and it is an unspeakably precious gift that can be offered to people of all faiths. The character of Jesus, we proclaim, provides humanity with a unique and indispensable guide for tracing the development of maturing images and concepts of God across human history and culture. It is the North Star, if you will, to aid all people, whatever their religious background, in their theological pilgrimage. The images of God that most resemble Jesus – whether they originate in the Bible or elsewhere – are the more mature and complete images, and the ones less similar to the character of Jesus would be the more embryonic and incomplete, even though they may be celebrated for being better than the less complete images they replaced.[5]

This is why we cannot simply say that the highest revelation of God is given through the Bible (especially the Bible read as a constitution, or cut and pasted to fit in the Greco-Roman six-line narrative). Rather, we can say that, for Christians, the Bible's highest value is in revealing Jesus, who gives us the highest, deepest and most mature view of the character of the living God.

Several passages of the New Testament affirm this very thing. In Colossians, for example, we do not read, 'The Bible is the image of the invisible God, the firstborn over all creation . . . For God was pleased to have all his fullness dwell in the Bible, and through the Bible to reconcile to himself all things.' Instead we read (1:15ff.), 'The Son is the image of the invisible God . . . For God was pleased to have all his fullness dwell in him, and through him to reconcile to himself all things, whether things on earth or things in heaven, by making peace through his blood, shed on the cross.'

Similarly, in Hebrews 1, we do not read, 'In the past God spoke to our ancestors through the Jewish prophets at many times and in various ways, but in these last days he has spoken to us through the Christian apostles. Their writings are the radiance of God's glory and the exact representation of his being.' No, we read (1:1–3), 'In the past God spoke to our ancestors through the prophets at many times and in various ways, but in these last days he has spoken to us by his Son, whom he appointed heir of all things, and through whom also he made the universe. The Son is the radiance of God's glory and the exact representation of his being, sustaining all things by his powerful word.'

Nor do we read in the Gospel of John, 'In the beginning was the Word, and the Word was with God, and the Word was God . . . The Word became the Scriptures and was published among us . . . The Bible is the light of the world and the way, the truth, and the life. If you have understood the Bible, you have seen the

Father. The Bible and the Father are one.' Instead, we read that the Word was made flesh in Jesus, that Jesus is the light, the way, the truth and the life, that Jesus and the Father are one. In fact, Jesus says (5:39), 'You study the Scriptures diligently because you think that in them you possess eternal life. These are the very Scriptures that testify about me . . .'

Of course, some will claim I'm dishonouring the Scriptures by saying these things, but in fact I'm trying to honour Jesus properly as the Word of God to which the words of Scripture bear witness. The Scriptures are indeed unique and precious – inspired by God, as Paul said, and profitable to teach, confront, correct and train us in right living so that we may be fully equipped to do good works. But just as the bronze serpent that had been an agent of healing in Moses' day could later become something of an idol (2 Kgs 18:4), so Christian individuals and communities can unwittingly become false trinitarians, worshipping Father, Son and Holy Scriptures.

When I am trying to communicate in front of a Christian group what it means to see the ultimate revelation of God not in the Bible but in Jesus, I often use a copy of the Bible to illustrate. To begin, I say that the first half of the Bible will represent the Hebrew Scriptures (or Old Testament), and the second half will represent the Christian Scriptures (the New Testament from Acts to Revelation). Then I say that the spine will represent Jesus, as presented to us in the four Gospels. Then I open the Bible and lay it flat on a table, face down. This represents what we could call a flat reading. In this approach, Jesus is simply in the middle of the book, flesh made words, on a par with all the other words, simply the source of a few more articles in an inspired constitution.[6]

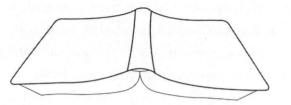

Next, I elevate the first half of the Bible so the open book slants downwards. Here the Hebrew Scriptures are the summit, describing the problem which Jesus and the New Testament are meant to solve, or creating the boundary conditions in which they must work. This reading favours the Law.

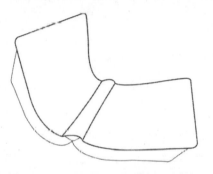

Then I elevate the second half of the Bible so the open book slants upwards, showing a progressive revelation that passes to and through Jesus to find its summit in Paul and perhaps John (in Revelation) as well. This reading favours the Epistles.

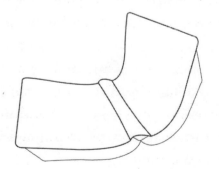

Finally, I angle both covers downwards, so the spine is at the summit, the top of an inverted 'V'. This, I suggest, can represent seeing Christ as the hinge of the biblical story, the spine or backbone of the narrative, the climax and focal point towards which the Old Testament points and ascends, and the peak from which the vigour and vitality of the New Testament flow. This is how Jesus can be seen, for Christians, as the supreme and ultimate revelation of God, with the Old and New Testaments pointing to him like dual spotlights.

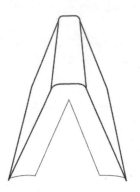

The character of God, seen in Jesus, is not violent and tribal. The living God is not the kind of deity who decrees ethnic cleansing, genocide, racism, slavery, sexism, homophobia, war, religious supremacy or eternal conscious torment. Instead, the character of the living God is like the character of Jesus. Don't simply look at the Bible, I am suggesting: look through the Bible to look at Jesus, and you will see the character of God shining radiant and full. Don't simply look at the many versions of Christian faith (or other religions), for they are full of distortions: look through even the best of our religious communities, and beyond them, to see Jesus.

For when you see him, you are getting the best view afforded to humans of the character of God. That profoundly important insight, of course, carries us to the next question in our quest.

FOUR

THE JESUS QUESTION

CHAPTER 12

Who is Jesus and Why is He Important?

When I celebrate Jesus as Word of God as I did in the previous chapter, some people get upset – and for opposite reasons. I've acknowledged some of these reasons in my previous books, and I will address some of them in upcoming chapters as well.[1] But, before going any further, I need to acknowledge that just saying the name *Jesus* doesn't mean much until we make clear which Jesus we are talking about. We must face the fact that many different saviours can be smuggled in under the name *Jesus*, just as many different deities can be disguised under the term *God*, or vastly different ways of living can be promoted under the name *Christianity*. Jesus can be a victim of identity theft, and people can say and do things with and in his name that he would never, ever do. Nobody has helped me see this more clearly than one of my most loyal and dedicated critics.

He was being interviewed a couple of years back about some of my friends and me, whom he described as 'some emergent types'. He claimed that my friends and I want to recast Jesus as a limp-wristed hippie in a dress with a lot of product in his hair, who drank decaf and made pithy Zen statements about life while shopping for the perfect pair of shoes.

Quite a way with words! The mischaracterisation of my friends and me was nothing, though, compared to the mischaracterisation of Jesus that came shortly thereafter: 'In Revelation, Jesus is a prize fighter with a tattoo down his leg, a sword in his hand and the commitment to make someone bleed. That is the guy I can worship. I cannot worship the hippie, diaper, halo Christ because I cannot worship a guy I can beat up.'

What would cause this articulate and highly committed Christian man to characterise Jesus as a prize fighter, armed with a sword, intent on harming, killing, inflicting violence, drawing blood?

By now, I hope you can anticipate my three-part answer. First, this fellow appears to be firmly lodged within the Greco-Roman narrative, with all its style and swagger. Second, he seems to be working from a constitutional approach to the Bible, which privileges him to pass judgement as if he were a Supreme Court justice. And, third, the view of God that he derives from those two sources causes him to interpret Jesus in a radically different way from the one many of us can accept – since we've lost faith in the constitutional and Greco-Roman paradigms.

A scene in the low-brow 2006 comedy *Talladega Nights: The Ballad of Ricky Bobby* captured the problem we face. Racing legend Ricky Bobby gathers his family – plus his father-in-law and best friend Carl – around the table and says grace for the food. 'Dear Lord Baby Jesus,' he begins, 'or as our brothers to the south call you, Hey-Zeus, we thank you so much for this bountiful harvest of Dominoes, KFC, and the always delicious

Taco Bell.' He continues praying to 'Dear Lord Baby Jesus' and 'Dear Tiny Infant Jesus', thanking him for 'my family, my beautiful two sons, Walker and Texas Ranger . . . and of course my red-hot smoking wife'. The prayer continues with Ricky Bobby asking the Lord to use his 'baby Jesus powers' to heal his father-in-law.

Finally, his wife interrupts: 'You know, Sweetie, Jesus did grow up. You don't always have to call him baby. It's a bit odd and off-puttin' to pray to a baby.'

Ricky Bobby replies, 'Well, look, I like the Christmas Jesus best . . . When you say grace, you can say it to grown up Jesus or teenage Jesus or bearded Jesus or whoever you want.'

At this point, his friend Carl pipes up with his preferences: 'I like to picture Jesus in a tuxedo T-shirt 'cause it says like *I want to be formal but I'm here to party too.* 'Cause I like to party, so I like my Jesus to party.'

Then one of the boys adds that he likes to think of Jesus 'as a ninja fighting off evil samurai', and Carl adds, 'I like to picture Jesus with angel wings. And he's singing lead vocals for Lynyrd Skynyrd and I'm in the front row hammered drunk.'

Ricky Bobby returns to his prayer: 'Dear eight-pound six-ounce newborn infant Jesus, you don't even know a word yet . . . just a little infant and so cuddly – but still omnipotent, we just thank you for all the races I've won and the 21.2 million dollars Woo! Love that money! – that I've accrued over this past season.'[2]

However ridiculous – or tasteless – the scene may be, it mirrors as only satire can a sad reality of Church history and of today's religious landscape. We are all tempted to remake Jesus into just about anything we like. We like a Jesus who (as Annie

Lamott has said) hates the people we hate and likes whatever we like, whether in terms of partying (like Carl), or fighting (like the son), or politics (of either left or right), or 'cuddly omnipotence' (like Ricky Bobby). At least Ricky Bobby seems somewhat aware of what he's doing, choosing the image he 'likes best'. In contrast, too many of us, whether as individuals or groups, honestly – and naïvely – believe that our view is 'objective' and 'true', with no distortion at all.

Among those who become more self-aware about the danger of distortion, an understandable fear arises: if all of us (not just 'all of *them*') are tempted to remake Jesus in our own image, then we should be extremely cautious about compromising, letting Jesus be re-imagined according to contemporary tastes. Thoughtful readers have probably already anticipated a problem with this otherwise well-founded caution. By holding a presumptive hostility to new views of Jesus which may indeed reflect contemporary biases, we may unwittingly preserve old views of Jesus which no less reflect dangerous and compromising biases – just biases of the past rather than the present.

So, in successfully rejecting an insipid 'hippie, diaper, halo Christ', we may unintentionally protect and uphold the white supremacist Jesus, the colonial Jesus, the Euro-centric Jesus, the Republican or Democrat Jesus, the capitalist or communist Jesus, the slave-owning Jesus, the nuclear-bomb-dropping America-first Jesus, the organ-music stained-glass nostalgic-sentimental Jesus, the anti-science know-nothing simpleton Jesus, the prosperity-gospel get-rich-quick Jesus, the institutional white-shirt-and-tie Jesus, the Native-American-slaying genocidal Jesus, the cuddly omnipotent Christmas Jesus, the male-chauvinist Jesus, the homophobic 'God-hates-fags' Jesus, the South African apartheid Jesus, the Joe-Six-Pack Jesus, the anti-Semitic Nazi Jesus, the anti-Muslim Crusader Jesus, and so on. Those who think they stand had better take heed lest they fall, and those who think they know may have some more learning to do.

As we noted earlier, the slippery-slope argument – that we'd better not budge on or rethink anything for fear we'll slip down into liberalism, apostasy or some other hell – proves itself dangerous and naïve even as it tries to protect us from danger and naïvety. First, it assumes we're already at the top of the slope, when it's just as likely that we're already at the bottom or somewhere in the middle. Second, it assumes that even if we were at the peak, there's only one side we might be in danger of sliding down, as if the mountain had only a northern liberal slope without an equally dangerous southern conservative slope, or an eastern 'new-age' slope without an equally dangerous western 'old-age' slope. You can back away from one danger and go smack over the cliff of another.

My loyal critic sincerely and passionately believes in the prize fighter, tattooed, sword-wielding Jesus because of his reading of Revelation 19:11ff.:

> I saw heaven standing open and there before me was a white horse, whose rider is called Faithful and True. With justice he judges and makes war. His eyes are like blazing fire, and on his head are many crowns. He has a name written on him that no one knows but he himself. He is dressed in a robe dipped in blood, and his name is the Word of God. The armies of heaven were following him, riding on white horses and dressed in fine linen, white and clean. Coming out of his mouth is a sharp sword with which to strike down the nations. 'He will rule them

with an iron sceptre.' He treads the winepress of the fury of the wrath of God Almighty. On his robe and on his thigh he has this name written:
KING OF KINGS AND LORD OF LORDS.

Now if we read this passage not as a constitutional document decreeing future events but as a crucial document in the biblical library, we need to place it in its historical context and genre. Clearly, this is a work of Jewish apocalyptic literature, which in turn is part of a larger genre known as the literature of the oppressed.[3] These kinds of literature worked in the first century in ways similar to the way science fiction works for us today. For example, when we read or watch *Planet of the Apes* or *Star Trek*, *The Matrix* or *Wall-E*, we don't think the writers and film-makers are trying to predict the future. We understand they are really talking about the present, and they are doing so in the hope of changing the future.

So *Planet of the Apes* turns out to be a way of talking about how nuclear war – a hot topic in the Cold War era in which *Planet of the Apes* was written – could destroy humanity. And it shines a light on prejudice and racism among contemporary humans by showing them at work in a future civilisation run by evolved great apes. *Star Trek*, over its various incarnations (the original with Captain Kirk, then *Next Generation* with Captain Picard, then *Voyager* with Captain Janeway, then *Deep Space Nine* and *Enterprise* – with more, some of us hope, to come), similarly reflected contemporary themes – dealing with difference and 'the other', finding a way beyond the Cold War us–them mentality, finding a way beyond the impasse of 'pure rationalism' and Romanticism, and so on. *The Matrix* and

Wall-E warn us about losing our humanity in a technological and consumerist culture. The depictions of the future given in these works of science fiction were not predictions or prognostications: they provided windows on the actual present from the perspective of an imagined future, and they did so in the hope of influencing us in the present to live and choose wisely, thus creating a better future than we otherwise would.

In the Apocalypse or Revelation, early followers of Jesus are in a similar moment of creative possibility. They must deal with the fact that they believe Jesus was right and his kingdom was true, yet they are being vilified and persecuted brutally. The emperor of Rome (maybe the sociopath Nero, maybe the ruthless dictator Domitian, depending on when we date the text) and his powers seem firmly in control, and nothing seems to be moving in the direction of the kingdom of God. In that light, what message do they need? Do they need to hear that soon they can forget about all that naïve peace and forgiveness stuff that Jesus taught – and soon they'll be allowed to pull out their swords, mount their war horses and kick some persecutors' hindquarters? Or do they need a message of reassurance, encouragement and confidence that the way of peace that Jesus modelled is indeed the good and right way, that it will triumph in the end, and so they shouldn't give up on it?

Apparently, the passage in question can be interpreted either way – one way that completely subverts the message of Jesus' Gospel life and message of peace making and reconciliation, and another way that reinforces it. For me, the latter approach is the only acceptable one. The passage in question isn't telling us that Jesus is a prize fighter with a commitment to make somebody bleed. Nor is it claiming that the Jesus of the Gospels was a fake-me-out Jesus pretending to be a peace-and-love guy, when really he was planning to come back and act like a proper Caesar, brutal, willing to torture and determined to conquer with crushing violence . . . more of a slash-and-burn guy.[4] Nor is it informing us that even God has to use violence to impose the divine will in the end.

Instead, this image of Jesus as a conqueror reassures believers that the peaceful Jesus who entered Jerusalem on a donkey that day wasn't actually weak and defeated; he was in fact every bit as powerful as a Caesar on a steed. His message of forgiveness and reconciliation, conveyed as a sword coming *out of his mouth* (not *in his hand*, as my loyal critic asserted – quite an important detail), will in the end prove far more powerful than Caesar's swords and spears. And the blood on his robe: that's not the blood of his enemies, it's his own blood, because the battle hasn't even begun yet, and Revelation has already shown us Jesus standing as 'a Lamb, looking as if . . . slain' (5:6). It may also recall the blood of the peaceful martyrs (6:9–11), since in attacking them, violent forces were also attacking Jesus, the Prince of Peace who taught them the way of peace.

To repeat: Revelation is not portraying Jesus returning to earth in the future, having repented of his naïve Gospel ways and having converted to Caesar's 'realistic' Greco-Roman ways instead. He hasn't become discouraged about Caesar seeming to get the upper hand after his resurrection and concluded that it's best to live by the sword after all (Matt. 26:52). Jesus hasn't abandoned the way of peace (Luke 19:42) and concluded that the way of Pilate is better, mandating that his disciples should fight after all (John 18:36). He hasn't had second thoughts about all that talk about forgiveness (Matt. 18:22) and concluded that on the 78th offence (or 491st, depending on interpretation) you should pull out your sword and hack off your offender's head rather than turn the other cheek (Matt. 5:39).

He hasn't given up on that 'love your enemy' stuff (Matt. 5:44) and judged it naïve and foolish after all (1 Cor. 1:25), concluding instead that God's strength is made manifest not in weakness but in crushing domination (2 Cor. 12:9). He hasn't had a change of heart, concluding that the weapons he needs are physical after all (2 Cor. 10:3–4), or that the enemies of the kingdom are flesh and blood after all (Eph. 6:12), which would mean that the way to glory isn't actually by dying on the cross (Phil. 2:8–9) but rather by nailing others on it.

He hasn't sold the humble donkey (Luke 19:28ff.) on eBay and purchased chariots, war horses, tanks, landmines and B-1s instead (Zech. 9:9–10). He hasn't climbed back to the top of the temple and decided that he made a mistake the first time (Matt. 4:1–10), or concluded that from now on he'd be smarter to follow Peter's Greco-Roman strategies 'of men' (Matt. 16:23). He hasn't decided that the message of the cross is a little too foolish after all (1 Cor. 1:18), or that Christ killing his foes is far more exciting than that lame, absurd 'hippie' gospel of 'Christ crucified' (1 Cor. 2:2).

He hasn't decided that my loyal critic was right, that nobody can be expected to worship a king they can beat up (Matt. 27:27ff.). He hasn't decided that a tattoo down his leg would look a whole lot tougher and more macho than scars on his hands, feet and side (John 20:27). He hasn't decided to defect to the Greco-Roman narrative since the majority of people who claim adherence to the religion that bears his name seem to frame their lives by it rather than by his good news of the kingdom of God.

The one I believe to be the real Jesus – the Jesus of Matthew, Mark, Luke and John, the Jesus of the Acts and Epistles and Revelation too (wisely interpreted) – cannot be understood and must not be trimmed to fit within the Greco-Roman framing story: he can only be crucified upon its violent right angles. Jesus matters precisely because he provides us with a living alternative to the confining Greco-Roman narrative in which our world and our religions live, move and have their being too much of the time. That's what Revelation actually tells us: that the humble man of peace is Lord. It confesses, in the midst of persecution and martyrdom, that the poor, unarmed Galilean riding on the donkey, hailed by the poor and hopeful, is the one to trust. It invites us to pledge allegiance to the one who rules by his own example of service and suffering rather than by making examples of others.

Revelation celebrates not the love of power but the power of love. It denies, with all due audacity, that God's anointed liberator is the Divine Terminator, threatening revenge for all who refuse to honour him, growling 'I'll be back!' It asserts, instead, that God's anointed liberator is the one we beat up, who promises mercy to those who strike him, whispering, 'Father, forgive them, for they know not what they do.' The suffering, serving one who bled on a cross, not the one with a commitment to make others suffer and bleed, is the King of kings and Lord of lords. In response to the crucified one's name, not Caesar's or any other violent human's, every knee will gladly bow.

If you don't want to worship someone you can beat up, then I might humbly suggest that you reconsider Caesar and the Greco-Roman narrative. It sounds like 'Christ and him crucified' is not for you. At least not yet.

CHAPTER 13

Jesus Outside the Lines

I am blessed, it turns out, with more than one loyal critic. Another one, even more well known than the first, in a widely disseminated radio broadcast (and in a book with a rattlesnake on the cover) contrasted his views of Jesus with my own: 'The only reason Jesus came was to save people from hell . . . Jesus had no social agenda . . . [He didn't come to eliminate poverty or slavery or] fix something in somebody's life for the little moment they live on this earth.'[1]

Now what could possibly cause this earnest and educated Christian man to assert that Jesus had no agenda regarding poverty and slavery? What could motivate a dedicated Bible teacher to minimise horrible social realities as minor inconveniences or pet peeves – 'something in somebody's life for the little moment they live on this earth'?[2] How could a pious and devoted believer ignore all of Jesus' words about the poor, all his deeds for the poor and oppressed, beginning with his first public sermon where he quoted Isaiah 61?

'The Spirit of the Lord is on me,
because he has anointed me
to proclaim good news to the poor.
He has sent me to proclaim freedom for the prisoners
and recovery of sight for the blind,
to set the oppressed free,
to proclaim the year of the Lord's favour.'
. . . 'Today this scripture is fulfilled in your hearing.'
(Luke 4:18–21, TNIV)

My faithful critic's statement is even more amazing in the light of the rest of the New Testament, where concern for the poor and oppressed remains strong page after page (see, for example, Gal. 2:10; Phlm. 16; 1 John 3:17–18; Jas 1:27; 3:14ff.). Yet for him, the *only* way we can understand Jesus is as the one who saves from hell (a subject to which we will return in a later question). For him, Jesus is not the one who saves from poverty, from captivity, from blindness or from oppression, even though these are Jesus' very words (borrowed from Isaiah in Luke 4) to describe his mission. I think you'll agree that my faithful critic's statement can only make sense, first, if we interpret Jesus within the confines of the Greco-Roman six-line narrative; second, if we predetermine to read the Bible as a constitution; and, third, if we construct and solidify our understanding of God before seeking to understand Jesus, rather than letting Jesus serve as the Word-made-flesh revelation of God's character.

In contrast, our quest allows us – and requires us – to put these pre-critical presuppositions aside and approach Jesus differently. Our quest invites us to understand Jesus in terms of the three-dimensional biblical narrative we introduced earlier, to see him in terms of the Genesis story of creation and reconciliation, the Exodus story of liberation and formation, and the Isaiah story of new creation and peace-making kingdom. We could choose any of the four Gospels to illustrate this alternative view, but let's choose the least likely of the four, John.[3]

John's Gospel is the one most often used to buttress the Greco-Roman story. Verses such as John 3:16, 5:24 and 14:6 are routinely interpreted to address a set of problems defined by the six-line narrative, namely how to remedy the 'ontological fall' and legally avoid eternal conscious torment, which (you'll recall) is the punishment for 'original sin' required (I suggest) by the Greco-Roman god Theos. But these verses and all the others in John's Gospel look very different when we read them in the three-dimensional biblical paradigm (creation, liberation, peace-making kingdom) rather than the six-line paradigm, starting with the Gospel's first words.

> In the beginning was the Word, and the Word was with God, and the Word was God. He was with God in the beginning. Through him all things were made . . . In him was life, and that life was the light of all people . . . the true light that gives light to everyone . . .
> (John 1:1–9)

With those first words, 'In the beginning', John clearly evokes the Genesis story. The story of Jesus is identified with the creative Word, the 'Let there be . . .' by which all things are created. He is associated with light, the first thing that God lets there be. He is associated with life, the life that God breathes into the clay of humanity. The psalmists tell us that all creation – the heavens and earth and all they contain – reflects the glory of God, and similarly, John tells us, 'We have seen [Jesus'] glory, the glory of the one and only' (1:14). Later we see Jesus creating wine from water, a creative act with clear echoes of the Genesis story. In fact, just as Genesis begins with the Spirit 'hovering over the waters', throughout John we have interwoven references to the Spirit and to water, most obviously when Jesus walks on (hovers over) the water, or when he tells the woman at the well or the crowd in Jerusalem about the living waters that he will give them, or when he tells Nicodemus he must be born of water and the Spirit.

His other miracles – healings, provision of food for hungry people, giving life to a dead man, conquering death himself – all suggest Jesus' life-giving, health-giving creative power. Together, these examples make clear that, from the first sentence, John is telling us that a new creative moment, a new Genesis, is happening in Jesus. The Genesis echoes keep resounding to the end of the book, where they ring out powerfully in the climactic account of the resurrection.

> Early on the first day of the week, while it was still dark, Mary Magdalene went to the tomb and saw that the stone had been removed from the entrance.
> (*John 20:1*)

Consider the imagery: the first day of a new week, the coming of light into darkness and of life into a void. The language evokes a new day, a new beginning, so the tomb becomes the womb giving birth to a new creation. Not only that, but if the book of Genesis ends with reconciliation as Joseph and his brothers are brought together, if it concludes with God's good intent overcoming evil human intent, then John ends in the same way, with a reconciliation among brothers. The risen Jesus could have been angry with his disciples for betraying, abandoning and disbelieving him, but he tells Mary, 'Go . . . to my brothers and tell them, "I am ascending to my Father and your Father, to my God and your God"' (20:17). Soon we see doubting Thomas being restored to his brothers and denying Peter being restored to his brothers. The Gospel fittingly ends not at a scenic sunset, but just after daybreak, around a breakfast cooking fire, the beginning, as it were, of the first day of a new world, a second Genesis.

In this light, Jesus' offers of 'life of the ages' and 'life abundant' sparkle with new significance. When Jesus promises 'life of the ages' (a far better translation of the Greek *zoein aionian*, I believe, than 'eternal life', the meaning of which is poorly framed in many minds by the six-line narrative), he is not promising 'life after death' or 'life in eternal heaven instead of eternal hell'. (John, it should be noted, never mentions hell, a highly significant fact.[4]) Instead, Jesus is promising a life that transcends 'life in the present age', an age that is soon going to end in tumult. Being 'born of God' (1:13) and 'born again' or 'born from above' (3:3ff.) would in this light mean being born into this new creation. So, again, Jesus is offering a life in the new Genesis, the new creation which is 'of the ages'   meaning it is part of God's original creation, not simply part of the current regimes, plots, kingdoms and economies created by humans in 'the present evil age' (a term Paul uses in Gal. 1:4). No wonder the risen Christ's first appearance is in a garden, and he is imagined to be a gardener (John 20:10ff.), just as Jesus has portrayed the Father as a gardener (15:1). John wants us to see in Jesus a rebirth of the original garden.

If these Genesis themes are strong, the prime Exodus narrative of liberation and formation resonates even more strongly in John's Gospel. Notice the obvious resonances to Moses in chapter 1:

> He came to that which was his own, but his own did not receive him . . . For the law was given through Moses; grace and truth came through Jesus Christ.
> *(John 1:11, 17)*

Just as Moses was initially rejected by his brothers (Exod. 2:14), so Jesus was initially rejected. Just as Moses led the way in liberation from Egyptian oppression, so Jesus leads the way in liberation from the social and spiritual oppression of his day. Just as Moses gave the Law, so Jesus does even more – as we shall explore in more detail shortly. In fact, although much attention has been given to the ways in which 'the Word' or 'Logos' of John 1 evokes Greek thought, we should also note that, for Greek-speaking Jews, 'Logos' evoked Law. The Law was understood not simply as a list of rules or requirements, but as a kind of inherent logic or wisdom that is woven into all creation – a way, a truth, a life, another resonance with John's Gospel (14:6).

In Exodus, God's presence was associated with the tabernacle, a sacred tent, and John says, 'The Word became flesh and made his dwelling [tent or tabernacle] among us' (1:14). Moses once asked to see God, but was permitted to see only God's aftermath, as it were (Exod. 33). John writes, 'No one has ever seen God, but the one and only [Son], who is himself God and is in closest relationship with the Father, has made him known' (1:18). Moses once asked God's name (Exod. 3:14), but was only told, 'I am,' and this is how Jesus habitually identifies himself in John's Gospel (see especially 8:58).

John the Baptist introduces Jesus as 'the Lamb of God, who takes away the sin of the world' (1:29). Here John the Baptist evokes not (or not only) the sacrificial lambs of Leviticus, but (or but also) the lamb that was slain at the Passover to protect the people from the tenth plague, the plague that finally persuaded the Egyptians to liberate their slaves. And the term 'Christ' or 'Messiah' literally means 'anointed one', suggesting a king or leader chosen by God to (like Moses) liberate the people from their oppression.

Jesus evokes Moses directly in his conversation with Nicodemus, saying that the Son of Man (a complex term drawn from Dan. 7, which I believe suggests a new generation or genesis of humanity) will be lifted up as Moses lifted up a bronze serpent in the wilderness (Num. 21). Jesus' provision of bread (John 6) and later fish (John 21) similarly evoke Moses' provision of manna and quail, suggesting that Jesus is leading the people on a new exodus journey. Even his walking on water (6:16ff.) evokes the crossing of the Red Sea.

Along with many other direct references to Moses and the Law (7:16–24; 8:5ff.), and indirect references to being liberated from slavery (8:31ff.) or leading the flock of God through the wilderness (John 10), we find Jesus giving a new command, one word (or *logos*) that in a sense will transcend and include the ten words (or *decalogue*) given by Moses: 'A new command I give you: Love one another. As I have loved you, so you must love one another' (13:34).

At the end of John's Gospel, we find Jesus telling his disciples that they will see him no longer, that the Spirit will guide them, and that they will now feed and tend his flock in his place – echoing, it appears, Moses' commissioning of Joshua to lead into the promised land the people Moses had led out of Egypt and through the wilderness. Just as they have followed Moses, they should now follow Joshua, Moses said; now Jesus says they should follow the Spirit, just as they have followed him. Interestingly, John ends his Gospel with the command Mark uses to begin his Gospel: 'Follow me' (21:19). It is as if Jesus is saying, 'OK. You've now been liberated from Egypt. My death and resurrection are like crossing the Red Sea. But our journey has only just begun: keep following now, through the wilderness and into the promised land. Just as fire and cloud guided your ancestors, my Spirit will guide you now.'

The promised land, of course, suggests the third dimension of the biblical narrative: the peace-making kingdom celebrated by all the prophets, but especially Isaiah. As we considered earlier, the narrative begins with the longing for a literal homeland – first, for Abraham, a home outside the Sumerian Empire, and later, under Moses, a place of freedom outside the Egyptian Empire, and later still, for the exiles, a return to their homeland, liberated from the Babylonian/Medo-Persian Empires. Gradually, the idea of a promised land morphs from a geographic reality to a social one; 'a land flowing with milk and honey' becomes a society where justice flows like water. This new society or kingdom is also described as a new era – a new time of *shalom*, harmony, social equity, prosperity and safety.

The key to this golden time is light (Isa. 2:5; 42:6–7; 49:6; 60:1–3), and, along with light, the healing of blindness (35:5ff.; 42:16ff.) and other maladies. So it's no surprise that John's

Gospel begins by telling us that Jesus is the light of the world that shines for all people in darkness (1:4; 3:19; 12:33–41), and that central to his Gospel is the healing of a blind man, with a lengthy reflection on the deeper meaning of this miracle (9:1–41, echoed in 12:37ff., where Isaiah is directly referenced).

Isaiah's vision of the peaceable kingdom includes bizarre imagery (to us, that is: we considered earlier the image of a child playing with a cobra, or of a lion living peacefully with a lamb), including pictures of geographical transformation (40:1ff.) like this one:

In the last days
the mountain of the LORD's temple will be established
as the highest of the mountains;
it will be exalted above the hills,
and all nations will stream to it.
Many peoples will come and say,
'Come, let us go up to the mountain of the LORD,
to the house of the God of Jacob.
He will teach us his ways,
so that we may walk in his paths.'
The law will go out from Zion,
the word of the LORD from Jerusalem:
He will judge between the nations
and will settle disputes for many peoples.
They will beat their swords into ploughshares
and their spears into pruning hooks.
Nation will not take up sword against nation,
nor will they train for war any more.
(Isa. 2:1–5, echoed in Mic. 4:1–4)

Obviously, the prophet isn't predicting a literal tectonic shift in which Jerusalem rises further above sea level and Mount Everest sinks, but rather a time when God's wisdom draws nations up to a higher level of relating, so disputes are settled non-violently, wisely, peacefully. (John may be echoing this global attraction in 3:14; 8:28; and 12:19). We find in Isaiah another set of geographical images associated with springs transforming the desert into a garden (32:1–2; 35:6ff.; 44:3). John picks up this water image in the conversation between Jesus and the unnamed woman at the well (John 4:1–42), where a dispute about mountains and a conversation about water gives way to a deeper insight: that God is seeking worshippers who come not to the correct mountain, but with the correct spirit.

Similarly, the thirst for physical water (Isa. 55) points to the present availability of living water (echoed in John 7:37ff.). Strikingly, Jesus says to the unnamed woman, 'A time is coming and has now come . . .' (John 4:23), echoing Jesus' words elsewhere (Mark 1:15; Luke 4:21) announcing that the long-awaited time of the peaceable kingdom has indeed arrived. Just as Isaiah's poetry is filled with images of war giving way to peace, Jesus makes clear to Pilate that in the kingdom Jesus represents, disputes aren't solved with swords (John 18:36).

Both Isaiah (1:11ff., 55, 58) and John's Jesus critique the religious establishment (implied in his use of ceremonial water jars for producing wine in 2:6, in the clearing of the temple in 2:13ff., in the interchange with Nicodemus in 3:10, in the marginalisation of Jerusalem in 4:21, in his healing on the Sabbath in 5:1–8, and in his subversion of a stoning in 8:5). And both Isaiah and John work with the rich imagery of a vineyard (Isa. 5:1–7; John 15) and emphasise the role of the Spirit of the Lord (Isa. 11:1–5;

Four: The Jesus Question

42:1; 61:1; John 14–16). John picks up Isaiah's theme of joy as well (Isa. 26; 35; 51; 55; 60; John 15:11; 16:22), along with Isaiah's use of wine imagery (Isa. 25; 55:1.; John 2). In Isaiah we see the precursors of Jesus' powerful shepherd imagery (Isa. 40:11; John 10:1–18; 21:15ff.) and childbirth imagery (Isa. 54; John 16:21), and even the precedent for calling God our Father (63:16; 64:8).

For Isaiah, the same 'day of the LORD' that will bring liberation for the oppressed will mean accountability for the oppressors (Isa. 5:8ff., 10:1ff.), a theme that John picks up again and again (5:22–30; 9:39; 12:31). And we can't forget Isaiah's striking theme of the Servant of the Lord (Isa. 42; 49; 50; 52), which John employs poignantly as Jesus literally costumes himself in the role of a servant (John 13). Just as Isaiah's Servant of the Lord liberates and heals through suffering (52:13 – 53:12), so John's Jesus goes through mockery and torture to the cross. And just as Isaiah predicts beauty beyond ashes, joy beyond mourning (61) and a new heavens and a new earth beyond the suffering and stress that must first be faced (65:17), so John presents us with a Jesus who raises the dead (11) and ultimately is raised from the dead himself (20:18), evidence of a new creation arising from the old (Isa. 66:22).

All of Isaiah's powerful images are interwoven with the dream of a peaceable kingdom, one that fulfils the unfulfilled promise of David's kingdom (9:7; 11:1, 10; 16:5; 22:22; 55:3). Of course, Isaiah is only one of many prophets who fund our imaginations with the peaceable kingdom dream, and John similarly draws from other prophets too (e.g. note how strikingly John 12:12 echoes Zech. 9:9ff.).

But even these few examples, selected from so many more,

make it clear that Jesus, contrary to my dear loyal critic's assertion, did not come merely to 'save souls from hell'. No, he came to launch a new Genesis, to lead a new exodus, and to announce, embody and inaugurate a new kingdom, as the Prince of Peace (Isa. 9:6). Seen in this light, Jesus and his message have everything to do with poverty, slavery and a 'social agenda'.

When we try to read John and also the other Gospels within the flat, six-line Greco-Roman narrative, the sandal just doesn't fit. But when we see Jesus in the three-dimensional Jewish narrative, we discover a gift from the Jews to the whole world: good news (that pregnant term being another powerful resonance with Isaiah, in 40:9; 52:7; 61:1) of a new Genesis, a new exodus, and a new kingdom come.

So many people are like my loyal critic: so utterly bought into the six-line, black-and-white, soul-sorting heaven-or-hell Greco-Roman narrative that it has become the pre-critical lens through which they see everything, causing them to see some things that aren't there and rendering invisible many things that are there. If they could only take off that set of glasses for long enough to see Jesus in full colour, in three dimensions, everything would look different. If only.

Thankfully, more and more people are realising that there's a renaissance under way regarding our understanding of Jesus. More and more of us are discovering Jesus as Word and Lord, coloured outside the conventional six lines. This Jesus, we discover, is far more wonderful, attractive, compelling, inspiring and unbelievably believable than the Jesus shrunk and trimmed to fit within them.

FIVE

THE GOSPEL
QUESTION

CHAPTER 14

What is the Gospel?

Like a lot of Protestants, for many years I 'knew' what the gospel was. I 'knew' that the gospel was the message of 'justification by grace through faith', distorted or forgotten by those pesky Catholics but rediscovered by our hero Martin Luther through a reading of our even greater hero Paul, and especially his magnum opus, the epistle to the Romans. If Catholics were called 'Roman Catholics' because of their headquarters in Rome, we could have been called 'Romans Protestants' because Paul's epistle to the Romans served as our theological headquarters. As its avid students, we 'knew' without question what it was about. To my embarrassment, though, about fifteen years ago I stopped knowing a lot of what I previously knew.

A lunchtime meeting in a Chinese restaurant unconvinced and untaught me. My lunch-mate was a well-known evangelical theologian who quite rudely upset years of theological certainty with one provocative statement: 'Most evangelicals haven't got the foggiest notion of what the gospel really is.' He then asked me how I would define the gospel, and I answered as any good Romans Protestant would, quoting Romans. He followed up with this simple but annoying rhetorical question: 'You're quoting Paul. Shouldn't you let Jesus define the gospel?' When I gave him a quizzical look, he asked, 'What was the gospel according to Jesus?' A little humiliated, I mumbled something akin to 'You tell me', and he replied, 'For Jesus, the gospel was very clear: *The kingdom of God is at hand*. That's the gospel according to Jesus. Right?' I again mumbled something, maybe 'I guess so'. Seeing my lack of conviction, he added, 'Shouldn't you read Paul in light of Jesus, instead of reading Jesus in light of Paul?'

I didn't admit it to the theologian as I stared deep into my hot-and-sour soup, but I had no idea what he was talking about. As a constitutional reader of the Bible, the words of Jesus and Paul were pretty much on a par for me. Beyond that, I had always assumed that 'kingdom of God' meant 'kingdom of heaven', which meant 'going to heaven after you die', which required believing the message of Paul's epistle to the Romans, which I understood to teach a theory of atonement called 'penal substitution', which was the basis for a formula for forgiveness of original sin called 'justification by grace through faith'. But my lunch-mate's questions unsettled all that. They bugged me so much that I started rereading the Gospels with new intensity, and it became clear that my knowledge needed to be doubted and at least some of my accumulated learning needed to be either unlearned or supplemented. Jesus' one-word preface to his gospel, 'Repent!', made sense to me as never before. 'Repent' means to become pensive again or have a change of mind and heart, and I needed to become pensive again about the gospel – its meaning for the world and for me.

The kingdom of God is at hand, or, in the words of my friend Rod Washington, *God's new benevolent society is already among us*.[1] I've devoted two entire books to understanding what that simple phrase meant and means, and I still feel there's so much more to discover.[2] Along with many others, I have written about how the phrase shimmers and glows in relation to the dominant social reality of Jesus' time: the kingdom of Caesar or the empire of Rome.[3] We've explored how the kingdom-orientated term *Christ* means *liberating king*, the one who will free God's people from oppression, confront and humble their oppressors, and then lead both into a better day. We've considered the radical – even treasonous – use of the term *Lord* by the early Christians: to declare *Jesus is Lord* meant – joyfully and defiantly – that Caesar wasn't.[4] This original three-word creed helps explain why so many people were willing to be martyrs in the early church: each martyrdom was a witness to the striking contrast between the two competing kingdoms and their lords – one who would gladly torture and kill to establish dominance via the *Pax Romana*, the other who would willingly suffer and die to establish reconciliation via the *Pax Christi*.

Increasing numbers of us, when freed from the constraints of the six-line Greco-Roman narrative and the associated constitutional reading of the Bible, gain courage to speak what has become joyfully clear to us in this fresh reading of the Gospels: Jesus didn't come to start a new religion to replace first Judaism and then all other religions, whether by the pen, the pulpit, the sword or the apocalypse. (In fact, in the light of everything we know about Jesus, doesn't it seem positively ludicrous to imagine him gathering his disciples to announce, 'Listen, guys. Here's my real agenda. We're going to start a new religion, and we're going to name it after me'?[5])

Instead, he came to announce a new kingdom, a new way of life, a new way of peace that carried good news to all people of every religion. A new kingdom is much bigger than a new religion, and in fact it has room for many religious traditions within it.[6] This good news wasn't simply about a new way to solve the religious problems of ontological fall and original sin (problems, remember once more, that arise within a different narrative altogether). It wasn't simply information about how individual souls could leave earth, avoid hell and ascend to heaven after death. No: it was about God's will being done on earth as in heaven for all people. It was about God's faithful solidarity with all humanity in our suffering, oppression and evil. It was about God's compassion and call to be reconciled with God and with one another – before death, on earth. It was a summons to rethink everything and enter a life of retraining as disciples or learners of a new way of life, citizens of a new kingdom.

More and more of us have begun to see what was incredibly obvious all along, if it weren't for our thorough Greco-Roman 'civilising' (or mind control): that the good news proclaimed by Jesus Christ wasn't primarily a way of integrating Plato and Aristotle, spirit and matter, perfect being and fallen becoming, or even law and grace – even though, in a sense, it does all these things. More essentially, it was a fulfilment of the three prime narratives of the Hebrew Scriptures.

First, to accept the free gift of being 'born again' into 'life of the ages' or 'life abundant' meant participation in a *new*

Genesis, a new creation, interrupting the downward death-spiral of violence and counter-violence, and joining an upward, regenerative movement. Second, to follow Jesus meant embarking on a *new exodus*, passing through the waters once again (this time, baptism instead of the Red Sea), eating a new Passover meal (the Eucharist) and experiencing liberation from the principalities and powers that oppress and enslave. Third, to enter or receive the 'kingdom of God' meant becoming a citizen of a *new kingdom*, the peaceable kingdom imagined by the prophets and inaugurated in Christ, learning its ways (as a disciple) and demonstrating in word and deed its presence and availability to all (as an apostle).

In this way, the most striking single element of Jesus' proclamation of the kingdom may have been, 'The time has come!' The kingdom of God is not a distant reality to wait for someday, Jesus proclaims; the kingdom is *at hand*, within reach, near, here, now (Mark 1:14ff.). Everyone agrees the poor and downtrodden should be helped someday, oppression and exploitation should be stopped someday, the planet should be healed someday, we should study war no more someday. But, for Jesus, the dream of Isaiah and the other prophets – of a time when good news would come to the poor, the prisoners, the blind, the oppressed and the indebted – was not 500 or 2,000 or 4,000 or 10,000 years in the future: the dream was being fulfilled *today* (Luke 4:18–21). The time has come *today* to cancel debts, to forgive, to treat enemies as neighbours, to share your bread with the hungry and your clothes with the naked, to invite the outcasts over for dinner, to confront oppressors not with sharp knives but with unarmed kindness. No wonder Jesus called people to repent: if the kingdom is at hand, we need to adjust our way of life and join in the joyful, painful mission of reconciliation right now, a.s.a.p.!

Now it's been tempting for those of us who are grappling with this message of the kingdom to try to minimise any implied discomfort for our good Christian sisters and brothers. Most of them are all, after all, quite comfortable in their padded pews, satisfied in their respectable denominations and non-denominations, entertained by 24/7 religious radio-TV-internet, and content and confident with their familiar but vastly different version of the gospel. It seems unconscionably rude to disturb anybody or perhaps incite them to hand out canary-yellow warning flyers.

After all, we're not importing any strange language into our theology: we're strictly working with what's always been there. We're not claiming some new revelation or new authority figure: we're following the best Christian tradition of going back to Jesus and the Scriptures, so our quest for a new kind of Christianity is, in fact, a most conservative quest. In our return to our roots, however, we're not writing off all the great sages, scholars and saints of Church history: we're simply going back to the original evangelists, apostles and especially Jesus and making sure we're as in sync with them as possible from this point forward. We're not trying to explain away anything in the Bible: we're simply trying to take seriously the central elements of the canonical texts that have been studiously marginalised for too long – the good news of the kingdom of God, and the biblical narratives that it consummates, integrates, celebrates and opens to all people everywhere.

So, being peace-loving people who don't want to upset any-one needlessly, we've thought, 'Maybe this new understanding can simply be added to what we already have, gradually, gently, so they won't even notice. Maybe it can enrich our existing understandings without upsetting them in any major way. Maybe we can simply add this kingdom-of-God stuff as fine print on the bottom of our existing theological contracts. Yes, those contracts presume the six-line Greco-Roman narrative, defend our constitutional reading of the Bible and leave our pre-Jesus view of God unchallenged and unchanged. Yes, it will be difficult and delicate to do so, but maybe we can bring this new wine into the old wineskins without upsetting anyone.'

Many are still working with this hope, and I wish them luck, but quite a few of us are coming to believe that the good news of Jesus the liberating King cannot fit into or co-exist with the Greco-Roman narrative. (If it did, Jesus would be neither liberator nor king.) Similarly, we're discovering that the more we let Jesus' message of the kingdom of God sink in, the more it begins to unsettle all our existing understandings and categories. It changes everything. Before this realisation, we are like lawyers trying to save an old contract, adding more and more fine print on page after page, until the provisos are weightier than the original contract. (This is good work, I suppose, and must be done for a generation or two, but it is not the work to which I feel called.) At some point, though, more and more of us will finally decide that it would make more sense to go back and revise the contract from scratch. And that process has begun. It is nowhere near complete, but the cat is out of the bag, imaginations are sizzling and exciting theological work is being done – by theologians, yes, but, equally importantly, by pastors, preachers, songwriters, screenwriters, producers, poets, dramatists, sculptors, photographers, painters, architects, youth leaders, community organisers, mums and dads and thoughtful readers like you.

But perhaps you're already anticipating the daunting problem that we all soon must face. Yes, our fresh discovery of Jesus' good news of the kingdom of God makes sense of the Gospels as never before. But what are we to make of Paul's writings, especially that pivotal epistle, Romans? I remember, eight or ten years ago, getting up my courage to re-read Romans now that I'd begun to reorientate my faith around Jesus' gospel of the kingdom of God. Would I uncover irreconcilable differences between Paul and Jesus, as some of my friends had done? Would I have to choose one over the other? Would I be able to fit my new understanding of Jesus into my old understandings of Paul and Romans, or vice versa? I got the idea of downloading the text onto my computer, and I started reading slowly and closely, keeping a journal of my responses as commentary to the text.[7]

What struck me first was the impression that Paul wasn't trying to define or explain the gospel at all – but rather he was trying to clean up a mess that Jesus had created through his gospel. By mess, I mean Jesus had quite effectively ruined the tidy, conventional categories of his religious community. In his mind, some prostitutes were closer to God than some Pharisees, and some tax collectors closer than some priests – and the greatest faith Jesus could find in all Israel was found in the heart of a political enemy of another religion.[8] Similarly, Jesus broke the rules about clean and unclean, and he kept raising wild and revolutionary new proposals – about the Sabbath, about what's kosher, about how to treat enemies and outsiders, about who's a true descendant of Abraham, and so on. In all these ways,

Jesus cracked opened the door for non-Jews to be accepted in the faith tradition that had previously been exclusively Jewish. First Philip (in Acts 8) and then Peter (in Acts 10) and then Paul would swing the door wide open and put a big 'All Are Welcome' mat on the front porch. How do you work out a deep shift like this in a community of faithful people who have always defined themselves in exclusive ways?

For example, what happens when a Gentile follower of Jesus invites a Jewish follower of Jesus over for dinner, and honours his guest by roasting his biggest, fattest, tastiest pig? What happens when Jewish followers of Jesus refuse to accept their Gentile counterparts until they start acting more Jewish (by dropping bacon from their diet, by observing all the right holidays, and by getting circumcised, for goodness' sake)? Even deeper, how do you help Jews and Gentiles stop seeing their counterparts as 'the other' and start seeing them as 'one another'? These are the kinds of messes Jesus' followers had to deal with through the rest of the first century.

As the Acts of the Apostles unfolds, the centre of gravity shifts from Jerusalem to Antioch and soon there seems to be no single geographic centre at all; the Church becomes a world-wide web, expanding from every node as little cells of believers are creating sites of *koinonia* and *diakonia* at every turn.[9] And Paul is, in a sense, right in the middle of the mess. He is the man simultaneously defending the right of the Gentile Christians to be different and struggling to keep Jews and Gentiles working together as one community.[10]

So, the more I read and re-read Romans and tried to make sense of its message, the more I became convinced that Paul never intended his epistle to be an exposition on the gospel. The

Gospels of Matthew, Mark, Luke and John would soon fulfil that exposition role quite well. Instead, Romans aimed to address a more immediate, practical question in the early Christian movement, less than twenty-five years after Jesus' death and resurrection: how could Jews and Gentiles in all their untamed diversity come and remain together as peers in the kingdom of God, without having first- and second-class Christians on the one hand, and, on the other, without being homogenised like a McDonald's franchise with the same menu, same pricing, same bathroom soap?

When we 'Romans Protestants' want to prove that Romans is an exposition of the gospel, we often quote these words from the letter's introduction (1:16):

> I am not ashamed of the gospel, because it is the power of God that brings salvation[11] to everyone who believes.

But, in so doing, we leave out the last eight words of the sentence: *first to the Jew, then to the Gentile.* Those words, it turns out, aren't filler: they're the point. Jesus' gospel of the kingdom must welcome Jews in their Jewishness and Gentiles in their Goyishness, and Paul wants to show how that can be. If you don't read Romans this way, you can with some wrestling twist chapters 1 – 8 so they fit together reasonably well. Then comes a strange interruption in chapters 9 – 11 that hardly fits at all, and then a somewhat mundane practical addendum in 12 – 16. But if you read Romans as a refusal to let Jesus' expansive and revolutionary gospel of the kingdom of God be shrunk back into the categories of anyone's exclusive religion, then the theme flows beautifully from beginning to end.

Now when I say the theme flows beautifully, it's important to note that Paul, like Jesus, is not a modern Western linear-argument type of guy. He's Middle-Eastern. He thinks in circles and speaks in parables. Paul is less the engineer and more the poet, maybe not the kind who doesn't comb his hair or clean his glasses or keep his shirt-tail tucked in, but at least the kind who understands the power of imagination and has a way with words. His letter (contrary to dominant readings) is no more of a well-reasoned, linear, logical, analytical argument than Jesus' sermons were. *And that's not a bad thing.* That's a good thing. Even though it frustrates modern readers. A linear prose argument may be the best way to teach engineering or refrigerator repair, but to teach matters of the spirit, literary forms work better – with all their twists and turns, their circlings and returns and refrains, their imagination and provocation, their spin and sneakiness (I mean that in the most positive way possible).

So as I read Paul, he will not address his one theme in a linear, lawyerly fashion. He will circle around it, again and again, from this angle and that, trying once, twice, again, again. He will throw down metaphor after metaphor – each of which works much like a parable in Jesus' repertoire, shedding some new light and furnishing the imagination with new images to see in a new and different way. But, once out of the bag, many of his metaphors will jump up on the table and claw the furniture – leading to unintended conclusions and creating new potential misunderstandings in the minds of unsympathetic or uncareful readers. So Paul will again and again regroup and qualify and correct potential misconceptions, creating an imaginary conversation partner who raises questions to which Paul responds.

Then, just when we think he might rest his case, he will abandon his current metaphor and reach for yet another to jolt the imagination in another way. (For an example of this kind of teaching on Jesus' lips, read Matt. 13.)

So, again, I suggest that Paul will explore his theme in a series of poetic moves, not in a linear argument that moves from point A to point B to point C. Rather, he will go from A (the gospel of the kingdom of God) to Z (for Jew and Gentile alike) several times, but not in a straight A-to-Z way. He will do something like this:

A, B, L, R, V, Z
A, F, R, W, Z
A, H, M, T, Z
A, D, S, Y, Z
A, E, G, N, O, X, Z
A, B, K, P, U, Z
A, I, J, Q, Z

Why does he do it like this? Why take this circuitous approach? Well, a one-question quiz will give a partial answer:

Q: WHO WROTE ROMANS?
A: Paul.
Q: Wrong. Try again.
A: What?

Of course, it's a trick question. Paul didn't write Romans; he dictated it. It was written by a scribe named Tertius (16:22). So, I'm suggesting that rather than imagining Paul sitting, as I am,

194

with a laptop on his lap, or even with a quill pen and parchment, instead we must imagine Paul sitting in a house, or perhaps outdoors in a courtyard, or perhaps on a rooftop, probably in Corinth. It's a sunny, Mediterranean day. Near him sits Tertius, head down, listening, scratching down Paul's words, perhaps holding up his left hand occasionally, signalling Paul to slow down until he can catch up.

So what we have is not a premeditated work of scholarly theology, edited and re-edited, complete with footnotes. Rather, Paul is dictating a letter to some people he loves on a subject he loves, expressing the honest, unedited, natural flow of his thoughts and feelings. Yes, I truly believe this flow is being carried along in a real way by the Spirit. But that doesn't mean (I must say this yet again) that the Spirit's inspiration turns Paul into a human DVR (digital voice recognition) device or transforms Paul's words into articles, sections and clauses in a constitution. If we read Romans keeping these realities in mind, I think we will become more sensitive than ever to the wonderful dance of the Spirit of God and the mind of a man . . . in the context of a community in crisis. Together, the Holy Spirit and Paul will make move after move towards the single goal of justifying the gospel as good news for Gentiles and Jews alike. Let's consider the moves one by one.

CHAPTER 15

Jesus and the Kingdom of God

Paul's first gospel move in his epistle to the Romans is downright brilliant. Its brilliance makes our abuse of it all the more tragic.

Move 1: Reduce Jew and Gentile to the same level of need (Rom. 1:18 – 3:20)

After his introduction, Paul describes Greco-Roman culture in graphic detail – going from moral catastrophe to moral catastrophe. He invites disgust as he details the horrible way pagan sinners suppress God's revelation in creation. They obsess over idols, indulge in sexual orgies and display a shocking range of depraved behaviour – including envy, strife, malice, deceit, greed, lack of compassion and gossip.[1] As his litany of their sins rises in intensity towards a condemning climax, he can imagine his pious readers shouting, or at least thinking, 'Amen! Amen! Those sinners deserve to die for what they've done!' Many of us have heard plenty of sermons that make exactly these points and stop exactly at this point, full stop, which is the tragedy I mentioned a moment ago.

Paul isn't hyping his readers into a moral frenzy against 'those people'. No: he's setting a tender trap for them, and at this moment, Paul springs it: 'You, therefore, have no excuse, you who pass judgment on someone else, for at whatever point you judge another, you are condemning yourself, because you who pass judgment do the same things' (Rom. 2:1). Unlike many contemporary preachers of Romans, he's not trying to create a blacklisted out-group who do things on the list he's just enumerated, in contrast to a righteous in-group who don't do those things. He's doing the very opposite: putting everyone in the same boat – all sinners. (Again, it's tragic how often his clear intent has been subverted by preachers using the Bible in constitutional ways.) Shortly after this, Paul mirrors his brutal litany of Gentile sins with an ironic litany of the 'righteousness' of members of his own religion. So, he says, you're the experts in the law, are you? You're the guide of the blind, the light for those in darkness, the professor of the ignorant, the teacher of little babies, are you? Once again, he turns on them: No, the truth is, you're just sinners like everyone else. The more you claim to know, the more guilty you are for failing to live up to your knowledge.

So, in Move 1, Paul asserts that God doesn't play favourites. All human beings are on the same level, whatever their religious background. All violate their own conscience, all fall short of God's glory, all break God's laws. Nobody can claim an inside track with God just because they have mastered a body of religious knowledge, avoided a list of proscribed behaviours, or identified themselves with a certain label. In this way, Paul renders every mouth silent and everyone accountable to God (3:19). There is no *us versus them*, no elite insiders and excluded outsiders. There's just *all of us* – Jews and Gentiles – and we're a rather pathetic bunch of sinners, united in our need of grace.

Move 2: Announce a new way forward for all, Jew and Gentile, the way of faith (Rom. 3:21–4:25)

Having convicted both Jews and Gentiles equally as sinners, Paul now points both Jews and Gentiles towards the way out: not a new doctrine, not a new religion, and not trying harder at the old religion either, but *faith*. Religious laws and practices are inherently exclusive: you're either circumcised or not, and you either keep kosher or you don't. But faith – having reverent confidence or dependence on God – is an option available to everyone. So, Paul concludes, God is the God of the Jews *and* the God of the Gentiles, and God has chosen, freely, through grace, to put everyone who believes in the same two categories: guilty sinners (in Move 1) and liberated/justified by grace through faith (in Move 2).

Paul now traces the role of faith back even further in Jewish history. What's more primal to Jewish identity than the Law of Moses? Circumcision, which began with Abraham. And what's more primal than circumcision? God's original call to Abraham. And to that core identity Paul now appeals. Abraham's relationship with God didn't depend on the Law or circumcision, since neither Jewish distinctive had yet been given. All that was expected of Abraham was that he believe – or have faith in – God's promise. So, Paul says, you may not be a Jew carrying the mark of circumcision, but you can still be a child of Abraham if you are marked by the same kind of faith Abraham had when he responded to God's call. On this common road of faith, Jew and Gentile can walk together in the gospel of the kingdom of God.

Move 3: Unite all in a common story, with four illustrations: Adam, baptism, slavery and remarriage (Rom. 5:1 – 7:6)

At the end of Move 2 and the beginning of Move 3, Paul does something beautiful as well as tactical. He stops talking directly about Jew and Gentile entirely for a while. Instead, words such as 'us', 'we' and 'our' provide the powerful unifying motif in this whole section. *Jew* and *Gentile*, *insiders* and *outsiders* have been left behind; the closest we get to recalling the problem between Jew and Gentile comes in the word *reconciliation* (5:11).

We've watched Paul's rhetorical instincts (guided by the Holy Spirit) take him back in history before the Law to Abraham, and now Paul goes back even further, in the most brilliant move possible: he goes back to Adam. Our diverse religious systems, he implies, have many points of departure that separate us, but if we follow any path back to its source, to the genesis of our common humanity, we come to the creation story of Adam where we are united. After unifying us in the story of our common ancestor Adam, Paul presents Jesus as a new Adam, a second Adam, the last Adam. His analogy appears a bit stressed in places as we watch him develop the analogy 'on his feet', so to speak, but the point is clear: Adam brought *death and condemnation* to all humanity; Jesus now brings *life and justification* to all humanity. So, we're all part of the story of the original Adam, and now we're part of the story of the new Adam, Jesus. That story is dramatised by baptism, where we die with Christ (as we are buried under water) and are raised with Christ (as we emerge from water). Baptism as death and resurrection provides Paul's second illustration of the common life we share.

Interestingly, Paul uses language in this illustration that evokes the narratives of both liberation and peaceable kingdom, suggesting that the members of our bodies – our arms, hands, legs, and so on – can be slaves to sin (evoking slavery under Pharaoh) and rebels against God's reign (evoking the dream of God's benevolent society). Or they can be liberated from slavery to sin and surrendered to God so they become instruments of God's reign. In baptism, Paul says, we die to the old life of sin-slavery and God-rebellion, and we rise to live free as agents of God's reign, as agents of God's restorative justice. Paul's third and fourth illustrations make the same point, employing slavery and marriage metaphors. We all – again, Jew and Gentile are implied even when not explicitly stated – have been enslaved by a cruel taskmaster, married to a stern (and impotent) husband. Through the death and resurrection of Christ, we die to those old relationships and we rise to a new kind of slavery and a new love affair. Like redeemed slaves, we are bound to our new master in service and fruitfulness; like a former widow newly wed, we are impregnated with our divine lover's goodness, bearing more and more good into the world.

Move 4: Unite all in a common struggle and a common victory, illustrated by two stories: 'the story of me' and 'the story of we' (Rom. 7:7– 8:39)

Several structural and thematic transitions come for Paul as he tries to anticipate and counter possible misunderstandings or misapplications of his previous point, and that's the case here.[2] As he backs off from any suggestion that the Law (the impotent first husband in our previous metaphor of marriage) is evil, he launches his next move. He begins by abruptly switching from the plural 'we' of the previous section into the singular 'I' and 'me', leaving interpreters ever since scratching their heads about how to read this section.[3] Interestingly, he will return to 'we' in the following section. In our Jews-and-Gentiles-united-in-God's-kingdom reading, Paul's strategy seems abundantly clear. Through 'the story of me' he shows how Jew and Gentile share a common experience of struggle as human beings ('in Adam', as he has explained it previously, 7:7–25), and through 'the story of we' he shows how Jew and Gentile can share a common experience of victory in the kingdom of God ('in Christ', as he celebrates in 7:25–8:39).[4]

In 'the story of me', Paul moves from the previous section's external imagery of Adam, baptism, slavery and marriage to the internal landscape of the human soul. This landscape is scarred by inner turmoil and frustration, the tension between high aspiration and low performance. It is dark with the despair of feeling fatally trapped in a no-win moral predicament and vicious cycle of self-examination, self-recrimination, self-defence, self-despair . . . as if he is experiencing exactly the kind of self-assessment he described in Move 1 (2:14), his thoughts 'now accusing' and 'now defending' him. Finally, in desperation, the 'I' in the story exclaims, 'What a wretched man I am! Who will rescue me from this body of death?' His answer: 'Thanks be to God, who delivers me through Jesus Christ our Lord!' (7:24–25). From this point, 'I' quickly fades away and Paul transitions briefly through a 'you all' to the unifying 'we' again.

The resonances here with previous circlings are obvious and strong (especially with 5:1–11), with one new metaphor added: adoption, rendering Jews and Gentiles siblings in God's one family as well as fellow citizens in God's one kingdom. Once again, Paul's mind naturally follows a course from forgiveness ('justified' in chapter 5, 'no condemnation' in chapter 8) to relationship ('peace with God' in chapter 5, 'sons of God' in chapter 8), to suffering ('rejoice in sufferings' in chapter 5, 'share in sufferings' in chapter 8), to victory and reward ('hope does not disappoint' and 'love poured into our hearts through the Holy Spirit' in chapter 5, 'share his glory' and 'the Spirit bears witness with our Spirit' in chapter 8). I find these parallels strong and moving. The points made in previous moves are truly glorious, but they shine even more brightly here, as Paul expands the scope of suffering and reward and glorification, seeing all of creation groaning in empathy and anticipation with this new humanity in Christ – one new humanity, one new kingdom, articulated in 'we' and 'us'.

> No, in all these things we are more than conquerors through him who loved us. For I am convinced that neither death nor life, neither angels nor demons, neither the present nor the future, nor any powers, neither height nor depth, nor anything else in all creation, will be able to separate us from the love of God that is in Christ Jesus our Lord.
> *(8:37–9)*

Once more we feel that Tertius could put down his pen. Another circling is complete. Paul has addressed and removed obstacles to unity yet again, and has once more (as he did in Move 3) described our shared experience in Christ in such glowing terms that one can't imagine the point being made any more powerfully. But, for some reason, Paul can't stop, so we can imagine him motioning for Tertius to continue inscribing.

Move 5: Address Jewish and Gentile problems, showing God as God of all (Rom. 9:1 – 11:36)

Yes, Paul has written powerfully, but unquiet thoughts and unanswered questions still lurk in his mind. They burst out in this next move:

> I am speaking the truth in Christ – I am not lying; my conscience confirms it by the Holy Spirit – I have great sorrow and unceasing anguish in my heart. For I could wish that I myself were accursed and cut off from Christ for the sake of my own people, my kindred according to the flesh. They are Israelites, and to them belong the adoption, the glory, the covenants, the giving of the law, the worship, and the promises; to them belong the patriarchs, and from them, according to the flesh, comes the Messiah, who is over all, God blessed for ever. Amen.
> *(9:1–5 NRSV)*

What is Paul's problem? This glorious new way of the Spirit that he has celebrated in the previous move is truly accessible to both Jew and Gentile. But Paul is broken-hearted because so many of his fellow Jews are not walking in the new way, not living the new life, not experiencing the 'no condemnation and no separation' of the kingdom of God. In the paragraphs that follow, he goes back and scans the stories of Isaac and Ishmael, Jacob and Esau, and finally Pharaoh and a metaphorical potter for clues as to why his countrymen haven't responded to the gospel of the kingdom of God. He brings to bear a variety of quotes from the Hebrew Scriptures, from Hosea, Isaiah and the Psalms. But he still can't seem to reach a final resolution. Why have so many Jewish people rejected Jesus and his good news of the kingdom of God?

Like someone who has lost something precious, he retraces his steps to see if he has missed something. Maybe Israel never heard the good news? No, that's not it. Maybe they heard, but didn't understand? No, that can't be it either. So he comes to the possible conclusion that God is responsible. God has hardened their hearts to achieve some greater good. Paul is finally comfortable with this conclusion, isn't he? No, not completely!

Something fascinating happens at this point. Paul realises that, just as the Jews may have been proud because they had the Law, the Gentiles might become proud now because they are coming to faith in Christ in greater numbers than his fellow Jews. Paul still can't conclusively explain the problem of widespread (though not universal) Jewish coolness towards the gospel of the kingdom of God, but, even though he can't explain it, he now decides to use it – to warn the Gentiles that if the Jews could wander from the path, so can they, so they shouldn't be proud; rather, they should be humble and careful – 'afraid', he says. Paul introduces a new term into his discourse at this point: *mystery*. Does it suggest some new insight, some new secret to disclose, that might lead to a breakthrough in understanding?

Just as you who were at one time disobedient to God have now received mercy as a result of their disobedience, so they too have now become disobedient in order that they too may now receive mercy as a result of God's mercy to you. For God has bound everyone over to disobedience so that he may have mercy on them all.

(11:30–32)[5]

These conclusive words, after this agonising journey in Move 5, seem too good to be true. Yet now, finally, his mind seems to be at rest. No, it is not at rest. Better than that, with this realisation, his mind is not at rest but is (I think a slang expression works best here) *blown*, as his final words in this move make clear:

Oh, the depth of the riches of the wisdom and knowledge of God!
How unsearchable his judgments,
and his paths beyond tracing out!
'Who has known the mind of the Lord?
Or who has been his counsellor?'
'Who has ever given to God,
that God should repay them?'
For from him and through him and to him are all things.
To him be the glory for ever! Amen.

(11:33–6)

Move 6: Engage all in a common life and mission
(Rom. 12:1 – 13:14)

A 'therefore' signifies a move now from the 'what' of God's amazing mercy to the 'so what' of how we should live in the light of that mercy. We should present our entire selves to God as 'living sacrifices', Paul says, a new kind of sacrifice in which Gentile and Jew can share equally. We shouldn't be conformed to the patterns of the world, but should be transformed by the renewing of our minds. We should use our gifts for the common good, loving others without hypocrisy, living the way Jesus lived and taught: sharing, giving, practising hospitality, breaking down class barriers, forgiving, reconciling, overcoming evil with good.

The resonances between this passage and the Sermon on the Mount are loud, strong and beautiful.[6] The Jew-and-Gentile-community-in-Christ, while radically 'non-conforming' to their culture, are not Zealots plotting violent revolution against the Roman Empire. They live and work as law-abiding, tax-paying citizens within the kingdom of Caesar, even though they are now citizens in God's kingdom. But they must remember that their highest law is neither the Jewish Law nor the law of Caesar: Paul describes it as 'the law of love', clearly echoing Jesus' teaching for disciples of the kingdom of God. This is the life to which 'we' – Jew and Gentile together – are called:

> Give to everyone what you owe: If you owe taxes, pay taxes; if revenue, then revenue; if respect, then respect; if honour, then honour. Let no debt remain outstanding, except the continuing debt to love one another, for whoever loves others has fulfilled the law. The commandments, 'You shall not commit adultery,' 'You shall not murder,' 'You shall not steal,' 'You shall not covet,' and whatever other command there may be, are summed up in this one command: 'Love your neighbour as yourself.' Love does no harm to its neighbour. Therefore love is the fulfilment of the law. *(13:7–10)*

Move 7: Call everyone to unity in the kingdom of God
(Rom. 14:1 – 16:27)

Having emphasised the importance of love, Paul gets down to grass-roots contemporary issues that put love to the test and that can easily alienate and divide Jews and Gentiles – dietary scruples, holy-day practices, and so on. Paul's message is not new or unique: it's exactly the message of Jesus. *Don't judge one another.* On these controversial matters, he says, everyone should do two things: first, be convinced in their own mind, and, second, keep their convictions to themselves. What they do regarding disputable matters *is important*, because it expresses their devotion to the Lord. But what they do *is not relevant* to what others do as their expression of devotion to the Lord. The kingdom of God (Paul mentions it explicitly now) will not be a community of uniform policies and practices. Only one policy will be universal: love. And on those central themes, love and the kingdom of God, Paul hangs his summation:

I am convinced, being fully persuaded in the Lord Jesus, that nothing is unclean in itself. But if anyone regards something as unclean, then for that person it is unclean. If your brother or sister is distressed because of what you eat, you are no longer acting in love. Do not by your eating destroy your brother or sister for whom Christ died. Therefore do not let what you know is good be spoken of as evil. For *the kingdom of God* is not a matter of eating and drinking, but of righteousness, peace and joy in the Holy Spirit . . .
(14:14–19, emphasis mine)

Paul seems to conclude the letter no fewer than four times with a succession of premature benedictions (15:5, 13, 33; 16:20). The first – emphasising unity – clearly resonates with Paul's grand theme:

> May the God who gives endurance and encouragement give you a spirit of unity among yourselves as you follow Christ Jesus, so that with one heart and mouth you may glorify the God and Father of our Lord Jesus Christ.
> *(15:5 NIV)*

Finally, Paul tells the Christian community in Rome how much he would like to come and visit them in person (which he will do about six years later, but as a prisoner, not a visitor). After offering a number of personal greetings, we can imagine Paul nodding as if to say, 'This is it, Tertius. I'm really finishing now.' He offers a fifth benediction, complete with a final reminder of his great theme: good news for all, both Jews and 'all nations', good news of a new way of life that reconciles people to one another and to God in trust and obedience:

> Now to him who is able to establish you by my gospel and the proclamation of Jesus Christ, according to the revelation of the mystery hidden for long ages past, but now revealed and made known through the prophetic writings by the command of the eternal God, so that *all nations* might believe and obey him – to the only wise God be glory for ever through Jesus Christ! Amen.
> *(16:25–7 NIV, emphasis mine)*

Tertius puts down his pen. Paul nods and smiles. The ink dries, and Tertius prepares the letter to be carried to Rome, where it will be copied and distributed and preserved, so that we can read it and ponder it today, just as we have done in this chapter. He has reduced Jew and Gentile to the same level of need. He has announced a new way forward for Jew and Gentile alike: the way of faith and grace. He has united Jew and Gentile in a common story, and in a common struggle and common hope as well. He has addressed specific controversial issues and called all to one common rule: non-judgemental love. And he has invited all to share a common life and mission – living out the restorative justice, peace and joy in the Holy Spirit that constitute the kingdom of God.

Through all these moves, Paul makes it clear: there is only one gospel, Jesus' good news of God's kingdom, available for all people. Paul's gospel, when we release him from the pre-critical assumptions of our conventional six-line Greco-Roman narrative, looks very different in Romans, and if you take these themes and approaches to his other writings, you will see that the same holds true there as well. The last picture we have of Paul in the Acts of the Apostles perfectly frames what we have seen of him here in his epistle to the Romans. It is AD 62 or so, about six years after he wrote his epistle to the Romans. Paul is, aptly enough, in Rome, under house arrest awaiting trial for disturbing the peace in Jerusalem, and a large number of inquisitive and open-minded people have come to hear about the 'sect' that Paul represents:

From morning till evening he explained and declared to them *the kingdom of God* and tried to convince them about Jesus from the Law of Moses and from the Prophets . . . For two whole years Paul stayed there in his own rented house and welcomed all who came to see him. Boldly and without hindrance he preached *the kingdom of God* and taught about the *Lord Jesus Christ.*

(Acts 28:23–31 NIV, emphasis mine)

In Rome, the headquarters of the kingdom of Caesar, Paul preaches the kingdom of God. In Rome, the seat of power of Lord Caesar the Emperor, Paul teaches about Lord Jesus the Liberator. As in his epistle to the Romans, Paul does not preach a different gospel: he is still carrying the same gospel he received from Jesus Christ in a vision, the gospel of the kingdom of God. Whether in person or by letter, he calls people everywhere to be reconciled in the kingdom of God: reconciled to God by grace through faith, reconciled within themselves, reconciled with others whatever their class, ethnic, cultural or religious backgrounds, and reconciled with all creation, because all creation groans in pain, waiting for humanity to become what God intends us to be.

Paul is a 'Jesus and the kingdom of God' guy from first to last.

This is the gospel of Jesus Christ, and of his servant/apostle Paul: *the kingdom of God is at hand.*[7] Repent and believe the good news. Be reconciled.

Add it as fine print to your existing theological contract if that's all you can manage right now, or fully rewrite the contract around this good news if you can. But, either way, repent. And believe the good news, for it is good indeed.

Book 2

Emerging and Exploring

I imagine some readers at this point are feeling liberated and energised. Having explored our first five questions, you may feel as if an Alka-Seltzer™ tablet has been dropped in the centre of your brain, and your imagination is fizzing with possibilities as relief comes to some of your theological indigestion. The Christian faith has never looked so good to you, and you're saying things like, 'Wow. Maybe I can be a Christian after all.'[1] Others are outraged, and what you're saying about this book and its author probably shouldn't be made public. (Although it probably will be.) A lot of readers are somewhere in between, maybe a little shaken and dizzy, with all kinds of ambivalence churning. You feel a lot like I did staring into my hot-and-sour soup at the Chinese restaurant I mentioned back in chapter 14 – disturbed, unsettled, baffled, maybe even guilty for entertaining new perspectives, but maybe a little hopeful too, and relieved, free, curious.

I'm sympathetic with your ambivalence. When I began asking

these questions, it wasn't simply an academic matter of inter-pretation and understanding for me, nor is it now. It isn't just a head thing; it's a heart thing, because I don't just aspire to believe in God or think correctly about God: I want to love God and worship God and serve and experience God. If my view of God changes . . . well, that changes everything for me. This quest stirs up all kinds of psychological issues for me too, because my theology and my biography are deeply integrated in my 'be-ology' – my sense of who I am and what I want to be as a human being.[2]

On top of all that, this is a social thing for me, and I know it's the same for you too, because this Sunday a lot of us will show up in churches where the ideas we've been considering would cause some people to choke. We could lose friends, and if we're pastors, professors or theological students, we could lose jobs or scholarships. And if we aren't careful, we could lose or divide communities that are precious to us, and to whom we are precious. As a lifelong churchgoer and a veteran pastor, I'm aware of all this as I write, and, frankly, it causes me pain, knowing that if I persuade you to join this quest for a new kind of Christianity, it will probably complicate your life.

So perhaps for some readers, this is as far as you need to go for now. But for those who are ready to go through the doors we've unlocked and opened, it's time to emerge and explore.

SIX

THE CHURCH QUESTION

CHAPTER 16

What Do We Do About the Church?

Many if not most of our churches are perfectly designed and well tuned to promote and support the five paradigms we have questioned so far: the Greco-Roman narrative, the constitutional approach to the Bible, the tribal and violent understanding of God, a rather flattened view of Jesus, and a domesticated understanding of the gospel. When we unlock the gates of those paradigms and begin to emerge into new territory, we find this question waiting for us: *What do we do about the Church?*

For a lot of people, the answer has been simple: they leave. Recent titles such as *A Churchless Faith, UnChristian, They Like Jesus but Not the Church* and *Quitting Church* tell the story.[1] Just this morning, I met another one – a dropout not only from Christian ministry but from the Church, and very nearly, truth be told, from Christianity entirely. 'They won't let you ask questions,' he said. 'How can you be alive if they won't let you think?'

Yet local churches and denominations, we must acknowledge, play a vital role in the lives of millions of people around the world – very literally, churches save lives.[2] Over the years I've seen this saving/unsaving drama playing out in the lives of many people.

I've heard stories of Catholics being saved from ritualism by becoming Pentecostal, Pentecostals being saved from emotionalism by becoming Presbyterian, Presbyterians being saved from rationalism by becoming Eastern Orthodox, Eastern Orthodox being saved from clericalism by becoming Baptist, and Baptists being saved from historical amnesia by becoming Catholic or Orthodox. Simple churches save people from complexity, and complex churches save people from simplicity; political churches save people from an overly personal religiosity, and personal churches save people from an overly politicised religiosity. Exciting churches save people from boredom, and quiet churches save people from hoopla and hype. Around and around the cycle goes.

The people who are successfully saved from something by a certain type of church or denomination generally stay in it, along with some others who get stuck there by birth or marriage or inertia or duty. (As a pastor, I always felt sorry for these poor people, and wished for their sake – and sometimes mine – that they could go elsewhere.) The people who don't find any particularly helpful kind of salvation from a church or denomination eventually leave, sometimes stomping out mad, or more often just drifting away bored. Sometimes they find a church that saves them from whatever their previous churches afflicted them with or disappointed them over, but, increasingly, they just drop out entirely, often swelling the hospitable ranks of the 'spiritual but not religious'. Younger generations especially have been choosing the latter option lately; they just can't figure out what they're being saved from . . . or for . . . enough to stay.[3] When enough church leaders wake up and smell the coffee, when they realise that their faith communities are shrinking and wrinkling and stiffening, they start to ask the church question very urgently: *What are we going to do about the Church?* Behind their question is the very real fear that their beloved congregation or denomination could soon find itself on the red side of a spread-sheet, and they find themselves seeking to save the beloved church that has saved them.

Those who dedicate themselves to be agents of change in our churches will require superhuman doses of courage, kindness, creativity, collaboration and perseverance. Thanks be to God: faithful change agents will find, like the little boy with his fish and bread, that they already have more resources for the journey than they realised. For example, Roman Catholics can rediscover the power of orders when diocesan structures are resistant or reactive to needed change. Episcopalians, Lutherans, Methodists and others with bishops can use the episcopacy to turn around their ocean liner, because just a few courageous bishops can do amazing things.[4]

Congregationalists of all sorts (including most Baptists and charismatics), who have no qualms about starting new congregations, can simply go ahead and do so (especially if the church-planters are willing to be bi-vocational and thus avoid the need to ask institutional headquarters for money).[5] Savvy denominations of all types (and newly forming collaborative networks too) will find ways to create 'free trade zones' and 'R&D departments' where old rules and strictures don't apply, and where emerging leaders can be given freedom (and maybe even some financial support) to experiment, learn and create new kinds of congregations to express a new kind of Christian faith.[6] These hopeful processes have already begun, and they continue the trajectory of development we see when we look at the big arc of Church history.

Consider this diagram depicting the evolution of early Christian churches.

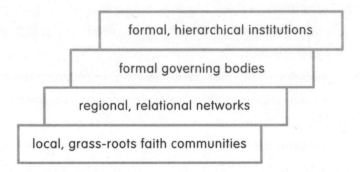

The first communities of disciples existed at the ground floor, so to speak, and over five centuries they developed increasing levels of organisation, institutionalisation, homogeneity and hierarchy – especially as their bishops decided to remake the Christian movement into a mirror image of the Roman Empire after Constantine.[7] By the sixth century, the first three levels had been completely engulfed within the fourth, as depicted in the following diagram. Over the last five hundred years (since the Protestant Reformation), the Christian faith has experienced 'downward mobility', expressing itself in less hierarchical, less centralised and less imperial forms, and recapturing its earlier plurality of forms.

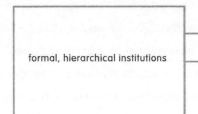
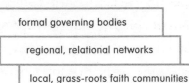

formal, hierarchical institutions

formal governing bodies

regional, relational networks

local, grass-roots faith communities

Some see this as a *division* to be remedied, but there's another way to see it: as *diversification* to be celebrated. What if the Christian faith is *supposed* to exist in a variety of forms rather than just one imperial one? What if it is more stable, more agile and more responsive to the Holy Spirit when it exists in these many forms? And what if, instead of arguing about which form is correct and legitimate, we were to honour, appreciate and validate one another, and see ourselves as servants of one grander mission, apostles of one greater message, seekers on one ultimate quest? That, I'd say, sounds like a new kind of Christianity.

But what would that one mission, message and quest be? Around what one grand endeavour can we rally?[8] What one great danger do people need to be saved from, and, more positively, what one great purpose do they need to be saved for? Around what melody can we harmonise without trying to homogenise? Of many possible answers, there is one to which I am continually drawn, embarrassingly obvious and simple to understand, but also embarrassingly challenging to do: the Church exists to *form Christ-like people, people of Christ-like love*. It exists to save them from the great danger of wasting their lives, becoming something less than and other than they were intended to be, gaining the world but losing their souls. When we ask, 'What do we do about the Church?' the first answer must be (it seems to me) to rethink our core mission, and to identify it in terms more or less like these.

When we are unlocked from our conventional paradigms regarding the biblical narrative, the Bible, God, Jesus and the gospel, the formation of Christ-like people of love naturally becomes the grand unifying preoccupation and mission of our churches. Churches, simply put, come to be communities that form Christ-like people who embody and communicate, in word and deed, the good news of the kingdom of God (or we could say the *shalom*, harmony, dance, sacred ecosystem, love economy, benevolent society, beloved community, or pre-emptive peace movement of God). And they do this, not within an isolated or withdrawn religious subculture, not simply to create an idealised spiritual country club for their own benefit, but rather in the world as it is and for the world as it could be, as transforming agents of transformation.[9] Churches seek to save us from the hell of becoming and staying the worst we can be, and to save us for what St Irenaeus of Lyons called *the glory of God – to be humanity fully alive*.[10]

That unifying vision requires not just careful strategy (although wise strategy would be a good thing), but a profound openness to the Holy Spirit. Putting it in Latin might make it sound a bit more official: *Nemo dat quod non habet*. You can't give what you don't have – which means, before anything else, we who lead must actually embody the Spirit-saturated, Christ-following, God-loving way of life we hope to pass on through our churches. To become like Christ, we need to have the Spirit of Christ within us, among us, before us, beside us, as the old Celtic prayer said. We need to be Spirit-saturated people.[11]

That sounds good, but it can certainly seem a long way from where and who we are. Yes, our churches are doing beautiful work, and they are sanctuaries of sacredness, beauty and kindness without which our world would be a much poorer place. But we must also acknowledge that our churches are divided, immature, confused about our purpose and identity, in danger of fragmenting our way into non-existence, all at once bending over backwards and straddling fences, stiff of neck and soft of spine, and otherwise twisted and contorted in compromise. We have financial troubles, sexual controversies, pride problems, schism threats, excesses in some forms of spirituality and deficits in others, and all manner of authority issues. And as soon as some of us point the finger at others, they hold up the mirror and show us that we're in as much mess as they are.

Rather than flogging ourselves with guilt over these characteristics on the one hand, or denying or minimising them on the other, perhaps we should simply acknowledge them with candour and humility. And then, perhaps, we should add that all these troubles taken together perfectly qualify us as authentic 'New Testament churches', since these are the very issues with which the original churches struggled, as Paul's first epistle to the Corinthians illustrates.

The 'church of God in Corinth' (1:2) to which Paul writes is a divided (1:10) collection of personality cults (1:12), each claiming superior wisdom and knowledge (2:4–5). As a result, its members are not maturing into truly spiritual Christ-like people, but are rather stunted – 'mere infants' (3:1) and 'mere human beings' (3:4). Paul urges them to see themselves as one field, planted by God (3:6), and one building project (3:10), but he sees their community as being destroyed (3:17) by competing factions, each claiming superiority based on wisdom and knowledge (3:18ff.). While they're boasting about superior wisdom and knowledge, they're tolerating gross immorality (5:1ff.; 6:16–18) and suing each other in court (6:1) rather than resolving their differences maturely (6:5) or willingly suffering wrong (6:7). (One recalls Jesus' words to the Pharisees about straining out gnats and swallowing camels.) He emphasises the urgency of the times to them (7:29), already in AD 55 anticipating the chaos that will come soon enough in AD 67–70 (7:31).

Then he bears down on the root issue, as he sees it. They have a whole tangle of arguments and disagreements (about marriage and sex in 7:1ff.; about dietary scruples in 8:1ff.; about leadership and politics in 9:3ff.; about disorderly public gatherings in 11:2ff.; about the use of spiritual gifts in 12:1ff. and 14:1ff.; about the timing and meaning of the resurrection of the dead in 15:12ff.). But all their controversies have one root problem: competing claims to wisdom and knowledge, especially around the issue of eating meat from the public markets – meat from animals sacrificed at pagan temples devoted to idol worship. Those who claim greater knowledge flaunt their freedom to eat this meat, since they know that the so-called gods that these sacrifices, idols and temples celebrate are really only illusions and superstitions.

Ironically, then, those with whom Paul agrees in theory are in practice wounding and hurting those with whom Paul disagrees. In response, Paul indulges in rather complex and sometimes scathing word-play around forms of the word *knowledge*:

> We *know* that we all possess *knowledge. Knowledge* puffs up, but love builds up. The man who thinks he *knows* something does not yet *know* as he ought to *know*. But the man who loves God is *known* by God.

So then, about eating food sacrificed to idols: We *know* that an idol is nothing at all in the world and that there is no God but one . . .

But not everyone *knows* this . . .

Be careful, however, that the exercise of your freedom does not become a stumbling-block to the weak. For if anyone with a weak conscience sees you who have this *knowledge* eating in an idol's temple, won't he be emboldened to eat what has been sacrificed to idols [i.e. to violate his conscience]? So this weak brother, for whom Christ died, is destroyed by your *knowledge*.
(1 Cor. 8:1–11 NIV, emphasis mine)

Perhaps evoking the primal story of Adam and Eve, who in a quest for knowledge sinned against God, Paul links knowledge with conceit and destruction. Far better, he says, to be 'known by God' as a person of love. Later, when he comes to the issue of spiritual gifts, he picks up the same language again, with some sharp irony: 'Now about spiritual gifts, brothers, I do not want you to be *ignorant*. You *know* . . .' (12:1–2 NIV). And then he identifies wisdom and knowledge not as attainments, but as gifts of the Spirit (1:7–8), given not for personal or sectarian advantage, but for 'the common good'. This Spirit forms everyone into one body (12:12–13) composed of many diverse parts (12:14ff.), each of which both belongs to the others (12:16) and needs the others (12:21ff.). God's goal is that there should be robust diversity without division, where each has equal concern for the others (12:25). In this way, Paul says, this community is not only the *ecclesia* of God (1:2) and the temple of the Holy Spirit (3:16; 6:19), but also the body or embodiment of Christ (12:17). And then, as if to celebrate the power of this insight, he says, 'And now I will show you the most excellent way.'

What is this way? It is not speaking in tongues or using other spiritual gifts (13:1–2). It is not mystery-fathoming knowledge or mountain-moving faith (13:2). It is not even a radical, non-conforming concern for social justice or courageous willingness to undergo martyrdom (13:3). These things, without love, Paul says, are worth nothing. If he were writing today, he might say:

> Though I interpret the biblical text with state-of-the-art herme-neutics and preach sermons with flawless homiletics, though all my theologies are systematic and all my books, blogs and podcasts are scrupulously orthodox, without love, I am static on a radio or an error message on a computer screen. Though I can show decadal church growth in double digits and raise millions of dollars in building funds, though I have files full of testimonials from people saved, healed, delivered and blessed through my ministry, without love, I'm just another clever, two-bit purveyor of goods and services in the religious industrial complex. Though I have worldwide impact, travelling by private jet and broadcasting on cable, satellite and the internet, though my budgets balance and my theological colleges are bursting with beautiful and handsome graduates (all of whom are above average in every way), and though powerful people stand beside me in photo opportunities and consider me a 'key person', without love, I am nothing.

The excellent way . . . no, the *more* excellent way . . . no, better than that, the *most* excellent way . . . is the way of love. Recalling his earlier juxtapositions of immaturity and maturity (3:1), of knowledge and love (8:2–3), he concludes,

For where there is knowledge, it will pass away. For we know in part and we prophesy in part, but when completion comes, the partial is cast aside. When I was an infant, I talked like an infant, I thought like an infant, and I reasoned like an infant. When I became a full-grown adult, I cast aside infantile things. Now we see but a poor reflection as in a mirror; then we shall see face to face. Now I know in part; then I shall know fully, even as I am fully known. And now these three remain: faith, hope, and love. But the greatest of these is love. Follow the way of love . . .
(1 Cor. 13:9–14:1, author's translation)

There's no maturity without love, Paul says. In comparison with love, other things seem childish, a partial reflection in a dirty mirror.[12] Paul makes a fascinating move as he concludes his epistle, recalling his very first play on the word *know*: 'For I resolved to *know nothing* while I was with you except Jesus Christ and him crucified' (2:2). The crucifixion seems to expose Jesus as foolish, weak, lowly and despised (1:21–3), a failure in the eyes of the wise, the scholar and 'the philosopher of this age'. But now we see that the lowly way of Christ, the vulnerable way of love, is the only way of life. And so in the end Paul brings us from the humbling theme of crucifixion to an inspiring celebration of the resurrection (15:1ff.), which anticipates the ultimate triumph of the kingdom of God (15:24, 50, 57) and which produces in us a constructive kind of knowledge:

Therefore, my dear brothers and sisters, stand firm. Let nothing move you. Always give yourselves fully to the work of the Lord, because you *know* that your labour in the Lord is not in vain.
(1 Cor. 15:58)

As is often the case with Paul, this seeming conclusion is one of many, followed by this one: 'Be on your guard; stand firm in the faith; be courageous; be strong. Do everything in love' (16:13–14). And then comes this one, as Paul takes the writing instrument from his scribe: 'I, Paul, write this greeting in my own hand . . . My love to all of you in Christ Jesus. Amen' (16:21, 24). In each case, love has the last word.

Love and knowledge are not opposed in Paul's mind: love and 'so-called' or pseudo-knowledge may be, but, for Paul, love seems to be the truest form of knowledge. Yes, you can know about something by critiquing it, by dissecting it and analysing it, by studying it as an object with you as the subject. But to truly know something, you must love it, bond with it, embrace it, not as an object, but as another subject. (Does anyone doubt that Jane Goodall knows chimpanzees more deeply through loving them than she could any other way?)[13]

The Church, then, in Paul's mind, must be above all a school of love. If it's not that, it's nothing. Its goal is not simply to pump knowledge into people, but to train them in 'the way of love', so they may do 'the work of the Lord', empowered by the Holy Spirit, as the embodiment of Christ. Perhaps school isn't the best metaphor, though, unless we think of a karate school or a dance school or a language school – not simply a community where you *learn*, or *learn about*, but where you *learn to*. Not simply a place where you hear lectures and amass information, but a community where you see living examples of Christ-likeness and experience inner formation. If taken to heart, this simple shift in metaphors – from house of worship or religious insti-tution to what my friend Mark Scandrette calls a 'Jesus dojo'[14] – could catalyse a true renaissance in our church life.[15]

What would it mean if we were willing to sacrifice – or at least subordinate – everything else for this one goal of forming Christ-like people, people who live in the way of love, the way of peace-making, the way of the kingdom of God, the way of Jesus, the way of the Spirit? Why should people go to the trouble of being part of a church if it does a thousand other things well, but falters in this one primary calling?[16] How does spiritual formation in the way of Jesus differ from religious education in the way of Christianity? How will this kind of spiritual formation take place in a pluralistic, high-tech, digital world of commuters and telecommuters? How does it engage with children, youth, young parents, older adults and senior citizens (a sky-rocketing demographic worldwide)? How does it work among the world's pre-literate poor and post-literate rich? What liturgies, lectionaries and church calendars will best support it? What rituals and symbols promote it? What kind of leaders can lead it, and what kind of post-college training models can develop those leaders?

Ah, more questions. And very good questions. These questions don't render us passive theorists about 'the future of the Church', producing and consuming speculations that we must compliantly prepare for or adjust to. These questions render us creative protagonists who have the power, through the Holy Spirit, to create a new future of the Church as a school of love – which means a school of listening, dialogue, appreciative inquiry, understanding, pre-emptive peace-making, reconciliation, non-violence, prophetic confrontation, advocacy, generosity and personal and social transformation. Anybody who thinks this is all soft and easy obviously has little experience in actually seeking to live this way and helping others to do so.

But understand this: I am not recommending we add to our to-do lists and pastoral job descriptions the burden of yet another crushing wish-dream or idealism – spiritual formation of Christ-like people who follow the way of love. Nor am I recommending we start arguing with others that *they* should be doing this, why don't *they* get this, and so on. Instead, I am recommending that some of us experiment with throwing out the other lists, and start over again, with this item as number one, knowing that there may be no need for a number two. Our quest for a new kind of Christianity, expressed on the local congregational level with this kind of mission, must then include a quest for new liturgies, lectionaries, calendars and music (with lyrics that celebrate and embed the new paradigm, not the old one); new heuristics[17] and curricula for children and youth as well as adults of all ages; new training and support structures for church leaders, and so on. If the current wineskins have been developed and fine-tuned to serve the old wine of a Greco-Roman, constitutional, tribal, non-kingdom-of-God-orientated Christianity, we shouldn't be surprised that new wineskins will need to be created – all in the service of the one thing that matters: forming people of Christ-like love.

The one grand calling, I suggest, tells us what the Church most truly is: it is a space in which the Spirit works to form Christ-like people, and it is the space in which human beings, formed in Christ-like love, co-operate with the Spirit and one another to express that love in word and deed, art and action.[18] Where that happens, I believe church is happening, whatever the forms or structures, whatever the history or pedigree.

I passed over what are probably Paul's best-known words in the epistle. Those words should conclude this chapter, because they paint the portrait of the kind of Christ-like person our churches are intended to form. They also describe the kind of Christ-like leader who can assist in the conception, birth and nurture of a new kind of Christianity, recalling, *Nemo dat quod non habet*:

> Love is patient; love is kind; love is not envious or boastful or arrogant or rude. It does not insist on its own way; it is not irritable or resentful; it does not rejoice in wrongdoing, but rejoices with the truth. It bears all things, believes all things, hopes all things, endures all things. Love never ends . . . And now faith, hope, and love abide, these three; and the greatest of these is love.
> *(1 Cor. 13:4–13, NRSV)*

SEVEN

THE SEX QUESTION

CHAPTER 17

Can We Find a Way to Address Sexuality Without Fighting About It?

I don't want to be closed-minded or judgemental, but in good conscience I simply can't approve of the lifestyle. I believe it's a choice, although upbringing and genetics may have a role. Freedom has limits — one limit being where others are hurt by a chosen lifestyle. And this lifestyle, there can be no mistake, is hurting a lot of people. Families are being torn apart by it, and churches too. There is absolutely no question about God's opinion on this lifestyle if we begin with the Bible. This orientation and the behaviours associated with it are thoroughly condemned, especially by Jesus. He was compassionate towards all kinds of people, but he had an absolute and uncompromising commitment to confront and expose one group: those who dishonour themselves and others by engaging in this lifestyle and its practices.

When people choose this lifestyle, they often cut themselves off from everyone who doesn't agree with them. They end up being assimilated and absorbed in closed communities where only their own voices and views are heard, and everyone who disagrees is mocked and condemned, often with very strong language. Some, after giving themselves over completely to the lifestyle, have a crisis of conscience. But when they want to leave, their leaders and peers depict their changing perspective as a betrayal and pressure them to stay, often using fear tactics to intimidate them and keep them in their gated community. Special ministries have formed to help people exit the lifestyle, recover from the abuse and pain the community has been known to impose, and be reorientated to a healthier life and perspective. But even with professional therapy, many people feel they have been wounded for life by their years in this lifestyle.

Advocates of this lifestyle are eager to recruit others into their 'love', as they call it. Through various organisations, they raise huge sums of money to recruit youth and children into their chosen way of life, and they have been extremely adept at using media – radio, TV and now the internet – to gain an aura of credibility and legitimacy. They organise huge events and mass rallies to celebrate their growing clout and demonstrate that they are proud of who they are and what they stand for. Everyone knows how much influence they have in our political system. But look at the countries where this lifestyle runs rampant, and you'll get an idea what your own nation will be like if some people don't have the courage to stand up and speak up. Wherever this lifestyle spreads, a whole host of social problems inevitably follows.

Yes, activists may use the word 'love' to justify their behaviour, but those who disagree with them are seldom treated with love. Many of us have already faced the scorn of the activists who promote this chosen lifestyle and defend it as legitimate and even godly. For doing so, we have received hate mail peppered with a wide range of threats and abusive speech. But even so, we have learned that we must not respond to hate with hate; we must hate the sin but still love the sinners.

The lifestyle I'm speaking of is *fundasexuality* (not, as you may have assumed, *homosexuality*), a neologism that describes a reactive, combative brand of religious *fundamentalism* that preoccupies itself with *sexuality*.[1] The term does not apply to the quiet, pious, respectful fundamentalism of straightforward, sincere people, but rather to the organising, angry, dominating fundamentalism that declares war on those who differ. Fundasexuality is rooted not in faith, but in an orientation of fear – fear of new ideas, fear of people who are different, fear of criticism or rejection from its own community, or fear of God's violent wrath on them if they don't fully conform to and enforce the teachings and interpretations of their popular teachers or other authority figures. It is a kind of *hetero-phobia*: the fear of people who are different. It comes in many forms – Christian, Muslim, Hindu, Jewish or even atheist.

Sociologists sometimes say that groups can exist without a god, but no group can exist without a devil. Some individual or group needs to be identified as the enemy, as evil, as a threat – so that the troops can be rallied, funds can be raised, internal questions and divisions can be suppressed, and boundaries can be maintained. If the 'devil' is the majority, then the group in question identifies itself as a persecuted, divinely favoured minority. If the group in question is a majority, it seeks a minority group on which to project its anxieties and anger. Gay, lesbian, bisexual and transgendered people are an ideal choice for this kind of fundamentalist scapegoating. Gay people appear to make up between 3 and 10 per cent of every society (although they are, in many parts of the world, still in hiding), just big enough but not too big to be scapegoated effectively. But more is going on in current controversies over sexuality than simple scapegoating. Our preoccupation with sexuality is a symptom, I believe, of our growing discomfort with conventional answers to the six questions we have already considered in this book.

(1) Regarding the Greco-Roman narrative in which we have framed the Bible, homosexuality stubbornly resists being explained by it for at least two reasons. First, the narrative assumes an inherent dualism in the universe – a bipolar world of matter/spirit, physics/metaphysics, natural/supernatural and male/female. This dualism portrays the human being as a ghost in a machine – a spirit or soul that indwells a physical body much as a driver indwells a car. If the car goes into a ditch, it's the driver's fault, and similarly if a person has sex with another person of the wrong gender, it's the soul's fault.

But this view is under assault from all sides. Medicine points to chemical imbalances, congenital defects and degenerative diseases that impair various functions we associate with the soul – reasoning, making moral choices, remembering, and so on. Psychology, psychiatry, neurobiology, evolutionary biology and related fields similarly blur the old distinctions between personality and chemistry or soul and body. As they do so, they additionally undermine the Platonic dualisms where maleness and femaleness are two absolute, eternal categories of being into which all people fit. In the light of additional biological complications like intersexuality (where children are born with some combination of male and female sex organs) and Klinefelter's syndrome (a genetic condition in which an individual has XXY chromosomes, rather than typical XY male or XX female chromosomes), it becomes clear that whatever we human beings are, we aren't simply metaphysical male or female souls riding around as passengers in male or female body-vehicles. This realisation is creating a far-reaching revolution in Christian anthropology.[2]

Second, in the perpetual high-noon sunlight of Platonic philosophy, words like *male*, *female* and *marriage* have timeless, perfect essences. No change in these essences can possibly occur, since they exist on the transcendent and eternal plane of ideal forms. Our job as fallen people stuck down here in the cave of illusion is to understand and conform to those unchanging, transcendent, absolute definitions as rigidly and faithfully as possible. True, faithful Bible readers struggle to reconcile this view with certain stubborn facts, such as the fact that marriage in the Bible was not always between one man and one woman, but rather evolved through stages where polygyny was not only permitted but in some cases required.[3] But, even so, the Platonic view has successfully rendered those facts strangely invisible, as if they weren't even there.

But now, as we move outside the Greco-Roman worldview, we are able to ask the same kind of uncomfortable questions about absolutist Platonic dualism that Jesus raised regarding the Jewish Law. Just as he asked, 'Was the Sabbath made for people, or were people made for the Sabbath?' we can ask whether humans were made to fit into an absolute, unchanging institution called marriage, or whether marriage was created to help humans – perhaps including gay humans? – to live wisely and well in this world.[4]

(2) Regarding the constitutional reading of the Bible, homosexuality today functions the way the retrograde motion of the

planets functioned in the late Middle Ages. It is a primary anomaly that the dominant paradigm can't explain. Copernicus and Galileo were pressured to label the observation of retrograde motion as a deceptive *appearance* – not a reality. And if a Christian today experiences gay friends, neighbours, colleagues or relatives as healthy, sincere and morally equal, she or he must similarly marginalise and discredit this experience; gay health, sincerity and equality must be deemed a deceptive *appearance*, because the *reality* demanded by the dominant paradigm is that they are rebellious and dangerous sinners, a twisted abomination, a deceptive moral aberrance.[5] In a sense, they are dangerous – dangerous to the constitutional reading of the Bible.

The constitutional reading of the Bible has been amazingly resilient. After vehemently rejecting the proposals of Copernicus and Galileo, its defenders learned to ignore the texts they had previously used against the astronomical innovators (Eccl. 1:4–6; Pss. 93:1; 104:5; 2 Kgs 20:11; Josh. 10:12–14). They also learned to forgive their leaders for being 'men of their times' – whether Luther (who called Copernicus 'an upstart astrologer' in a 1539 'table talk'), or Melanchthon (who accused the 'pernicious' defenders of Copernicus of being deluded by 'a love of novelty, display of ingenuity . . . a lack of honesty and decency'), or Calvin (who asked, 'Who will venture to place the authority of Copernicus above that of the Holy Spirit?'), or the Congregation of the Index of the Roman Catholic Church (who in 1616 banned Copernicus's ideas as 'false and altogether opposed to Holy Scripture' and incompatible with 'Catholic truth' – a ban which was not reversed until the nineteenth century).

Practitioners of the constitutional approach have gone through a similar four-stage pattern regarding several appearances that turned out to be reality: the discovery of fossils indicating an ancient earth, Darwin's theory of evolution, slavery and segregation and apartheid, and the rights of women to vote and lead in state and Church. First they oppose, condemn and reject. Then they modify and make small concessions. Then they go silent for a while. Finally, they tolerate and accept.[6]

There's evidence that this pattern is at work regarding homosexuality today. Many of us remember when nearly all conservative Christians said homosexuality was simply a perverted choice and therefore a damning abomination. Case closed – oppose, condemn, reject. Then more and more leaders modified their previous view by acknowledging that there is an unchosen orientation at play – *orientation* being a category completely unrecognised in Scripture, by the way. During this stage there was a lot of 'love the sinner, hate the sin' talk. Initially, these Christian leaders asserted that the orientation must be healed through prayer and therapy. But then, when a large percentage of purported healings proved temporary, religious authority figures capitulated to a 'cross to bear' approach where the orientation must be borne through celibacy. Now some have begun to reduce the vehemence or frequency of their pontifications on the subject and many have gone silent altogether. Many leaders have told me they privately dissent from the conventional view, even though their silence maintains the appearance of supporting it. During this latency period, the abomination-become-orientation is being de-stigmatised, so gay unions are increasingly seen as inevitable in one form or another, to one degree or another.

(3) The image of God as violent or even genocidal comes into play when people claim that God chooses one tribe and

rejects or considers inferior other classes or types of people simply for being who they are – whether they're Gentiles, Jews, women, non-whites, non-Christians or gay. Although this kind of favouritism may seem unfair, the line or argument goes, *God is God, and so whatever God does is automatically fair. Who are you to question it?* This 'might makes right' kind of argument may seem suspicious, but it's simple, and it can be defended by a constitutional reading of the Bible.

You won't find many motivations more visceral than the fear of an angry God, especially the fear of being demoted by God from the high, bright status of the elect and elite to the low, dark status of the apostate and damned. And if your view of God involves a lot of smiting, it's all the more risky to change it. So if God considers homosexuality a smiteable abomination, sympathising with the damned takes either a lot of courage or a lot of stupidity. Either way, under the influence of that vision of God, it's much easier to stay loyal to the lucky heterosexual tribe favoured by the tribal God, letting the chips fall where they may for those so unfortunate as to have been born different.

But if our view of God is transformed by seeing Jesus the crucified as the image of God in whom the fullness of God dwells in human form (as Paul does in Col. 1), and as the radiance of God's glory and the exact representation of God's person (as in Heb. 1), then God has been best self-revealed not in the smiter but in the one being smitten. In a crucified man, God demonstrates supreme solidarity not with the rejecter and excluder, but with the ones who are rejected and excluded, not with the humiliator and shamer, but with the ones who are humiliated and shamed. And in that light it becomes more difficult to cast the first stone at the 'sexually other'.

(4) The issue of Jesus' identity as ultimate Word of God comes into play as well. If Jesus' life and example are simply textual data on an equal par with Leviticus, and if Jesus can make no claim to be Lord and teacher over Paul, then perhaps the conventional approaches win.[7] But if Jesus represents the zenith of God's self-revelation and the climax of a dynamic biblical narrative rather than simply one article in a flat and static constitution, Jesus' treatment of the marginalised and stigmatised requires us to question the conventional approach. We have many examples of Jesus crossing boundaries to include outcasts and sinners, and not a single example of Jesus crossing his arms and refusing to do so.[8]

(5) The meaning and purpose of the gospel also come into play. If the purpose of the gospel is to solve the problem of original sin so souls won't go to hell, and if homosexuality is seen as a heinous symptom of original sin and therefore a hell-qualifying offence, then homosexuality is indeed a problem that must be solved. But if we discern the purpose of the gospel through Exodus, Genesis and Isaiah, we discover the dynamic story of God as liberator, creator and reconciler. From this vantage point, homosexual and heterosexual stand equally in need of liberation, because God is equally the Creator of both, and God's kingdom has room for both, calling both to repentance and reconciliation with God and one another. The question is developed from 'Is homosexuality right or wrong?' to 'How should gay and straight people understand and treat one another in God's kingdom?'

(6) As we saw in the last chapter, the previous five questions have a radical bearing on what the Church will be and do. The conventional set of answers postures the Church as an inherently conservative and change-averse community; the other set

241

as an inherently creative and change-catalytic community. As a change-averse community, the Church sees the increasing acceptance of gay people as yet another slide down a slippery slope towards moral relativism and decay. As a change-catalytic community, the Church sees this increasing acceptance as yet another step up in removing the old dividing walls of Jew/Gentile, slave/free, male/female, and so on.

This creative and catalytic spirit, it turns out, was the way of the gospel in the very beginning. It is the true tradition, and we are being conservative in the best sense of the word to conserve it faithfully. Just as the parable that began this chapter can be read in two ways, our whole faith can be expressed in two ways, depending on the questions we raise and the responses we give.

As we said in the previous chapter, it's not easy forming change-catalytic disciple-making communities. Take your first few steps in that direction, and a dozen complexities throw themselves in your path. But it's never been easy or simple, as an under-appreciated passage in the Acts of the Apostles makes clear. As the story begins, Jesus says that the gospel of the kingdom of God will be proclaimed through his followers 'in Jerusalem, and in all Judea and Samaria, and to the ends of the earth' (Acts 1:8). By Acts 8, it has transcended geographical boundaries again and again, spreading through Jerusalem, Judea and Samaria, and now it is about to be spread to the first of the 'ends of the earth' – Africa. And it will happen through a most unlikely person.

Philip, one of the early leaders in the *ecclesia* in Jerusalem, has been sent by angelic vision to walk 'the wilderness road' that leads to Gaza. Along comes a chariot carrying an official of the Ethiopian government, returning to his nation after a visit to Jerusalem. The man is described as a eunuch – a castrated male, an odd designation to us, but less so in the ancient world. In many ancient cultures, certain males were chosen for castration so that they would never marry and have a family. Without a family, they would have no loyalty to anyone other than their king, which would suit them well for sensitive positions in the court – including manager of the king's harem, taster of the king's food (an important 'homeland security' job), or overseer of the king's (or, in this case, the queen's) treasury, which was this eunuch's position.[9]

He had visited Jerusalem to worship – perhaps a way of showing political solidarity between the two nations, or perhaps an expression of his own religious hunger, or both.[10] The Spirit prompts Philip to run alongside the chariot, and Philip hears the Ethiopian reading aloud these words from the prophet Isaiah:

> He was led like a sheep to the slaughter,
> and as a lamb before its shearer is silent,
> so he did not open his mouth.
> In his humiliation he was deprived of justice.
> Who can speak of his descendants?
> For his life was taken from the earth.
> *(Acts 8:32–33, from Isa. 53:7–8)*

After Philip asks if he understands what he's reading, the eunuch invites Philip to join him in the chariot, to explain the text's meaning. The eunuch raises this poignant question: 'Who is the prophet talking about, himself or someone else?' (v. 34).

Now, given this man's unique identity, we should ask why this particular passage would so seize his attention, and why this particular question would arise. Would the image of cutting – a sheep about to have its neck slit, or a lamb about to be sheared – have special significance to a eunuch? Would humiliation and the denial of justice strike a responsive chord with him? Would the word 'descendants' (or 'generation') have special meaning to a man incapable of producing a next generation?

Philip responds by telling him 'the good news about Jesus' (v. 35), using this passage as a starting point. This good news, we must remember, is not the version shaped by the Greco-Roman narrative: it is the good news of the kingdom of God, the message proclaimed by Jesus and shaped by the Jewish narratives of creation, liberation and reconciliation. It is the message embodied in a man who was stripped naked and publicly humiliated, despised, rejected and misunderstood, a man without physical descendants, a man who was cut and scarred for ever. The eunuch obviously feels that this good news relates powerfully to him personally, and so as the chariot passes by a stream along the Gaza road, he says, 'Look, here is water. What can stand in the way of my being baptised?' (v. 37).

Perhaps you feel the profound pathos of his question, especially if you imagine it being asked in a high-tenor, testosterone-deprived voice. The pathos becomes all the more intense in view of the small detail that Luke has already mentioned: this man is returning from Jerusalem where he had been hoping to worship. What would have happened to him there? As an Ethiopian – a 'person of colour', we might say – he was obviously not Jewish, which would exclude him from full participation in temple worship. (Remember that a riot will break out in Acts 21 simply because Paul is accused of bringing a brown-skinned Greek man into the temple precinct. Think what would have happened if a coffee-coloured Ethiopian dared to enter.) But there was a 'court of the Gentiles' in the temple. Perhaps he could at least have worshipped there, from a distance? Sadly, though, even second-class participation would have been forbidden, because for the Jews, castration was considered a 'defect'. The defect disqualified a person from priesthood, and this disqualification was specified to be in effect 'for the generations to come'.[11]

But, even more sweeping, Deuteronomy graphically extends the exclusion beyond the priesthood to everyone: 'No one whose testicles are crushed or whose penis is cut off shall be admitted to the assembly of the LORD' (23:1, NRSV). So our castrated official has come to worship in Jerusalem, but he has undoubtedly been turned away: both his racial and his sexual identities have prevented him from inclusion in the worshipping community. In this light, do you feel the full pang of the question he asks as the chariot passes some water? *I have just been rejected and humiliated in Jerusalem, but you have told me of a man who, like me, has no physical descendants, a scarred and wounded man like me who has been humiliated and rejected. Is there a place for me in his kingdom, even though I have an unchangeable condition that was condemned for ever by the sacred Jewish Scriptures?*

Philip doesn't speak. Nor does he leave for Jerusalem to consult with the apostles there, nor does he convene a five-year committee to study the subject. Instead, he simply acts. The audacity of his action is seldom appreciated, I fear. As the horses are reined in and the chariot comes to a stop in a cloud of dust, he leads the eunuch down from the chariot and into the water, and there he baptises him. The sign of the kingdom of God that began in Jesus – a place at the table for outcasts and outsiders – continues in the era of the Acts of the Apostles. The poor are accepted, and the sick. Samaritans are accepted, and Gentiles, including Africans, and here, even the 'sexually other', those considered 'defective' who will never have a place in traditional religion or in the traditional culture based on the 'traditional family'. The old 'other-excluding' sanctions, against the uncircumcised, against the 'defective', even though they were claimed to be in effect 'for the generations to come', have been buried in baptism, left behind as part of the old order that is passing away. As Philip and the Ethiopian disciple climb the stream bank, they represent a new humanity emerging from the water, dripping wet and full of joy, marked by a new and radical reconciliation in the kingdom of God.

Not only does this represent an acceptance of a member of God's creation (from the Genesis narrative), and not only does it represent liberation for one who has been deprived of justice within an oppressive social system (the Exodus narrative), it is also an expression of the peaceable kingdom, in direct resonance with the prophetic narrative of Isaiah (56:1–7):

This is what the LORD says:
'Maintain justice
and do what is right,
for my salvation is close at hand
and my righteousness will soon be revealed.
Blessed are those who do this –
who hold it fast,
those who keep the Sabbath without desecrating it,

and keep their hands from doing any evil.'
Let no foreigners who have bound themselves to the LORD say,
'The LORD will surely exclude me from his people.'
And let no eunuch complain,
'I am only a dry tree.'
For this is what the LORD says:
'To the eunuchs who keep my Sabbaths,
who choose what pleases me
and hold fast to my covenant –
to them I will give within my temple and its walls
a memorial and a name
better than sons and daughters;
I will give them an everlasting name
that will endure for ever.
And foreigners who bind themselves to the LORD
to minister to him,
to love the name of the LORD,
and to be his servants,
all who keep the Sabbath without desecrating it
and who hold fast to my covenant –
these I will bring to my holy mountain
and give them joy in my house of prayer.
Their burnt offerings and sacrifices
will be accepted on my altar;
for my house will be called
a house of prayer for all nations.'

These, of course, are the evocative words quoted by Jesus when he 'cleansed' the temple – which for him didn't mean cleansing it of 'sinners', eunuchs and Gentiles – or of homosexuals and undocumented aliens – but of money-changers whose religious-industrial complex excluded many and embedded the faith in the economy of the empire and vice versa. If there could be any question that God might soon change plans and revert from this campaign of gathering and including – hearkening back to a more traditional rejecting and excluding that religions seem to prefer – Isaiah adds these words: 'The Sovereign LORD declares – he who gathers the exiles of Israel: "I will gather still others to them besides those already gathered"' (v. 8).

And so the tension between exclusion and inclusion continues to today. When I was a young Evangelical, the issue was racial segregation. Then it was 'those hippies' with their blue jeans, hairstyles and rock'n'roll music. More recently, in the US, it was Democrats, and now it's gay people. Those who feel they must, to be faithful to Scripture, maintain a conventional policy of exclusion regarding gay people may not be convinced by this line of thinking, but I hope they will at least see that it is not the 'throw out the Bible and anything goes' caricature that is often presented as the only option in a classic false dichotomy.

I experienced the power of this kind of inclusive in-gathering many years ago in my early days as a pastor. Our little church had outgrown our living room and was meeting in an elementary school cafeteria in a poor part of town, not too far from the University of Maryland where I had been a tutor. I had recently met a Kenyan graduate student named Moses at a party and invited him to church. This was his first Sunday visiting. Moses had suffered from polio as a child, so he walked with braces, his muscular upper body poised like a robust triangle on his shrivelled lower body, and I remember after the service, after nearly all the metal folding chairs had been stacked away, seeing Moses folded over on a lone chair in the middle of the room. He was gently shaking, his face buried in his hands, his forehead touching his knees.

I touched his shoulder. 'Moses, are you OK?'

He raised his face, tears streaming down his coffee-brown cheeks. 'Oh, dear brother, these are tears of joy,' he said.

'I don't understand,' I replied. 'What happened?'

'This is my first time celebrating the holy supper,' he said, referring to the Eucharist.

'But, Moses, I thought you told me that you had been a Christian since childhood.'

'Oh, yes, but until today, I have never shared in the holy supper,' he replied. 'You see,' he added, as if his explanation would make perfect sense to me, 'I am a child of the third wife.'

He went on to explain that the Anglican Church in Kenya, of which he was part, had made a policy for polygamous converts. Only the children of the first wife could participate in the Eucharist. 'When I came here today, Brian,' he said, 'and when you said that all were welcome to the table, I realised that here I am not a child of the third wife. Here I am simply Moses, a Christian, and I am welcome at the table.'

Welcome in the waters of baptism, welcome at the table . . . tax collectors and sinners, impure Samaritans, uncircumcised Gentiles, de-sexed eunuchs, children of the third wife, but surely not gay or transgendered men and women, right? Right? And surely not people who suffer from birth defects, Down's syndrome, bipolar disorder or schizophrenia, right? And surely not communists, Marxists, liberals, libertarians or convicted felons, right? Right?

Scripture tells us that the Ethiopian eunuch was accepted and baptised that day by Philip, but tradition tells us more – that this 'sexually other' person brought the gospel of the kingdom of God back to Ethiopia. Think of that: a non-heterosexual in missional leadership from the very beginning of the Jesus movement.[12]

Having spent many pages talking about homosexuality, I need to add that I actually think we have many other significant sexual issues on our front doorstep – issues that may in the long run be no less important and even more difficult to address. In particular, what we have called traditional marriage – one virgin man and one virgin woman becoming the only sexual partner the other will ever have for life – isn't working as it's supposed to for heterosexuals. In fact, it's surprisingly rare, nearly an endangered species in the US and in many other places as well. Before marriage, premarital sex is the norm, not the exception, for Christians as well as non-Christians, and for evangelicals as well as other brands. And it is the norm not by a few percentage points, either: the average 'sexual debut' for an American evangelical, for example, is just after his or her sixteenth birthday.[13] Even teens who make abstinence pledges, the research shows, only forestall premarital sex by about eighteen months on average. As might be expected, the pledgers are less likely to use contraceptives when they have sex, increasing the likelihood of pregnancy and STDs. So, while American evangelical teenagers uphold abstinence as their ideal by a strong majority – 74 per cent – most of them end up living with varying degrees of cognitive dissonance and guilt.[14]

But the problems aren't only *before* marriage: divorce rates are startlingly high for Christians as well. It's hard to square the frequently heard argument that tolerance of homosexuality weakens the institution of marriage when heterosexual church-goers are having divorces at rates not very different from (and sometimes higher than) their less religious neighbours. And ironically – or predictably, depending on your assumptions – some subgroups with the highest divorce rates can be the most strongly vocal against homosexuality.[15]

I share these observations not to load more guilt on already guilty people: it's not easy being a red-blooded human being who is simultaneously blessed with hormone-producing gonads and fidelity-inspiring spiritual commitments. And being a human being at this time in history makes it all the more difficult to navigate our sexual lives. The opportunities for promiscuity may never have been greater, and the supports for chastity and fidelity have seldom if ever been weaker. Consider these realities:

- We've moved from villages where 'everyone knows your name', and where nearly everyone is committed to the same moral standards, to cities where we're all virtually anonymous and where anything goes. So sex and community are less connected than ever before.[16]
- We're the first humans to have low-cost, readily available birth control, making sex and pregnancy less connected than ever before.
- We're the first humans to have condoms and antibiotics readily available, making sex and disease less connected than ever before.
- We've created an economic system that increasingly requires both men and women to work outside the home, in company with members of the opposite sex, thus increasing the possibilities for extramarital attractions to develop and become sexual.

- We've created an economic system that rewards education and punishes early marriage, pushing the average age of marriage higher and higher. As a result, we've put the biological peak for sex and reproduction further out of sync with the cultural norms for marriage than ever before.
- Meanwhile, a number of factors are bringing the average age of puberty lower and lower, leaving more years than ever during which sexually mature people are likely to be single, and therefore likely to engage in sex outside marriage.
- The internet has made pornography ubiquitous, the advertising industry continuously exploits onscreen sex to sell everything from hamburgers to lawn mowers, and the entertainment industry uses sex to sell films, books, TV shows, magazines and related products and services. As a result, sexual stimulation has become increasingly virtualised and universalised.
- The print, onscreen and online ubiquity of 'perfect' bodies in 'virtual reality' – fully or nearly fully exposed, often cosmetically and digitally enhanced – can create images of sexual perfection compared to which nearly all actual partners will disappoint, thus increasing sexual tension in actual relationships.
- The combination of poverty, unemployment and life in refugee camps or slums puts millions of people together with literally nothing to do, day after day, increasing the likelihood of casual sexual contact among people without the resources to raise the children they conceive.

When I consider these and the many other factors that are working against sexual sanity and health, I'm amazed that we're doing as well as we are. Which brings me back to the subject of homosexuality. By coming out of the closet regarding their *homosexuality*, gay people may help the rest of us come out of the closet regarding our *sexuality*.[17] And that is important, because the longer we hide from the truth of our sexuality – in all its beauty and agony, in all its passion and pain, in all its simplicity and complexity – the sicker we will be, as religious communities, as cultures, and as a global society.

As in so many areas, we must blaze a new trail into that terra nova beyond the binary and reactionary ideals of sexually repressive fundasexuality on the one hand and sexually unrestrained hedonism on the other.[18] We must pursue a practical, down-to-earth theology and an honest, fully embodied spirituality that speak honestly and openly about our sexuality, in all its straight and gay complexity.

Catholics need this quest, as they come to terms with the problems of an unmarried and all-male clergy and of a lingering historical ambivalence in some quarters about sex in general.[19] Evangelicals need this quest, as they come to terms with the gap between their ideals and pledges and their actual performance – not just in their young people, but in their middle-aged pastors and celebrities who keep slipping into scandals made all the more delicious by their claims to represent morality. Mainline Protestants need this quest, as they face the negligible difference between the sexual behaviour of their young people and those outside the Church. Parents and Christian educators need it so they won't damage their children's full human development as they try to steer them away from damaging sexual behaviours. Single adults need it so they won't be tempted to lead double lives. Everyone needs it as rates of divorce, births to single mothers and STD infection remain high, leaving great human suffering in their wake.

Perhaps our anxiety about this needed quest provides one more reason why we're focusing so much displaced energy on gay people and on our disagreements about how to treat them. It's a lot easier to make them the problem than to face the deeper problems we all face as sexual–spiritual creatures, women and men, straight and gay, married and single, celibate and sexually active. A new kind of Christianity must move beyond this impasse and begin to construct not just a more humane sexual ethic in particular, but a more honest and robust Christian anthropology in general. To do that, some of us at least will need to start talking and walking and working together as never before, even when we disagree.

EIGHT

THE FUTURE QUESTION

CHAPTER 18

Can We Find a Better Way of Viewing the Future?

Some us are terribly familiar with the theological term *eschatology*, the study of the *eschaton* or the future and end towards which history moves.[1] We grew up in fundamentalist, Pentecostal or restorationist churches that loved to hold prophecy conferences, to preach sermons about the coming last days, to publish garish magazines and illustrated tracts about 'the LITERAL FULFILMENT of biblical predictions TODAY', and to speculate about the impending apocalypse (initiated by godless communism in Russia? China? Iraq?). Our preachers often speculated according to a theory of eschatology called *dispensationalism*. Although dispensationalism was invented somewhat recently – in the 1830s – among the rather eccentric Plymouth Brethren (the fascinating tradition in which I was raised), it has been popularised worldwide through the Scofield Reference Bible since 1909, and is now considered absolute historic orthodoxy by millions of Christians around the world.

Those of us raised in dispensationalist circles can regale one another with stories about scary 'left behind' sermons, some-times illustrated through huge and serious wall charts and dramatised in B-rated films. These sermons would climax with warnings about the second coming, when Jesus will return like 'a thief in the night', initiating 'the rapture' when 'born-again Christians' will (we were told) be miraculously evacuated to heaven and the rest (including the children of 'saved' parents) will be left behind for a nightmare apocalypse. As a boy of about eight, having come home from school and found the doors locked and nobody home, I once spent nearly an hour sitting on my back porch, deeply dejected and with rising panic, sure that the rapture had occurred and I was a child left behind. Who knew that a young child could feel such terror and despair?

To the uninitiated, this all might sound pitiful or laughable, like wild conspiracy theories shared on strange websites or middle-of-the-night radio. But surprising numbers of mainline Protestants and Roman Catholics have also been thoroughly catechised in this eschatology through televangelist broadcasts and books (and newer B-rated films) in the 'Left Behind' series, which have broken sales records around the world.[2] If they only focused on speculation about who is the antichrist (I remember hearing it was Khrushchev, then Henry Kissinger, then Saddam Hussein, and now, apparently, odds are being placed on Barack Obama!), their eschatological hobby might be harmless enough – like a crazy uncle obsessed with UFOs.[3] But, in recent decades, dispensationalism and its eschatological cousins have become significant factors in the foreign policy of the richest, most consumerist and most well-armed nation in the history of history – and that's where things get even scarier than a B-rated film.[4]

If the world is about to end, why care for the environment? Why worry about global climate change or fuel resources? Who gives a fig for endangered species or sustainable economies or peak oil or global poverty if God is planning to incinerate the whole planet soon anyway? If the Bible predicts the rebuilding of the Jewish temple (or requires that rebuilding for its prophecies to work in a dispensationalist framework), why care about Muslim claims on the Temple Mount land? Why care about justice for non-Jews in Israel at all – after all, isn't it their own fault for being on land God predicts will be returned in full to the Jews in the last days? If God has predetermined that the world will get worse and worse until it ends in a cosmic mega-conflict between the forces of Light (epitomised most often by the US) and the forces of Darkness (previously centred in communism, but now, that devil having been vanquished, in Islam), why waste energy on peace-making, on diplomacy, on inter-religious dialogue? Aren't those simply endeavours in rearranging deckchairs on the *Titanic*? And since even Jesus can't set the world right without taking up the sword and shedding swimming pools of his enemies' blood (recalling our discussion under the Jesus Question), what's so bad about another war, and maybe even a little torture and genocide now and then? If God sanctions it, why can't we?

Maybe now you see why I believe that a new kind of Christianity demands a new kind of eschatology, a new way of viewing the future.[5] And maybe you can anticipate ways in which we have already opened up new possibilities by questioning the theological paradigms we've examined so far. Most importantly, the Greco-Roman narrative offered us a vision of history as a timeline, which forced us to think of past, present and future as flat, narrow, linear and predetermined. In that paradigm, we were driven from the past into the future at a constant pace on a flat plane, from left to right.

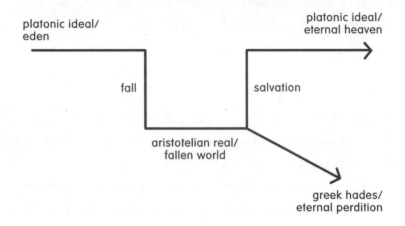

But we have begun exploring the future in the light of the dynamic and spacious biblical narrative rather than the flat, linear and predetermined Greco-Roman one. In that context, we see the future not as a *timeline* on a flat plane, but as a *time-space* in three dimensions. In that expanding space, millions of good stories can unfold and be told. Suddenly we find ourselves not in a one-dimensional determined universe with a fixed future, but in a deep, expanding universe with a future full of widening possibilities. At every moment, creation continues to unfold, liberation continues to unshackle us, and the peaceable kingdom continues to expand with new hope and promise.

This continual unfolding, expanding and opening all flow from a generous, creative and liberating God, a God as far different from the static Theos of the Greeks as three wild dimensions are from a perfectly flat line. So let's think of creation as height, liberation as length, and peaceable kingdom as depth. When we do, we quickly realise that we're not in theological flatland any more.

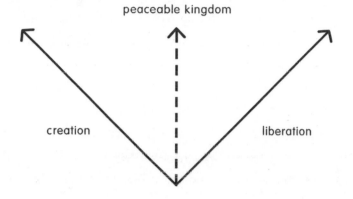

To live in this three-dimensional universe does not mean we're just stuck in static cycles like gerbils on a wheel. Nor are we spurting around aimlessly in an anything-goes universe like a deflating balloon, with one direction no better than another. No, there is a trajectory to history, a flow to creation, a moral arc to the universe that slowly but surely tends towards justice, as Dr King used to say. If we think of the moment of creation at the bottom of our diagram, we can think of God's light shining from above, calling all things from chaos, void and darkness towards order, fullness, life and light. Evil actions resist the flow. They turn away from the light and revert towards the darkness of destruction (anti-creation), oppression (anti-liberation) and violence, hatred and fear (anti-reconciliation). Good things grow upwards and outwards, like seedlings from soil, like the branches of a tree reaching towards the light.

That means that, contrary to dispensationalism and many other conventional eschatologies, there is no single fixed end point towards which we move, but rather a widening space, opening into an infinitely expanding goodness, like the air and sunlight into which a tree spreads out its branches. Creation branches out into an ever-widening sphere of goodness, justice and peace. This understanding, to me, is glorious, and I want to get up and shout and sing and dance around my little office today as I sit here writing about it.[6]

But imagine what it would be like to live in this deep three-dimensional universe while still thinking you were living in the flat six-line universe. That, I believe, is the condition many of us find ourselves in, and it explains why many of us find our religion limiting, cramped and unlivable. This three-dimensional approach provides a spacious and hopeful alternative to secular as well as religious determinisms – visions of the future which are set in stone, determined by either laws of physics or decrees of the Almighty. Secular scientists typically offer us two possible futures: in one, the universe is doomed to a final white-hot collapse of gravity (a big crunch), and in the other, to an eternal dark cold freeze of entropy (a big freeze). Either way, in the end, no meaningful residue or memory of our lives, or of life and our world in general, will be left – nothing. Nothing.

Religious determinists have offered us another determinism we could call the 'big-sort' universe: everything that exists will be sorted into either the destruction/damnation or the redemption/salvation bins. Everything, everyone, is pretty much determined to end up in one bin or the other. That sounds good if you're one of the chosen few, but, then again, how could good and generous people rest in peace or celebrate in bliss when they know the majority of their ancestors, friends, family members and descendants are experiencing eternal conscious torment in hell? The big-sort determinism may be an improvement over big crunch and big freeze, but then again, it may not.

This three-dimensional approach, I believe, offers a better vision of the future than any of its deterministic alternatives. We might say that in it, the future is *undoomed* – undoomed from the crunching or freezing annihilation of secular determinisms on the one hand, and undoomed from burning destruction and eternal conscious torment on the other. It is undoomed to eventual healing and joy, undoomed to ultimate liberation, resurrection and (in the fullest sense of the word) salvation, because the living God will never forsake or forget this beloved creation.

In this three-dimensional view, God is not *in control* in the sense of being a machine operator pulling levers or a chess-master moving bishops and pawns. Nor is the universe *out of control* in the sense of being chaotic, random and purposeless. Instead, God and the universe are *in relationship*. That *in-relationship* vision is captured in a number of metaphors in the Bible. For example, God is like a rider guiding a horse with a will of its own, or God is like a parent guiding a child with a will of her own.

The universe, in this view, isn't just an object upon which God acts by dominating *fiat*; it is a subject endowed by its Creator with millions of real minds and wills, a community with which God relates intersubjectively. All creation is harmed when humanity pulls or drops or drifts *out of relationship*, like a moody child pouting in the corner, or like a rebellious teenager running away to a distant country far from home. All creation (try thinking of this ecologically) groans for humanity to re-enter a right relationship with God, so that we can fulfil our God-given calling as creation's stewards, students and creative partners – and cease being its abusers, exploiters and plunderers.

Conventional eschatologies, whether pre-millennial, post-millennial, a-millennial, preterist, and so on, tend to argue about different arrangements or lengths of the lines in the Greco-Roman narrative. That's what makes this new approach so different and difficult to label, because it dispenses with the linear approach altogether. We could borrow from Hans Kung and others and call it an 'improvisational eschatology'.[7] We could also call it *participatory*.[8] In a participatory eschatology, when we ask, 'What does the future hold?' the answer begins, 'That depends. It depends on you and me. God holds out to us at every moment a brighter future; the issue is whether we are willing to receive it and work with God to help create it. We are participating in the creation of what the future will be.'

If you explore this three-dimensional participatory eschatology for a while, you might feel a little naughty or even rebellious at first, because you'll soon be in tension with things that your six-line tutors have always taught you. But once you allow yourself some space to experiment with it, to try it on for size for a while, you'll start seeing and noticing so much that you've been taught to ignore. Once that happens, I don't think you can ever go back.[9] And, maybe more disturbing, you'll realise that along with being taught *not* to see things that *are* there in the biblical text, you've been taught to see things that *aren't* there at all. We've already seen how this is the case with the term *the fall*, and when it comes to eschatology we'll have to make a similar discovery regarding the term *the second coming of Christ*.

Regarding the second coming, our best Bible scholars are largely united in realising that the New Testament writers were not anticipating the 'end of the world' and the destruction of the space–time universe.[10] They were anticipating 'the end of the world as we know it' and the beginning of a new spiritual–historical age or era. For them, 'the blessed hope' outlined in the Gospels focused on several soon-to-be-fulfilled historical realities, not one far-distant history-ending one.

1. From Holy Thursday to Easter morning, gospel hope focused on Christ's resurrection, which was fulfilled.
2. From the resurrection until Pentecost, it focused on the coming of the Holy Spirit, which was fulfilled.
3. For about the next forty years (during which nearly all the epistles were written), it focused on the survival and rebirth of God's people through an anticipated catastrophe, which came to fruition in the destruction of Jerusalem in AD 70. In this light, it turns out that Jesus was right after all when he said, 'Not one stone . . . will be left on another,' and, 'This generation will certainly not pass away until all these things have happened,' and Paul was right when he said, 'This world in its present form is passing away' (see Matt. 24:2, 34; 1 Cor. 7:29–31).[11]

The question remains: was *everything* they anticipated fulfilled by AD 70, or was there something more? To this many reply, 'The second coming of Christ wasn't fulfilled, of course.'[12] When you point out that the term 'second coming of Christ' never appears in the Bible, they will then point to a Greek term that does occur: *parousia*. That word was formed by adding the prefix *para*, meaning *alongside*, to the root *ousia*, meaning *substance*. Its primary meaning as *presence* is even clearer in contrast to its opposite, *apousia*, meaning absence. Although it is often used in the New Testament simply to refer to the arrival or presence of a friend or associate (see, for example, 2 Cor. 7:6 or 1 Cor. 16:17), Paul uses it to refer to Jesus eight times (once in 1 Cor. and seven times in 1 and 2 Thess.). James also uses it referring to Jesus twice, 2 Peter twice, and 1 John once. Jesus himself only uses it four times, all in one single passage (Matt. 24). According to scholar N. T. Wright, the term, like the Greek words for 'kingdom', 'gospel' and even 'church', often had political connotations, being used 'in relation to the visit of a royal or official personage'.[13]

Whatever *parousia* meant in the apostolic era, it's clear that New Testament writers believed it was coming in the immediate future, and my bias is to assume, at least provisionally, that they were in some sense right. If that's the case, if the New Testament writers were in fact correct in their expectations of a close-at-hand *parousia*, then how should we understand the term? If we aren't restricted to think and work within the old Greco-Roman six-line narrative, the term could mean the arrival or manifestation not of a Platonic eternal state of Greco-Roman perfection and damnation, but rather of a new age or era – a new season of growth. It could mean not the full arrival of 'the end of the end', but the full arrival of 'the beginning of a new beginning'.[14]

Parousia, in this way, would signal the full arrival, presence and manifestation of a new age in human history. It would mean the presence or appearance on earth of a new generation of humanity, Christ again present, embodied in a community of people who truly possess and express his Spirit, continuing his work.[15] This would be the age of the Spirit and grace rather than law and law-keeping. It would be the age of God's presence in a holy people being formed in all cultures rather than God's presence localised in a holy temple centralised in one city. It would be the age of love rather than circumcision or other in-group markers as the prime identification of the people of God. It would be an age where the cult of animal sacrifice and related atonement mechanisms would be passé.

If this alternative understanding has merit, the *parousia* – the arrival or presence – of the new era or covenant began after an in-between time during which the old era or covenant co-existed with the new. In other words, the age of the new covenant had been *conceived* in the birth, life, teaching, good works, death and resurrection of Jesus. Then, after Easter, the new era continued *gestating* in the community of his followers through several decades of struggle and persecution, culminating in a time of great tribulation, when persecution and danger intensified like *labour pains*. During these years, the new age, like a gestating baby, was *already* here, but *not yet* fully born.[16] During this time, the old system of animal sacrifice, priesthood, temple and holy city had *not yet* ended, yet the new system (or covenant) that would outlast it was *already* developing in secret.

When the Romans came to Jerusalem and crushed a Zealot-led rebellion in AD 70, the temple was destroyed, the sacrificial system ended, the priesthood was disbanded, and the old era came to its last day. With the cataclysmic last days of the old era ended, the new age, new covenant, new testament or new era was brought to full term, and its *parousia* had come.[17] Our call, in this view of things, is not to wait passively for something that is not present (*apousia*), but rather to participate passionately in something that is present (*parousia*) – fully present, but not complete in its development, and so calling for our whole-hearted participation.

This is a participatory eschatology. Within it, we are not frantic to get this world and its history over with as soon as possible so that a perfect forever can begin – any more than a musician is frantic to get to the last note of a beautiful song: we understand that every note of the song is precious and should be played with all we can give it. The point of history, like a song, is not in the ending or finishing of it, but in the passionate playing of it, every moment. To say that the kingdom of God is fully born and fully present, of course, does not mean that it is fully grown or fully mature, any more than a president, for example, has completed his or her work and term in office on inauguration day, the date on which he or she and the new administration are fully present. (The previous few sentences may deserve a second read.) So we who follow Jesus, embody his Spirit and continue his work could be said to serve – or *participate* – in his administration. We are misled if we expect a quick end to this project, because Jesus himself said the kingdom would spread its influence gradually like yeast in bread or seeds in a field. And we lack faith and hope if we expect it to fail, ending in the destruction of all things rather than the renewal of all things.

While conventional eschatologies have inspired resignation (God's in control; whatever is predestined will occur), fear (the world is falling apart, so we'd better circle the wagons and protect ourselves), apathy (the world is getting better, so let's relax and party on), and aggression (God's agenda is our agenda, so we have a mandate to impose our agenda on others, using any means necessary), this new participatory eschatology inspires the opposite. It inspires, instead of resignation, a passion to do good, whatever the suffering, sacrifice and delay, because of a confidence that God will win in the end. It inspires courage, rather than fear, because God's Spirit is at work in the world and what God begins

God will surely bring to completion. It inspires a sense of urgency, rather than apathy, because we are protagonists in the story, not mere pawns in a divine chess game or observers of a show whose outcome is already determined. And it inspires humility, not arrogance, because we are aware of our ability to miss the point, lose our way and play on the wrong side.

This eschatology of *participation* produces an ethic of *anticipation*: we seek to have our present way of life shaped by our vision of God's desired future.[18] This anticipatory ethic prompts us to live less as hold-overs from an idyllic past, and more as time-travellers or spies from the future (like Joshua and Caleb after spying out the promised land), returning to the present with a good report of better possibilities ahead.

Jesus' death and resurrection, in this light, aren't merely doctrines to affirm or meanings to celebrate in creed and song. They are a paradigmatic summons to participation and anticipation. True, the transformed future desired by God isn't achieved by human effort, strategy or wisdom apart from God.[19] But neither is it achieved by God working apart from humanity via miraculous skyhooks. No, a better future comes as we join Jesus first in dying (metaphorically by dying to our pride, our agendas, our schedules, our terms – or literally through martyrdom as witnesses for God's kingdom and justice), and then in rising, through the mysterious but real power of God.[20] In this cruciform way, we participate in the ongoing work of God, and we anticipate its ultimate success.[21]

But we can refuse to participate as well. That's what makes a participatory eschatology so different from pessimistic determinisms (like those of pre-millennialism[22]) on the one hand and from triumphalistic determinisms (like those of post-millennialism[23]) on the other. In a participatory approach, God is always present to lead and accompany us in a more hopeful direction, but we are also free to spurn God's leading and presence. The view is ultimately hopeful because God's persistent grace will surely prove more durable and vigorous than our persistent stupidity. But that ultimate hope leaves no room for complacency or smugness in the present moment, because human stupidity can and does produce true and great suffering and sadness.

An odd but fascinating biblical story cleverly and unforgettably illustrates this participatory eschatology, this anticipatory ethic, and our general resistance to embracing it: the story of Jonah. Jonah is often perceived as a cute children's story about a gentle magic whale who serves as a living submarine for a runaway prophet. Actually, it could win an award as the most subversive document in the biblical library. Its one home-grown character, Jonah, is rebellious, pouty and wrong nearly 100 per cent of the time, while all other characters in the story – from pagan sailors, to ocean waves, to Ninevites, to a vine and a worm, to the great swallowing-and-vomiting sea creature himself – respond to God beautifully.

The story begins with the word of the Lord coming to Jonah: 'Go to the great city Nineveh and preach against it, because its wickedness has come up before me' (Jon. 1:1).[24] Jonah declines the assignment and jumps on a ship that will carry him to the opposite end of the Mediterranean world (meaning contemporary Spain instead of Iraq). God intervenes with a major storm to block Jonah's escape. Jonah ends up getting thrown overboard by a remarkably kind group of sailors who, after doing everything they can to save both him and their own skins, in the end capitulate to Jonah's death wish and toss him into the sea. Enter the whale, or great fish, who dutifully swallows Jonah, and whose stomach provides a kind of prayer chamber – a symbol, to my interpretive eye, of the Jewish experience of conquest and exile. When cued by the Lord, the fish vomits Jonah onto the shore, and when cued by the Lord a second time to go to Nineveh, Jonah complies. Jonah arrives in Nineveh and starts preaching that the city will be destroyed in forty days, and, right on cue, everyone repents, from the least to the king himself. The king calls everyone to fast and pray, to 'give up their evil ways and their violence' (3:8), for this reason: 'Who knows? God may yet relent and with compassion turn from his fierce anger so that we will not perish' (3:9).

And that's all it takes for God to drop the 'destroy in forty days' forecast. At this point, Jonah is furious. He vents, 'Isn't this what I said, LORD, when I was still at home? That is what I tried to forestall by fleeing to Tarshish. I knew that you are a gracious and compassionate God, slow to anger and abounding in love, a God who relents from sending calamity' (4:2). In other words, Jonah says, 'I didn't want to come to Nineveh, our enemy and the axis of evil, for fear that you would be gracious and compassionate to them.' He wants no part in sharing his tribe's 'secret defence' or 'secret weapon' – the grace and love of God – with the enemy. He wishes God would remain more to his liking – suitably tribal, exclusive and xenophobic.

Jonah then, in his second suicidal moment, begs for God to kill him, as if to say, 'I'd rather be dead than have to live in a world where you love both our enemies and us', a remarkably common sentiment among religious people still today, it seems. God tries to reason with Jonah, using first words and then a kind of experiential learning programme involving a vine and

271

a worm, but Jonah keeps sulking and wishing he were dead. God twice asks Jonah what right he has to be so angry. The first time, Jonah just walks away without saying anything, although one can imagine him muttering something under his breath like a cheeky teenager. The second time, he claims he does have a right, and (once again) he'd rather be dead, thank you very much. God replies:

> You have been concerned about this vine, though you did not tend it or make it grow. It sprang up overnight and died overnight. But Nineveh has more than a hundred and twenty thousand people who cannot tell their right hand from their left, and many cattle as well. Should I not be concerned about that great city? *(4:10–11 NIV)*

And that's the end – the only document in the biblical library that ends with an open question and with no sense of closure to the plot.[25] This openness presents us with great hope.[26] Even though Jonah rebels and runs away from his calling, his rebellion is not the end of the story. Even though Jonah asks to be thrown overboard, his death wish is not the end of the story. Even though Jonah is swallowed by a whale, the whale's potent stomach acids are not the end of the story. Even though Jonah has a snarky attitude and stomps away from God in a huff, his temper tantrum isn't the end of the story. And so on. Whether you're Jonah or the Ninevites or us, wherever you turn, you keep bumping into a gracious and compassionate God, slow to anger and abounding in love. Again and again, God opens up another chance to repent, and so the story ends without really ending. Instead of closure, the story leaves us with aperture.

Should God not be concerned? Should God not be 'a gracious and compassionate God, slow to anger and abounding in love' – both towards the Ninevites and towards his reluctant, recalcitrant prophet? Should God not care? Our answers to these questions, I believe, shape our vision of the future. The future is open because the compassion and care of God are unconstricted, open wide for us to turn and find a better life than we're now experiencing by taking a better path than we're now walking.[27]

What of final judgement? The reality of judgement seems to be a central theme across the biblical library, because in God's presence all pretence and hypocrisy, like all hidden virtues and goodness, are brought to light and our true colours shine through. This means that the true accounting, evaluation or assessment of our lives, our works, our nations, our world cannot help but happen.[28] This true accounting, evaluation or assessment is what *judgement* means. But, sadly, that word has been defined for us – and thoroughly spoiled for us – in the old Greco-Roman big-sort narrative.

As a first step in seeing judgement in our new eschatological context, we must stop defining it as condemnation. God's judgement in the three-dimensional biblical context is not merely retributive – seeking to punish wrongdoers for their wrongs and in this way to balance some sort of cosmic equation. No, God's judgement is far higher and better than that: it involves 'putting wrong things right'. It means reconciling, not merely punishing; healing, not merely diagnosing; transforming, not merely exposing; revaluing (or redeeming), not merely evaluating.

Second, we must realise that final judgement will not be merciless or graceless, as many assume, because in God what we

273

may think of as opposites – grace and truth, justice and mercy, kindness and strength – are beautifully and fully integrated.

And, third, we must see the life and way of Jesus – not a list of laws, rules or beliefs – to be the high and gracious standard by which history's events and our own lives will be valued and evaluated.[29] To see Jesus as God's paradigm for judging or evaluating our lives means that it's not the powerful and dominant who will be deemed history's heroes, but the humble and poor in spirit, like Jesus. It's not the pleasure-satiated hedonists who grabbed for all of life's gusto who will be judged winners, but those who mourned the tragedy of injustice and who hungered and thirsted for a better day, like Jesus. It's not the victors in war, but the makers of peace who will be seen as bearing God's family resemblance – those like Jesus.

Whatever the final judgement will be, then, it will not involve God (please pardon the crudeness of this) pulling down one's pants to check for circumcision, or scanning one's brain for certain beliefs like products being scanned at the supermarket checkout. No, God will examine the story of our lives for signs of Christ-likeness – for a cup of cold water or a plate of hot food given to one in need, for an atom of mercy shown to one who has been unkind or unthoughtful, for a visit to a prisoner or an open door and warm bed for a stranger, for a generous impulse indulged and a hurtful one denied, like Jesus. These are the parts of a person's life that will be deemed worthy of being saved, remembered, rewarded and raised for a new beginning. All the unloving, unjust, non-Christ-like parts of our lives – and of our nations, tribes, civilisations, families, churches, and so on – will be burned away, counted as unworthy, condemned (which means acknowledged for what they are) and forgotten for ever.[30]

So when we say, with the writer of Hebrews, that 'people are destined to die once, and after that to face judgment', we are not saying, 'and after that, to face condemnation'.[31] We are saying, with John, that to 'see God', to be in God's unspeakable light, will purge us of all darkness:[32]

> See what great love the Father has lavished on us, that we should be called children of God! And that is what we are! . . . Dear friends, now we are children of God, and what we will be has not yet been made known. But we know that when Christ appears, we shall be like him, for we shall see him as he is. All who have this hope in him purify themselves, just as he is pure.
> (1 John 3:1–3)

Since 'what we will be has not yet been made known', it is hard to say anything more, except this: in the end, God will be all in all, and all shall be well, and all manner of things shall be well.[33] This view may not contain all the details and terror of the old end-times charts, but I think it brings something better: hope and confidence to walk the path of Jesus. Dr King had this hope and confidence:

> To our most bitter opponents we say: 'We shall match your capacity to inflict suffering by our capacity to endure suffering. We shall meet your physical force with soul force. Do to us what you will, and we shall continue to love you. We cannot in all good conscience obey your unjust laws, because non-cooperation with evil is as much a moral obligation as is cooperation with good. Throw us in jail, and we shall still love you. Send your hooded perpetrators of violence into our communities at the midnight

hour and beat us and leave us half dead, and we shall still love you. But be ye assured that we will wear you down by our capacity to suffer. One day we shall win freedom, but not only for ourselves. We shall so appeal to your heart and conscience that we shall win you in the process, and our victory will be a double victory.'[34]

That vision of a double victory – one that reconciles rather than conquers and one that eliminates opposition by gently converting it rather than cruelly torturing it – seems to be the vision most worthy of the gospel. Lutheran theologian Jürgen Moltmann reached the same conclusion:

> The Message of the new righteousness which eschatological faith brings into the world says that in fact the executioners will not finally triumph over their victims. It also says that in the end the victims will not triumph over their executioners. The one [Jesus] will triumph who first died for the victims and then also for the executioners, and in so doing revealed a new righteousness which breaks through the vicious circles of hate and vengeance and which, from the victims and executioners, creates . . . a new humanity.[35]

This is a new kind of eschatology – not an eschatology of determinism and acquiescence, but an eschatology of hope, anticipation and participation. It probably won't produce much in the way of scary B-rated films and end-times prediction charts that map the future. But, instead, it will produce vision and motivation to help us participate in the creation of a better future – for ourselves and for the world, in this life and history and in the glorious mystery beyond.

NINE

THE PLURALISM QUESTION

CHAPTER 19

How Should Followers of Jesus Relate to People of Other Religions?

I'm not sure which of the ten questions in our quest is most important. I suppose it depends on our criteria for importance. But if our list of criteria includes saving lives from war and genocide and terrorism, this question may draw the others together in a way that puts it at the top of the list. For we all woke up again today in a world where Christians, Muslims and Jews (along with adherents of many other religions) are either killing one another or planning new ways to kill one another, and many believe that in doing so they are obeying and even pleasing and honouring God. Each group points at one of the others as the prime offender, and the pointed-at group tends to point back. But, whoever the biggest offender may be, all of us share in the danger and opportunity of this moment – and in the responsibility to turn it towards a better future.

Christians of all types add up to about 33 per cent of the world's population, Muslims about 21 per cent and Jews less than 0.25 per cent, but in the light of their past sufferings, it's no surprise that they possess a disproportionate number of weapons. Together the three Abrahamic faiths make up more than half the people in the world. If Christians, Muslims and Jews are at each other's throats, nobody in the world is safe. And if Christian, Muslim and Jewish belief in one Creator God inspires more violence than peace-making, all three religions are losing ground as they sling mud at one another.

It's no wonder, then, that in my travels around the world questions about religious pluralism are among the most common I receive, especially from younger people. Christians seem ambivalent when they ask these questions. On the one hand, they seem to want a less hostile approach to other religions. They feel uncomfortable with the win–lose, 'it's either us or them' mindset they have inherited, because they know this mindset too easily descends into prejudice, dehumanisation and violence towards the other. But they also feel uncomfortable with the 'whatever you believe is fine, as long as you're sincere' approach. Just as the former fuels fear, resentment and even hatred towards 'them', the latter undermines commitment and identity among 'us'. I share this ambivalence, because I think both dangers are real.

So in our quest for a new kind of Christianity, we must address this pivotal question of a Christian approach and attitude towards people of other religions, remembering that this is not simply a religious question: it carries profound political, military and humanitarian implications, and millions of human lives could be saved or taken depending on our response. Theologians, denominational leaders, pastors and other religious leaders too seldom remember that their work, if taken seriously, literally becomes a matter of life and death.[1]

If we want to get on the right side of the life-and-death divide, we need to start with some sober, serious, old-fashioned repentance, starting with this admission: *Christianity has a nauseating, infuriating, depressing record when it comes to encountering people of other religions (and a not much better record when encountering people of other brands of Christianity either)*. It's unpleasant to have to say this, because most of us Christians are nice enough people and we would never even think of forcing conversions at swordpoint, ghettoising unbelievers, or in any way shunning or victimising the religiously other, much less of engaging in pogroms, genocides, torture or execution for religious infidelity. But these things have been done, and not just a few times.[2]

Take the story of westward expansion in the so-called 'Christian nations' of North America in relation to the Native peoples, or the treatment of Aboriginals and Maori in Australia and New Zealand, or the story of Pizarro and Atahualpa in the Andes of South America. Take the constant, brutal, catastrophic warfare between Catholics and Protestants in Europe between 1618 and 1648. Take inquisitions and witch burnings and crusades. Take segregation and apartheid, and, more recently in the US and elsewhere, growing animosity among some Christians towards Muslims. It's not a pretty picture, and claiming that these assaults on the other were isolated incidents perpetuated by a few bad apples rings of cluelessness and denial, not honesty and repentance.[3]

So how do we find a better approach to the religiously other in our quest for a new kind of Christianity? We could begin by a survey of Scripture. We might look at John 1:9; 3:17; and 12:32;[4] not to mention 21:22, where Jesus responds to an inquiry about someone else's spiritual status with, 'What is that to you? You must follow me.' We could then turn to Paul's epistle to the Romans. In 2:1–29, Paul makes clear that people are never judged based on knowledge they don't have, and that God will bless 'those who by persistence in doing good seek glory, honour and immortality'. 'There will be . . . honour and peace for everyone who does good . . . For God does not show favouritism,' Paul says. He adds that when people of other religions 'who do not have the law, do by nature things required by the law, they are a law for themselves . . . [since] [t]hey show that the requirements of the law are written on their hearts, their consciences also bearing witness, and their thoughts now accusing, now even defending them'.[5]

We could also look at Romans 5:12–21, where Paul says that the impact of Jesus' obedience will be as far-reaching as the impact of Adam's disobedience, reaching 'all people' and 'the many', because 'where sin increased, grace increased all the more'. And in 11:25–36, as we saw in chapter 14, Paul almost seems to surprise himself when he concludes, 'God has bound everyone over to disobedience so that he may have mercy on them all.' We could trace Paul's line of thought in 2 Corinthians 5, where he says that because Christ died for all (5:14–15), God is not holding the sins of humanity against them (5:20) – not just the sins of Christians, we must note, but the sins of all humanity. This realisation causes us, Paul says, to see others in a new way – including, no doubt, others of other religions. 1 John offers a similar challenge to conventional us–them categories: not those who share our creed, but those who do what is right and just demonstrate that they are God's children (2:29; 3:7); those who love show that they have passed from death to life and are part of God's family (3:14, 24; 4:7, 16–21).

We could follow the theme of the 'righteous outsider' in the Hebrew Scriptures – where 'outsider' characters such as Melchizedek, Jethro, Rahab, Ruth, Uriah and several others prove themselves more just and godly than the religious insiders. The Scriptures don't minimise their goodness, but rather celebrate it. The story of Jonah, as we've seen, doesn't sanitise the wrong of religious insiders or downplay the goodness of outsiders (such as the sailors who don't want to do the wrong thing, even at risk to their lives), and it celebrates the compassion of God for 'our' enemies.

We could pay special attention to the writings of the prophets, such as Amos, where the Lord says (9:7ff.), 'Are not you Israelites the same to me as the Cushites [Ethiopians]? Did I not bring Israel up from Egypt, the Philistines from Caphtor, and the Arameans from Kir?' Yes, God liberated and guided the Jewish people, but they shouldn't become proud as if they had some elite status, because God also guided and preserved the Philistines and the Arameans. I'd take special note of the context in which Isaiah says that God's thoughts and ways are higher than ours (Isa. 55:8–9). In context, Isaiah refers to God's desire to welcome outsiders – 'nations you know not . . . nations you do not know' (55:5). God's higher thoughts and ways transcend our arrogant, exclusive, low-level religious supremacy and tribalism, and God invites us to transcend as well. To this we could add all the Scriptures that say God does not show favouritism.[6]

We could go to the book of Acts and notice how Paul expresses a similar conviction in a conversation held in Athens, where he says (Acts 17:24–8):

The God who made the world and everything in it . . . made all the nations, that they should inhabit the whole earth; and he marked out their appointed times in history and the boundaries of their lands. God did this so that they would seek him and perhaps reach out for him and find him, though he is not far from any one of us. 'For in him we live and move and have our being.' As some of your own poets have said, 'We are his offspring.'

In those few words, Paul shatters the typical Greco-Roman us–them mindset (and its corresponding Western Christian us–them mindset). People of every language, culture and religion are given a place in God's world, and no nation is given permission to crush, annihilate, dominate or assimilate others. In so doing, Paul unifies everyone in a singular 'us' – people created by God, people who have a God-given right to life and land, people who are being invited to seek God right where they are, people to whom God is already near, people who are already living and moving and having their being in God, people who are already God's children. We could also go back to the original calling of Abraham in Genesis 12, noting that God does not choose some to the exclusion of others, but some *for the benefit of others.*

We would eventually need to look at Jesus, considering in detail, say, his attitudes towards a Samaritan woman, or a Roman centurian, a Syro-Phoenician woman, or some Greeks who wanted to see Jesus and went through Andrew and Philip. We could even look at Jesus' birth narrative in Matthew, noting how the Magi – what we might call New-Age practitioners – are drawn to Jesus through their own religious arts.

When I'm asked about pluralism in my travels, I generally return to Jesus' simple teachings of neighbourliness such as the Golden Rule, saying something like this: 'Our first responsibility as followers of Jesus is to treat people of other religions with the same respect we would want to receive from them. When you are kind and respectful to followers of other religions, you are not being unfaithful to Jesus; you are being faithful to him.'

Then I ask them how they would want people of other religions to treat them. They typically say things like this: 'I would want them to respect my faith, show interest in it and learn about it, not constantly attack it; find points of agreement that they could affirm, respectfully disagree where necessary – but not let disagreement shatter the friendship; talk about their faith with me without pressuring me to convert, invite me to share my faith with them, include me in their social life without making me feel odd, and so on.'

After each reply, I generally say, 'That sounds great. Go and do likewise.'

But then, as often as not, someone, like a gunslinger going for his revolver, will reach for John 14:6 and draw it in a flash. 'But didn't Jesus say he was the way, truth and life and the only way to the Father?' they ask, implying that if Jesus is 'the only way', then we cannot show Christ-like love and respect to our neighbours of other traditions.[7] When this happens, I wonder: *Why do so many sincere, well-meaning and well-trained Christians put aside a hundred other relevant verses and pull out this one? Why do they respond to this issue with the identical script, in a kind of quotation reflex, as if they've been struck by a rubber hammer on the patellar tendon?* The answer, I've come to believe, is that this pluralism question – about making room for 'the other' in a multifaith world – taps into a key point of tension between the mind of Jesus and the Greco-Roman mind.[8] Since we've been so well tutored in Greco-Roman thinking, the few passages that can most effectively be quoted (or misquoted) to bolster it are the ones best programmed into our response reflexes, instantly rendering thousands of other passages invisible, insignificant, non-existent.

At least four characteristics of the Greco-Roman, imperial mind contribute to the problem. First, if you're Greco-Roman, you're in a dominant position, which renders you inherently anxious. As the group perched highest atop the ladder of success, you have the greatest fear of falling. You're always worried about what you will eat, what you will drink and what you will wear.[9] You're always driven for more, more, more – more money, more land, more influence, more power, more pleasure – because you believe that just a little bit more will make you safe at the top, and thus cure your anxiety once and for all. (If you're Greco-Roman, you think this is a normal and universal expression of the human condition.) But, like just one more hit of crack or heroin, it never works.

Second, your perpetual anxiety makes you vulnerable to paranoia. 'They' aren't neighbours; they're enemies because they represent a threat – competitors for your profit share, rebels to your stable regime, obstacles to your anxiety-driven strategies. So the world is inherently divided between civilised 'us' and barbarian 'them', between 'good' insiders and 'evil' outsiders.

Third, if you live by Greco-Roman anxiety and paranoia, you only have one logical hope for the future: a world (here or after death) where 'they' are gone for ever, and where the only ones left are 'pure us'. You simply can't imagine a future of harmonious diversity and neighbourly otherness: the other must be banished or gone.[10] Ultimately, then, 'we' are normative and belong here; others are anomalies and don't belong. They don't really have the same right to exist that we do. So when it comes to 'them', you have only five options:

- You can convert and assimilate them, so that 'they' become part of 'us', and their otherness is eliminated.
- You can colonise and dominate them, making 'them' subservient to 'us', and maybe even useful to 'us', so less of a threat.
- You can ignore, exclude or otherwise distance yourself from them, keeping 'them' at bay from 'us'.
- You can fight, persecute, shame and keep 'them' off-balance and intimidated by 'us'.
- You can 'cleanse' the world of them through mass murder, leaving only 'us'.

Fourth, if you are driven by economic anxiety, social paranoia and an unconscious will to assimilate, dominate, eliminate, persecute or distance, life is an unending, all-out war. With the army of 'us' there is goodness, civilisation, reason, absolute and ultimate truth, liberal progress, conservative faithfulness. (Forms of liberalism and conservatism actually reside in the two hemispheres of the same Greco Roman mind.) In the army of 'them' there is evil, chaos, delusion, relativism and nihilism, liberal embrace of decadence and conservative preservation of ancient superstition. Because everything is at stake in this profound battle between the forces of us and them, any means are justified in the heat of battle.[11]

Blaise Pascal said, 'Can anything be stupider than that a man has the right to kill me because he lives on the other side of a river and his ruler has a quarrel with mine, though I have not quarreled with him?'[12] But that stupidity is sanity in the Greco-Roman mind. Perhaps now you can see it: *If the Christian religion were ever to be recast to fit within the Greco-Roman mind, it could become something very different from what Jesus intended, and something very dangerous.* Perhaps you will also agree that this is precisely what has happened: Christianity has a persistent problem with pluralism not because of Jesus or his Jewish roots, but because of its Greco-Roman captivity. Psychologists and sociologists have uncovered powerful syndromes in which former victims later become victimisers and in which former hostages end up identifying with their captors. We might hypothesise that, after centuries of persecution by the Romans, the Christian religion fell prey to this syndrome and has not yet recovered.[13]

As Christians raised in the Greco-Roman tradition of faith, increasing numbers of us feel like Peter after the crucifixion: we have been part of a massive betrayal of our Lord.[14] What happens now? Will we be sent away in disgrace? Or will we be invited with Peter to repent and get back to our original calling in the kingdom of God – to feed, tend and care for people instead of trying to conquer, dominate and control them? Thankfully, Peter's experience tells us what to expect. And this is good news for at least two reasons. First, for all its flaws (which must not be understated), the Greco-Romanised version of Christian faith has invaluable spiritual treasures (which also must not be understated) and remains profoundly redeemable. In fact, a humbled, repentant, reborn religion surely has more value to the world than either an arrogant, unchallenged one or an innocent, naïve one. So I would rather see Christianity humbled, healed and liberated from its imperial captivity than discredited, scarred and discarded because of it. (I could say the same about every other religion too.)

And, second, my fellow Christians raised in various versions of Greco-Romanised Christianity currently control most of the world's wealth, consume most of the world's resources, produce most of the world's waste, and sell and use most of the world's weapons. As I mentioned earlier, a recent study in the US said that certain types of Greco-Roman Christians are most likely to support state-sponsored torture, and other studies have shown them to be more likely to be racists than their non-religious neighbours.[15] So, if we do not repent of our imperial, kingdoms-of-this-world ways, and move firmly in the direction of the way of Jesus, I fear what we will do in the future, especially in the light of what we have done in the past.[16]

If we could break free from the Greco-Roman soul-sort narrative, think of what could change: we Christians could offer Jesus (not Christianity) as a gift to the world, and we would no longer consider it a requirement of faithfulness to insult other religions and call their founders demonic. We would no longer envision a day when all other religions would be abolished and only our own will remain. We would no longer consider ourselves as normative and others as 'other'. We would stop seeing the line that separates good and evil running between our religion and all others. We would be freed from the tendency always to think 'insider/outsider' and 'us/them'. We would learn to discover God in the other, and we would discover a bigger 'us' in which people of all faiths can be included.[17]

We would consider it a matter of faithfulness to show the

same respect to other religions and to their founders that we would wish to be shown to our own. We would envision a day when members of all religions, including our own, learned to be reconciled with God, one another and all creation. We would see that Jesus and his message of peace and service were right and true after all, and that Jesus was not a gift to one religion, but to the whole world. We would consider all people God's beloved, as neighbours in God's world, loving them, serving them, enjoying them. We would practise the kind of Christ-like hospitality that welcomes the outcast outsider in.

Evangelism would cease to be a matter of saving souls from a bad ending in the Greco-Roman, soul-sort narrative. It would cease to be a proclamation of the superiority of the Christian religion. It would no longer require hell-fire-and-brimstone scare tactics or slick promotional campaigns, as if Jesus and his gospel were products under exclusive proprietary licence to the Christian religion, to be sold to customers using religious infomercials and catchy jingles and, if all else fails, threats of ECT.[18]

No, instead, a reborn, post-imperial evangelism would mean proclaiming the same good news of the kingdom of God that Jesus proclaimed. It would mean seeking to do so in the manner Jesus proclaimed it – in word and deed, through art and teaching, in sign and wonder, with clarity and intrigue, with warning and hope.[19] It would mean recruiting people to defect from destructive ways and join God in the *missio dei*, a decentralised, grassroots, spiritual–social movement dedicated to plotting goodness and saving the world from human evil – both personal and systemic. It would invite people into lifelong spiritual formation as disciples of Jesus, in a community dedicated (as we've seen) to teaching the most excellent way of love, whatever the new disciple's religious affiliation or lack thereof.

This kind of evangelism would celebrate the good in the Christian religion and lament the bad, just as it would in every other religion, calling people to a way of life in a kingdom (or beautiful whole) that transcends and includes all religions. Yes, it would welcome people into communities of faith in which they would experience formation in the way of Jesus, and, yes, you could call these communities Christian churches if you'd like, although you could call them other things too. But whatever you call these communities, they would be interested in breaking out of the cocoons of Christianity that were spun within the Greco-Roman narrative, governed by a constitutional reading of Scripture, orientated around violent and tribal views of God, and so on.

To get there, we will have to take a fresh look at the 'reflex verses' that are used to justify the dismissive or combative attitude of many Christians to their neighbours of other religions – beginning with John 14:6.[20] If we do so, we will see the painful but liberating irony that John 14:6 has nothing – absolutely nothing – to say to the questions it is commonly quoted to answer. One would think that the context reads like this:

'You should be very troubled, because if you believe in God, but not me, you will be shut out of my Father's house in heaven, where there are a few small rooms for the few who have correct belief . . .' Then Thomas said to him, 'Lord, what about people of other religions or no religion at all? Will they go to heaven after they die?' Jesus said to him, 'I am the only way to heaven, and confessing the truth about me is the

only truth that will get you to life after death. Not one person will go to heaven unless they (a) personally understand and believe a clearly defined message about me, (b) personally and consciously ask me to come into their heart, (c) disavow any other religious affiliation, and (d) affiliate with the new religion I'm starting and naming after myself. Nobody can come to God unless they get by me first.'
(Not John 14:1–6)

But Jesus' actual meaning is very different, because it comes in response to a very different question. The question is not a cosmic, doctrinal question like 'What about people of other religions?' or 'Is Jesus the only way to heaven?'[21] Rather, it's an urgent, practical, down-to-earth question: 'Jesus, where are you going?' (see John 13:36; 14:5; also 16:5). If you don't understand Jesus' answer in the context of this question, you're not interpreting his words: you're misappropriating them, twisting them, abusing them.

John 14:6 comes in the middle of a particularly long conversation that begins in the previous chapter, throughout which the disciples are constantly confused and troubled because Jesus has said he's going somewhere they cannot come.[22] It's understandable that they would feel this way: their identity is wrapped up in being his *followers*, but Jesus says he is going somewhere they cannot *follow*. So, where is he going and why can't they follow? The context makes it clear: he is going to be glorified and return to his Father – and this glorification will occur, paradoxically, through suffering and death. Meanwhile, even though they're still traumatised by this 'you cannot follow' statement, Jesus is making another point, his main point. He moves from what they now *cannot do* (follow with him to suffering and death) to telling them what they now *must do*:

A new command I give you: Love one another. As I have loved you, so you must love one another. By this everyone will know that you are my disciples, if you love one another. *(13:34–5)*

Now all the Gospels seem to take delight in pointing out how the disciples just don't get it, and here's a great case in point. Jesus has just said they are to love one another, and he has highlighted these words dramatically by suggesting that they are among his last words to them before departing from them. In addition, he has used the provocative phrase 'new command' – which suggests that he's consciously mirroring Moses, inaugurating a new era as law-giver with one overarching commandment in place of ten. He has demonstrated his love for them in deed (by washing their feet, taking the role of a humble servant) and now translates his teaching by example into a clear verbal command: 'Love one another.'

But Peter treats all this as a distraction and returns to Jesus' troubling words about going somewhere they cannot go. It's as if a man creates suspense for his sweetheart by saying, 'I went to a jewellery shop the other day and bought something for you. I have a very important question to ask you. Your answer will change both of our lives for ever. Would you be my . . .' But the woman interrupts, 'Just a minute. Which jewellery shop did you go to? And which car did you drive to get there? And what route did you take?' She's oblivious to the fact that he's about to propose to her. She just doesn't get it, and neither does Peter.

Simon Peter asked him, 'Lord, where are you going?'

Jesus replied, 'Where I am going, you cannot follow now, but you will follow later.'

Peter asked, 'Lord, why can't I follow you now? I will lay down my life for you.'

Then Jesus answered, 'Will you really lay down your life for me? Very truly I tell you, before the rooster crows, you will disown me three times.'

(13:36–8)

So Jesus says, 'Someday you may indeed follow me into suffering and death, but not now. Now – this very night – you will deny me.'[23] No wonder Jesus' next words are words of reassurance:

Do not let your hearts be troubled. Trust in God; trust also in me. My Father's house has plenty of room; if that were not so, would I have told you that I am going there to prepare a place for you? And if I go and prepare a place for you, I will come back and take you to be with me, that you also may be where I am.

(14:1–3)

Many assume that 'my Father's house' means 'heaven', which sets up John 14:6 to explain how to go to heaven. But, before we make that assumption, we should recall another episode from earlier in John's Gospel (a strange passage for several reasons[24]) where Jesus also referred to his Father's house (2:13ff.).

So he made a whip out of cords, and drove all from the temple courts, both sheep and cattle; he scattered the coins of the money-changers and overturned their tables. To those who sold doves he said, 'Get these out of here! Stop turning my Father's house into a market!' His disciples remembered that it is written: 'Zeal for your house will consume me.'

(2:15–17)

Here, 'my Father's house' doesn't mean heaven above; it means the temple down here on earth. A fascinating discussion of the temple follows this incident, in which Jesus says, quite shockingly, really, 'Destroy this temple, and I will raise it again in three days'. John even intrudes into the narrative to explain that Jesus is cryptically referring to his body.[25] The temple will soon be irrelevant, Jesus will say shortly (4:21); his body will become the new temple.

So what does Jesus mean here in John 14 by 'my Father's house'? Wouldn't it make sense for us to assume, unless there's contrary evidence, that he has the same thing (the temple, not heaven) in mind – especially because he's about to enter a three-day period in which the temple of his body is destroyed and then raised? An era of faith centred on a single temple in a single holy city is coming to an end. A new era will begin (after three days) when the one temple will be replaced by another: the many human lives who will constitute 'the body of Christ', 'the household of God' and the 'living stones' of the new temple.[26] Jesus, then, wouldn't be telling them that there is a place for them in heaven after they die (although, thankfully, there is). He would be telling them that there will be a place for them in the new people-of-God-as-temple that Jesus is preparing the way for over these next three days. In this way, then, it appears clear that the term *my Father's house* – like the terms *life, abundant life* and *life of the ages* – is, like Jesus' core message of the *kingdom of*

God, not about the afterlife but about this life.[27] The close relationship or equivalence between *my Father's house* and *kingdom of God* becomes clearer if we compare *the house of my Father* with *the kingdom of my Father*, or *God's home* with *God's kingdom*. All these phrases suggest the same reality: life lived in loving relationship with God and others so that God's will is joyfully done on earth as it is in heaven, and so that God's presence spreads throughout the world in Spirit-inhabited human lives.[28]

So we could paraphrase 14:1–4 like this: *Don't be worried, my friends, even though I've told you I'm leaving you. Trust God, and trust me. By going away, I'm going to make it possible for you to be with me again, where I am now at this moment:*[29] *dwelling in the presence of God, living in the kingdom of God, bearing the presence of God to this world. There's plenty of room for you in this venture! So don't worry. You know the way to the place I'm going.*

It's that last sentence that so bothers Thomas that he can't keep quiet for another moment. He asks a question, and it is a thousand miles away from 'What about people who never heard about you? What about people of other religions? Will they go to heaven?' He says, no doubt with some exasperation (14:5), 'Lord, *we* don't know where you are going, so how can *we* know the way?' (emphasis mine).

What is Thomas asking here? It's absolutely clear that Buddhists, Hindus, Muslims, Zoroastrians, followers of indigenous religions in Africa or South America, much less modern secular atheists or sceptics, couldn't be further from his mind. Thomas and his fellow disciples, in their dismay that their leader will now go somewhere they can't follow, are thinking about one thing: *themselves*, and only themselves. When Jesus says they know the way to meet him beyond their impending separation, they haven't a clue what he's talking about. So Thomas speaks out. And that is the context for Jesus' oft-quoted words, *I am the way and the truth and the life. No one comes to the Father except through me. If you really know me, you will know my Father as well. From now on, you do know him and have seen him.*[30]

At the risk of overfeeding a thriving horse, let me say it again: Jesus isn't making an abstract statement about the fate of unbelievers at the final judgement, but he is telling his disciples (specifically Thomas, but this is generalised to all the disciples) how they will get from *here* (with Jesus visibly present) – through *a little while* (when his body is in the grave) – to *there* (with Jesus present in a new way). Thomas's question seems to be as much an expression of frustration and confusion as a plea for some specific information.[31] In that light, we can read Jesus' response as a repetition and reinforcement of what he has just given them (14:1–4): *reassurance*.

He has just said, 'Don't be troubled. Trust God. Trust me.' Now he repeats the reassurance, saying in essence, 'Listen, Thomas, your head is spinning. You don't need to understand all this. You simply need to trust me. Don't look for a way apart from me. Don't look for a route or destination – some concept or technique or system of thought that will get you through the tough time that is coming. I'm not trying to give you information or instructions so you no longer need me and can instead depend on the information or instructions. No – just trust me. Everything you need is in me. I will be gone, but then I will be back again and we will be together. "The way" or "the truth" or "the life" aren't things separate from me. *I am these things, so you'll find them in me!* Whether or not you know what I've been talking about, if you know me, you know the Father, you know the way, you know the truth, you know the life.'

But what of the statement, 'No one comes to the Father except through me?' Clearly, taken in context, these words are not intended as an insult to followers of Mohammed, the Buddha, Lao Tsu, Enlightenment rationalism, or anybody or anything else. Rather, the 'no one' here refers to Jesus' own disciples, who have just been told that he is leaving them for a while, and who want, in his absence, to trust some information – a plan, a diagram, a map, instructions, a technique – so they can get to God or the kingdom of God on their own.[32] But the reassurance once again falls on deaf ears; the 'non-get-it-factor' continues. Next, following in the clueless tradition of Peter and Thomas, Philip speaks up. Jesus has just mentioned coming to the Father, and so Philip interrupts:

> Philip said, 'Lord, show us the Father and that will be enough for us.'
>
> Jesus answered, 'Don't you know me, Philip, even after I have been among you such a long time? Anyone who has seen me has seen the Father. How can you say, "Show us the Father"? Don't you believe that I am in the Father, and that the Father is in me? The words I say to you I do not speak on my own authority. Rather, it is the Father, living in me, who is doing his work. Believe me when I say that I am in the Father and the Father is in me; or at least believe on the evidence of the works themselves.'
> *(14:8–11)*

To me, the dynamic core of this passage leaps out here in verse 9, not back in verse 6: *Anyone who has seen me has seen the Father*. Here the irony becomes nearly unbearable (to me at least), as we contrast this statement with the conventional interpretation of verse 6. Jesus says in verse 9 that the invisible God has been made visible in his life. 'If you want to know what God is like,' Jesus says, 'look at me, my life, my way, my deeds, my character.' And what has that character been? One of exclusion, rejection, constriction, elitism, favouritism and condemnation? Of course not! Jesus' way has been compassion, healing, acceptance, forgiveness, inclusion and love from beginning to end – whether with a visit-by-night Pharisee, a Samaritan woman, a paralysed man, a woman caught in adultery or a man born blind.

But our conventional interpretation of verse 6 seems to say, 'Forget all that. Forget everything you've seen in me – the way I've lived and treated people, the way I've accepted prostitutes and tax collectors, the way I've welcomed outsiders and rejects. Forget all that. Believe instead that God will reject everyone except people who share your doctrinal viewpoints about me, because I won't let anyone get to the Father unless they get by me first by joining my new religion.' It makes me want to cry, or groan, or scream.[33]

'If you have seen me, you have seen the Father,' Jesus says, but our conventional interpretation of John 14:6 turns this all upside down: 'Reinterpret me in the light of your old, tribal, chauvinistic, exclusive, elitist views of God and religion. But instead of circumcision and dietary laws to exclude the outsiders, now substitute mental markers or belief markers about me.' Once this alternative understanding hits you, once you see it, it's truly heart-breaking that John 14:6 can be used in the way it so commonly is.

Of course, we haven't even begun to resolve all the issues of living in a multifaith world as deeply committed Christians seeking a new kind of Christianity. But I hope this much is clear: there is a way to be a committed follower of Christ that doesn't require you to be flatly and implacably against other religions and their adherents. And not only that: there are reasons to believe in and love Jesus beyond having him save you from the bottom line of the Greco-Roman soul-sort narrative.[34]

How wonderful if lovers of Jesus, re-reading John 14:6, would discover that Jesus, outside the conventional narrative, is even more desirable, profound, mysterious, gracious and indispensable than he appeared within its confines. How wonderful if they could discover that he didn't simply come to save us within the terms and conditions of the Greco-Roman framing story. Instead, he saves us from that whole sad story itself and introduces us to a new and better story – a story that sends us into the world with Christ-like love for our neighbours of other religions, not suspicion; with humility and respect, not disdain; with a desire to understand, serve and know, not a desire to conquer and colonise; with a passion to share – both receiving and giving – because we each have been given treasures for the common good. May it be so, before it is too late, because even now, some people are loading their weapons and enriching their uranium in the name of God.

TEN

THE WHAT-DO-WE-DO-NOW QUESTION

CHAPTER 20

How Can We Translate Our Quest Into Action?

In the time of Jesus and the apostles, there was a Jewish sage and Pharisee named Gamaliel (Acts 5:36ff.). Many of his colleagues saw the new Jesus movement as a threat, so they were hatching plots to stamp it out. Gamaliel dissented. Give this thing some time and space, he counselled, and if it's only of human origin, the wheels will fall off and it will swerve into the ditch on its own. But if it is from God, he warned, it will be unstoppable; to fight against it will mean fighting against God. Looking back on what we've considered so far in this quest for a new kind of Christian faith, some of us will feel like Gamaliel's colleagues – wondering how to stamp this damned thing out before it spreads. Others, like Gamaliel, will be more open-minded, willing to give it a chance. But either response raises the same question: Is this quest only of human origin? Or – in spite of and alongside all the human frailty and stupidity inherent in this quest – is God at work in it?

I have been somewhat shy about speaking of God's agency so

far in these pages. In part, my shyness flows from a temperamental preference for understating rather than overstating.[1] Sadly, few things are more common in some religious circles than people claiming that God is at work in their endeavours. As evidence of divine involvement, they may testify about thousands being saved, healed, delivered, transformed, added, touched, etc. (Some friends of mine call these numbers *evang-elastic*.) These statistics are often followed by an inspired plea for tax-deductible donations, which are *desperately needed now* for this vital work to continue. Making these claims may have some motivational value (at least for the ones making them!), but, based on my observations, the loudness and frequency of the claims may be inversely proportional to their validity.

But there's an equal and opposite ditch on the other side of the road. We can back away so far from the ditch of overstating God's support for our work that we fall into the opposite ditch of minimising the agency of God altogether. That's the deeper and slimier ditch, I think, and the one towards which contemplative/reflective types like me may be more prone to veer. We can so successfully avoid the danger of overstating God's power in our work that we become content to have God's blessing on our talk. We can be so concerned about appearing spiritually manic that we become spiritually catatonic.[2] Neither condition will serve this quest for a new kind of Christian faith.

In the end, if this quest leads only to a reformation in our thinking, it is not a new kind of Christianity at all, but just a variation on an old kind. The end of our quest is not simply better concepts or beliefs in our heads or hearts, although both will have some instrumental value. The end of our quest is a better world in which God's will is increasingly done. Similarly, stopping the dropout and decline rates among young people in the Church will have instrumental value, but our quest must aim higher: for those young people to put a vital, radical faith into vital, radical action – action for and with the poor, action on behalf of the planet, action that makes for peace.[3]

So our quest calls us first and foremost to nurture a robust spiritual life – not only a deep commitment to serve God, but also a deep desire to know and love God, to make room, as Gamaliel said, for God to be truly in us and in our quest. That means that we need as our models more than great thinkers and theologians: we also need great saints, women and men of the Holy Spirit, women and men who are full of God. Thankfully, we can look back in our tradition for the examples we need as we move forward.

For example, in the tradition of St Patrick and the Celts, we can learn to arise each day in the real presence of the Father, Son and Holy Spirit, knowing Christ beside, above, before, behind and within us. And, like Patrick, we can find and nurture a lifelong passion to bring the liberating good news of Jesus Christ to everyone we can, and to do so, like Patrick, outside the bounds of the Roman Empire, so to speak.

Similarly, in the tradition of St Francis and St Claire, we can nurture an interior life with God that awakens our kinship with brother sun, sister moon, brother fox and sister bird – not to mention brother leper and sister Muslim, Buddhist or Jew.

In the tradition of Martin Luther, we can find sustaining inner strength so that we will not recant when under pressure, because our conscience is captive to God's Word.[4] Like Luther, we can learn to struggle with the versions of the faith we inherited without giving up on faith altogether, and we can discover what he called 'a totally other face of the entire Scripture'.[5]

In the tradition of Menno Simons and the Anabaptists, we can learn to proceed less by loud disputation and bitter polemics, and more by quietly building communities of peace and practice rooted in the teaching and example of Jesus.

In the tradition of Julian of Norwich and St Teresa of Avila and all the other mystics, we can learn to render ourselves vulnerable to the 'favours of God' – those indescribable experiences that mock our dualisms and so saturate our imagination with abundance that they transcend our ability to convey the joy and wonder. In the tradition of St John of the Cross, we can learn to survive and derive benefit from the soul's dark night.

In the tradition of the Wesleys, our hearts can be 'strangely warmed' and we can refuse to pit head, heart and hand against one another. When head, heart and hand come together (the intellectual, the experiential and the volitional; the mind, the soul and the strength), then faith, reason and tradition will come together too, and personal and social holiness will be for us two expressions of one great love.

In the tradition of the early Pentecostals, we can experience the fire of the Holy Spirit so powerfully that the dividing walls between races, classes and denominations will burn away. Like them, we can create new forms and expressions of worship (whether or not we call them *liturgies*) and new spontaneous networks of rapid expansion (whether or not we call them *denominational structures*) to express our overflowing passion and our joy in the Lord.

So, although I've been shy about speaking of it, I must here emphasise that for me this quest has not simply come as a result of thought and study, although I've done a lot of both. It has equally arisen from prayer, worship, devotional reading, fellowship, solitude, fasting, soul friendship and other spiritual practices that render me porous and thirsty for the living, loving, holy and present God. At various turns in this quest, I have stumbled into moments or even seasons of insight so moving that I can only use the word *ecstatic* to describe them. I've felt my soul opening up, my mind being bathed in God's holy joy, my vision being transformed so that everything looks fresh and new and rooted and ancient, all at the same time. *God, you are so wonderful!* I find myself praying again and again. *Your good news is even better than I've ever imagined! Why didn't I see it before?* Through many milestone experiences, then, I have become convinced that this quest is not simply an intellectual or theological one: it is also a personal and spiritual one.

For thousands and thousands of us, this personal, spiritual quest is part of our participation in the ongoing human quest that Paul described to the Athenians (Acts 17:24ff.): God made and arranged all things, 'so that [humanity] would seek him and perhaps reach out for him and find him, though he is not far from any one of us. For in him we live and move and have our being'.

This essential emphasis on spirituality reminds us, then, that *a new kind of Christianity* is not simply new – in the sense of a new tree being planted at some distance from an old one. It is rather the green tips growing out on many of the fragile branches of the ancient tree of faith and spirituality that has been growing through history.[6] In recent years, a number of macro-historians have been trying to look back to describe the general trajectory of this ancient–contemporary quest.[7] They have discerned a number of phases or stages to the quest, not unlike the stages of human development – from pregnancy to birth to infancy to childhood to adolescence and so on.

Typically (and, to some, annoyingly), macro-historians use complex schemes of numbers or colours to describe the stages or zones of the quest. For our purposes, the colours of the spectrum (red, orange, yellow, green, blue, indigo and violet) provide a good organising schema for reasons that will become clearer soon.[8]

Our human adventure began with the quest for *survival*. This was the life of our most ancient ancestors travelling in little bands of hunter-gatherers. In this stage, God (or the gods or spirits) provided (or, some thought, withheld) what we needed: especially water, food and land. (Think of the stories of Genesis and Exodus and their focus on these essentials of survival.) God or Spirit may even have been identified with parts of the land-scape, and spirituality was still too primal perhaps to be called religion; in fact, people in some later stages would probably call it *superstition*. We'll call this the red zone – the passionate quest for survival.

Second came our quest for *security*. As we developed tribes, clans and chiefdoms, and as we farmed our own lands to support our survival, we lived with a new anxiety: our survival anxiety was replaced by security anxiety. Will our neighbours come and attack us? Will we win our next battle? Will the rains come, or will the crops fail? God (or the gods) became our Warrior, our Protector, our Provider. We looked for magical ways to get God (or the gods) miraculously to protect and provide for us, so shamans and priests – with all their mysterious God-appeasing and God-recruiting rituals – became our combined Department of Homeland Security and our Department of Agriculture. In this insecure stage, we began to be afraid of God, since failing to appease or honour God properly might result in our being cursed with drought, plague, locusts and other calamities. Our search for physical security, we might say, produced a by-product of insecurity. We'll call this the orange zone – the challenging quest for security.

Third came our quest for *power*. We found ourselves in a world of competing city-states governed by powerful warlords. Each group needed a competitive advantage over neighbouring groups. Many of us found a competitive advantage in an understanding of one God – ours – as superior to or supreme over all others. God became wedded to our national politics. As we developed kingdoms, we saw God as king; as we developed empires, we saw God as emperor; as we developed totalitarian regimes, we saw God as absolute dictator. Such views of God promoted civil order: who dares defy a dictator ruling by the decree (or divine right) of the Almighty? One might dare the risk of temporal torture for differing with a dictator, but who dares face God's own threats of eternal torture for civil disobedience? Along with fear and political compliance, these views of God also promoted a sense of awe and transcendence; we imagined a God as far above humanity as a king is above a serf or slave. We'll call this the yellow zone – the quest for power.

Fourth, there was the quest for *independence*. Something predictable had happened to us in the age of powerful kings: we increasingly felt that the more power they had, the more corrupt they typically became. The more powerfully they protected us from other kings, the more they became a threat to us themselves. So we began to feel as exploited as we were protected by our rulers. We searched for something even higher than a human ruler: we searched for laws – principles, absolutes, universals – to which even dictators must submit. And now God became for us less the magical intervener or national protector (as in the orange and yellow zones) and more the rational architect of universal laws or principles. Put differently, God became less the *king* who rules by wish and whim (as in the yellow zone), and more the *judge* who enforces laws, mandates punishment and negotiates settlements. For some of us, the laws, principles or mechanisms eclipsed any role for God at all. The universe was rendered a giant eternal machine, comprehensible without reference to any supreme being, and God became either its distant and non-interfering engineer or an unnecessary hypothesis altogether. This we'll call the green zone – the quest for independence.

Fifth, there was the quest for *individuality*. Once the world had become for us a rational machine – operating according to physical, biological, social, moral and spiritual laws or mechanisms – we were free to discover and express ourselves as autonomous or independent individuals, joyfully exercising our personal freedom through competition for goods and services. We gained individual grades in school, salaries in work, degrees in education, ranks in the military and even mansions in heaven: personal success and individual winning became everything to us. No wonder God became our personal Saviour, and no wonder the spiritual life often involved mastering techniques for earning (or otherwise obtaining) God's favour and blessing on our ambitious plans for personal prosperity and individual achievement. We formed voluntary associations – denominations, political parties, unions, ideologies – with others who shared our sense of which techniques best guaranteed individual success, both temporal and eternal. We'll call this the blue zone – the quest for individuality.

Sixth came the quest for *honesty*. The mid-twentieth century hit many of us like a heart attack: What had we done? What had we become? What went wrong with us? We – meaning inhabitants of our enlightened Western civilisation – had launched two world wars, a holocaust, segregation/apartheid. We – meaning participants in our bigger-faster-more-driven military–industrial complex – were covering the earth with cement, burning rainforests, turning fossil fuels into greenhouse gases, driving unprecedented extinctions and multiplying high-tech weapons across the world. We – meaning children of the Enlightenment – had used 'pure reason' to defend the extinction or debasement of native peoples through colonisation, to justify the African slave trade, to maintain the subordination of women, to send six million Jews to the ovens, and to create and drop atomic bombs, twice. We – meaning beneficiaries and defenders of capitalism – had (a) created enclaves of unimaginable prosperity while leaving behind the majority of people in ghettos of poverty and often squalor, and (b) had created short-term profit for ourselves at the expense of the planet that we would bequeath to our children.

And even though we had stopped doing some of these things (at least to a degree, at least temporarily), we were barely beginning to come to terms with how our Western, 'civilised', military–industrial, Enlightened, capitalist system had so disastrously malfunctioned. Much less had we even begun to figure out what to do about it. So we at least wanted to be honest about our failures. Some of us called this quest for honesty *deconstruction*, some *relativism*, some *pluralism*, and some of us called it *repentance*. 'Let's at least be honest,' we said, 'that there are many ways to see things, that our way isn't the only way, that we who were so confident about being right about everything have been tragically, dangerously, criminally wrong about many things.' Just as kings solved some problems and then created others, our individualism and confidence had begun demonstrating dangerous unintended consequences, leading us into the indigo zone – the quest for honesty, and perhaps even humility.

Now we face the seventh quest, the quest to *heal* what we have so disastrously broken, the quest to *unify* and *liberate* what we've tragically divided and conquered, the quest to *(re)discover* a larger and more beautiful whole rather than pit part against part in deadly conflict. I don't know what to call this quest, but I think it is a quest for what is named and sought in every language and culture:

Saalam, pace (Arabic, Italian)

Sidi, shanti (Tibetan, Hindi)

Mir, tutkium, soksang (Russian, Inuit, Khmer)

Rongo, amani (Maori, Swahili)

Elohe, he ping (Cherokee, Chinese)

Sula, pokoj, shalom (Persian, Polish, Hebrew)

Ukuthala, vrede (Zulu, Afrikaans/Dutch)

Lumana, irene (Hausa, Greek)

Ashtee, amniat (Farsi, Pashto)

Wolakota, amahoro (Lakota, Kirundi/Kiruanda)

Runyara, santiphap (Shona, Lao)

Heiwa, paix, qasikay (Japanese, French, Quechua)

We could call it *peace*, but in the light of Western dominance and its discontents, I think it is better to use a non-Western name – perhaps *ubuntu* from Africa, a rich word meaning one-another-ness, interconnectedness, joined-in-the-common-good-ness, and profound commitment to the well-being of all. We in the twenty-first century have practical reasons for this quest, reasons that, interestingly enough, bring us back to the red zone, because our survival as a species now depends on the transformation of 'the other' into 'one another'. We'll call this the violet zone – the quest for *ubuntu*.

This isn't the last stage, no doubt. Beyond our quest for survival (red), protection (orange), power (yellow), independence (green), individuality (blue), honesty (indigo) and *ubuntu* (violet), I imagine there could be an ultraviolet quest for *sacredness*, a desire to live in a growing conscious awareness of the presence of God and the goodness of God reflected in all things. And, beyond that, we can only begin to imagine what our quest might entail.

But here's the rub: we are all at different places in this quest. Most of us – especially most of us in the Christian faith – are in quests for protection (consider the prosperity gospel and certain magical forms of Pentecostalism) and power (consider some forms of strict hyper-Calvinism and other fundamentalisms, with their view of divine sovereignty as deterministic control exercised on behalf of the elect few). Or we're in quests for independence (consider the many kinds of systematic theologies that pursue mastery of mystery through doctrinal systematisation in almost the same way that scientists pursue mastery over mystery through the scientific method), and individuality (consider the self-help focus of many mega-churches, with their emphasis on 'personal salvation' and its close cousins 'personal spirituality' and 'personal success'). That means that most of us really aren't interested in a quest for 'inconvenient truths' that might obstruct or interfere with our more immediate quests for protection, power, independence and individuality. Just as a young boy longing for a football kit or a bicycle isn't interested in a girlfriend or a college degree yet, we aren't ready for the higher zones of our quest yet – which is why I call those truths *inconvenient*.

The situation is made unintentionally worse by the small but growing minority of us who are entering the quest for honesty (many in the emergent conversation of which I am part would fit in this category).[9] This book itself – with its 'quest for truth' – obviously grows out of the indigo range of the spectrum. But the indigo zone, while it's great for raising honest questions, is not so great at reaching conclusions. In fact, indigo people generally seek honesty by critiquing the previous stages and by questioning the adequacy of their conclusions – something we have spent a good many pages doing in this book. But, as any PhD-holder can attest, honest inquiry and thought do not necessarily lead to wise action. Sometimes (recalling Paul's words about knowledge 'puffing up') our honest inquiry simply leads to conceit and a critical spirit.

So those of us in the indigo zone commonly look down on red-, orange-, yellow-, green- and blue-zone people and groups, calling them primitive, backward, immature, conservative, fundamentalist, and so on. We often 'explain' their behaviour with a kind of cool and elitist detachment, and in so doing we objectify and dehumanise them (as some of us may have been doing while reading this chapter so far). We in the indigo zone feel comfortable casually critiquing, relativising and deconstructing the very systems, structures, doctrines and institutions that red-to-blue cultures have worked, lived, fought and died to build and defend. So no wonder indigo people see others as obstructionists, and the others see them as terrorists or nihilists.

In short, we in the indigo zone – just like those in the earlier zones – want to transcend and distance ourselves from everyone in earlier zones. And, in so doing, we resist our transcendence into the violet spirit of *ubuntu*, which seeks to close up distances and be joined with others. So, in many ways, the quest that we have pursued through our first nine questions in these pages cannot be fulfilled in the zone that inspired it. Our quest must transcend itself, rising from an indigo quest for honesty into a violet quest for reconciliation, integration and *ubuntu*. And entering a new zone is never an easy thing.

An *ubuntu* or violet faith will require us to stop seeing the earlier ranges as inferior, wrong or bad. Rather, we must see them as necessary. Each is an essential part of the process – an essential band of full-spectrum light. And, contrary to honest indigo thinking, the ideas and beliefs of the other ranges in the spectrum aren't actually *dishonest* for the people who hold them: they are simply the way reality honestly looks from that vantage point. From red, the world honestly looks red; from orange it looks orange, and so on. Theologically, we could say that people in a certain zone of a religion or denomination are seeing God in the only way they *can* see God, and as only *they* can see God. Yes, it is ultimately a mistake for green, yellow or blue people to say that God is only green,

315

yellow or blue – although this is what people at these stages will always say. But that is no greater a mistake than for indigo people to attack them for doing so, which is what indigo people will always do.

So, although the indigo quest for honesty is important, it creates problems that can be resolved only at the next level.[10] You may have noticed, or you may go back and notice now, that the same is true for each level: each level resolves issues created by previous levels, but then creates conditions and problems that must be transcended by rising to the next level. And that's what makes the violet level so important, so urgent, so utterly needed now at this moment. We have oranges, yellows, greens and blues threatening and killing each other, often in the name of their gods and more often in the name of (supposedly) the same God (but seen from different perspectives), battling for dominance in an unholy war that produces only losers. And we have indigos critiquing them all from a position of superiority which only alienates people in other zones, making them defensive and thus increasing their resistance to moving forward.

We desperately need violet Christians – along with violet Muslims, Jews, Hindus, Buddhists, atheists and others – who can create a zone of *ubuntu* that welcomes all people to mature and advance in the human quest. If more of us don't grow violet, our world will grow more violent. We might picture it using the following diagram. We used to put ourselves in the appropriate religious column. But perhaps now we need also to put ourselves in the appropriate row – and perhaps the row says more about us than the column.

	christian 33%	muslim 21%	non-religious 16%	hindu 14%	buddhist 6%	other 10%
A						
B						

Let's say that row A represents 'the old kind of Christian, Muslim, Buddhist' (and so on), and that by 'the old kind' we mean the kind that approaches the other with the red-to-indigo attitudes of domination (us over you), elimination (us without you), assimilation (us taking you over), isolation (us at a distance from you), victimisation (us under you), revolution (us displacing you), supremacy (us superior to you) and competition (us competing with you). And then let's say that row B represents 'a new kind of Christian' (and so on), the full-spectrum kind we have tried to imagine in these pages, a new way of being human that sees 'us in you' and 'you in us' and 'some of us for all of us'.

Perhaps now you see why I love Jesus so much. I didn't have this kind of terminology for it, but in this book's first pages, when I described my feeling as a pastor of living in the tension between something good and something wrong, the something good was this inescapable awareness that in Jesus there wasn't simply a red, orange, yellow, green, blue, indigo or violet light. In Jesus I saw and see not only the coloured light of a particular religion at a particular stage, but the full-spectrum light of God.[11] Through him, in him, everything looked . . . brighter, more glorious, more holy and alive and meaningful. As the apostle John said, *In him was life, and that life was the light of all people. The light shines in the darkness, and the darkness has not overcome it* (1:4–5). He was radiant with a kind of full-spectrum light that included and transcended all others, but couldn't be contained by any of them.

Include and *transcend*: those are the key words that mark the difference between being violet and being violent. If we celebrate and defend a yellow Christian faith or a green Christian faith or a blue Christian faith, that's certainly OK for a while, especially because we are generally defending it against the attacks of those defending previous stages from the threat we pose as innovators. But eventually more and more of us (or our children) will outgrow the current stage, whatever it is, and either we will have to leave Christianity-as-we-know-it, or we will have to find a new expression or zone of Christian faith.[12]

If we refuse to transcend a stage or zone when 'the fullness of time' requires us to, we get ugly, tense, dishonest, defensive and mean. Then the orange quest for protection degenerates into Christian magic and voodoo; the yellow quest for power sours into inquisition and colonialism and culture wars in the name of God; the green quest for independence shrivels into an arid and sterile set of doctrines or propositions devoid of spirit and life; the blue quest for individuality decays into spiritual narcissism and Christian consumerism; and the indigo quest for honesty lapses into relativism where one thing is as good as another, which means one thing is as bad as another – and from there, the slide into nihilism and apathy constantly lies underfoot like ice at every step.

If we don't transcend a stage in the fullness of time, we experience a kind of stagnation. We're stuck, and we only look backwards, congratulating ourselves on our superiority to those who came before, but never looking forwards to see the next stage before us. Our pride thus prepares us for a regression. If we do transcend the previous stages but then judge and exclude all that has gone before, we will remain stuck in the indigo moment of stage six, unable to continue the quest. To cross from indigo to violet, we must include as well as transcend. The violet zone challenges us, then, to learn to see in a completely new and unpractised way: to see previous stages not in the old dualistic terms of good/evil or right/wrong.[13] As we become acclimatised to the violet zone, we learn to see all previous zones as appropriate and adequate for their context, just as we consider infancy, childhood or adolescence as appropriate and adequate to their time, not bad, evil or wrong. Similarly, the new stage into which we are growing isn't *right*; it's simply *appropriate and adequate* for the challenges we now face.

When we climb a ladder, we can see things from higher rungs that we couldn't see from lower rungs, but we never would have reached the higher rungs if it weren't for the lower ones. So just as we can say that every rung is good, we can say that every zone in our quest is good, but none is good enough to stay there for ever. This approach isn't *absolutist*, then, claiming that one zone is right and others are wrong; nor is it *relativist*, claiming that all zones are equally good (or bad). It is holistic or integral and, in a sense, *hierarchical*, affirming that all zones are partial and greater wholeness is better than lesser wholeness.

Jean Daniélou demonstrates how this integral, evolutionary mindset was inherent in the thinking of one of early Christianity's most fertile theological minds. Gregory of Nyssa lived from AD 335 to after 394, exactly the uneasy period in which early Christianity (Harvey Cox's 'Age of Faith') was morphing into what we've been calling Greco-Roman Christianity (Cox's 'Age of Belief'). Gregory had a complex and non-compliant relationship with that process, reflected in the fact that the

Roman Catholic Church conferred upon him neither the status of doctor of the church nor the status of sainthood, nor did she commemorate him with a feast day. Reflecting on Gregory of Nyssa's conception of the stages of the soul's growth, Daniélou writes:

> Thus each stage is important; it is, as Gregory says, a 'glory'; but the brilliance of each stage is always being obscured by the new 'glory' that is constantly rising . . . And the laws of the soul's growth are parallel with those of man's collective history. And yet this is by no means to depreciate the value of each particular stage – all are good, all are stages of perfection. But the mistake would be to try to hold on to any one of them, to put a stop to the movement of the soul. *For sin is ultimately a refusal to grow*.[14]

Paul seems to agree. He said:

When I was a child,
I spoke and thought and reasoned like a child.
But when I became an adult,
I put childish ways behind me.
Now we see in a mirror, dimly.
But later we will see face to face.
Now I know in part.
But later I will understand fully,
Even as I have been understood.
So . . . faith, hope and love abide, these three.
But the greatest of these is love.
I will show you the most excellent way.
Follow the way of love.[15]

This way of love, this quest for *ubuntu*, this violet, full-spectrum way of seeing and relating, is virtually impossible to imagine for people who haven't reached the violet zone; they are likely to mock it or condemn it as something naïve, silly or even evil (which is exactly what we would expect from people in other zones). Even when we have imagined it, it requires habits and skills of the mind and heart that are profoundly hard to learn and master.[16]

But eventually we will learn and master them – and that's really the point of this book. When I began by saying that Christianity in all her forms was pregnant, that something was trying to be born from Christian faith, what I meant (without really realising it then) was that orange Christian faith was pregnant with yellow Christian faith, which is pregnant with green Christian faith, which is pregnant with blue Christian faith, which is pregnant with indigo, which is pregnant with violet, which will eventually become pregnant with something that is currently beyond our ability to see but is no doubt there. Why am I so confident that people of faith in yellow, green, blue and indigo zones will keep moving forward? For two, no, three reasons, which bring us back to my comments about the agency of God at the beginning of this chapter.

First, I am confident because of the reality and presence of the Creator with creation. This is God's world. It is now clearer to us than ever that God created a universe of expansion and evolution. To resist growth and transcendence in God's universe, then, goes against the grain of the universe; again, to recall Gregory and quote Jean Daniélou: *sin is ultimately a refusal to grow*. All living things repeatedly face the choice between adaptation (or growth) and extinction, because this is not the static, sterile neo-Platonic universe of Theos; this is the dynamic, fertile creation of the living God. Where sin abounds – where the resistance to growth, transcendence and inclusion abounds – what abounds more? God's grace, God's invitation to grow into ever-increasing aliveness, goodness and love. So I cannot help but have hope because God is present with us.

Second, I have hope because of Jesus. We are stuck with Jesus, and he won't go away. Yes, we can try to tie him up or cage him in with any number of absolute Greek lines. Yes, we can crucify him with Roman power and bury him in a rich man's tomb. Yes, we can seal that tomb with the heavy marble stones of institutions, traditions, legalisms and systems of thought. Yes, we can post armed guards in the form of theological thought-police who try to keep Jesus in and us out, or we can practise identity theft and use Jesus' name to do our own bidding in a thousand ways. Yes, we can do all these things, but Jesus cannot be contained. He rises again. He keeps coming back. We have been given a full-colour portrait of Jesus in the Gospels, against the backdrop of the Law and the Prophets, lighted by the rest of the New Testament. And that portrait is so beautiful that it always transcends (and includes) every attempt to contain it in one colour or zone. So, as long as we listen to the stories of Jesus told in Matthew, Mark, Luke and John, we will be prodded out of our current zone and summoned by love to continue our quest.

But we do not just have a portrait of Jesus, and that is my third reason for hope. We also have the presence of Jesus, the Spirit of Jesus, the Spirit and Breath and Wind and Fire of God, alive and active in us and all around us. We might even say that the call to transcend and include is a call that comes from the

Holy Spirit in whom all of us live, move and have our being. So we cannot escape. We can throw a temper tantrum. We can sit in the corner and pout. We can cower in the closet in fear. But then we hear music from another room playing faintly. Gradually, eventually, we are enticed and magnetised by the Spirit's jazz . . . and we have to come out of our closet and dance, to join in the unending improvisation and lively rhythm of the Father, Son and Holy Spirit.

So this quest is not just our little quest. It is part of the big quest – the quest of the Christian faith and, bigger still, the quest of humanity in general. And, even beyond that, perhaps we could also say that we are participating in the quest or adventure of God: God is seeking, adventuring, questing to create (with us) a universe that will become his eternal dancing partner, his delight, even his lover. The quest is a dance, and the dance is in fact a holy, cosmic, unending romance into which we are all invited. Perhaps this is a window into the vision given us in the last few pages of the Bible, as a wedding banquet is prepared, a glorious banquet to celebrate the consummation of the love affair between humanity's true God and God's true humanity.[17]

As Gamaliel said, if our 'purpose or activity is of human origin, it will fail'. But if our purpose and activity are from God . . .

CHAPTER 21

Living the Questions in Community

Our quest will probably be a lot easier for people who engage with it in ten years' time: easier because some of us have pioneered the early paths and taken the brunt of the first rounds of unfriendly fire from people who, like Gamaliel's colleagues, want to 'stop this thing from spreading any further among the people' (Acts 4:17). Fifty or seventy years from now, this episode of the quest may have run its course and this surge of struggle and creativity will be largely fulfilled (with new ones, no doubt, taking its place). By then, more and more followers of Christ will be spiritually formed within the new framing story or paradigm that is now being born through us. By then, some of the paradigms that currently dominate will be studied in theological history books and preserved only in small defensive enclaves. They will no longer be normative, and some of the ideas that we now pay a price to hold will be the new norm.

For now, however, we need to acknowledge that, among the many forms of spiritual suffering, there is a kind of intellectual and theological suffering, a painful death of old ways of being Christians and a joyful resurrection into new ways that some of us are called to undergo. *Martyrdom* might not be too strong a word for this agonising process. If you are one of those called on this quest, blazing rough trails now so that others will more easily follow in the future, then, please, be a friend to yourself.[1] Understand how hard this process is, and provide yourself with the kind of care you would want for a friend so engaged.[2]

When I started talking openly about my quest for a new kind of Christianity, I quickly learned that some people weren't safe to talk with. Much could be said about their reactions, but what mattered more was my response to their reactions. Sometimes I felt hurt: *Why don't others see how beautiful and good this quest is?* At other times I felt angry: *These people are so closed-minded and narrow!* Sometimes I got nasty: *You call me a heretic, do you? Well, I'm not the heretic – you are!* Sometimes I was tempted to withdraw: *I guess I'm just not wanted around here. I've had it with organised religion.* But eventually I'd get over these initial reactions and, instead of getting bitter and cranky, I prayed and struggled to get better and creative.

Through this process, I learned to hold in tension two indispensable elements of our quest. First, without what my friend Mabiala Kenzo calls 'the courage to differ', I felt insecurely that I must pretend to agree with the yellow-, green- or blue-zone versions of faith, even when I didn't.[3] Second, without a sufficient dose of 'the grace to differ graciously', I felt that I must convert everyone to see things my way before I could confidently live out my new perspectives. As a result, I embroiled myself too often in fruitless contention instead of generative conversation. In so doing, I harmed others, myself and the quest to which I had become committed. As I learned to combine the courage to differ with the grace to differ graciously (which I'm still learning, and in pursuit of which I have no doubt stumbled at times in these pages), I gradually learned to share with those who either 'get it' or want to get it, and not to bother – or look down upon – those who don't. As a result, now I'm far less disappointed in the number of people who are uninterested in or opposed to this quest than I am amazed by the number of people who are dying to join in the journey.

How do you know which people might be interested in 'getting it'? I've found a simple way: to say as little as possible and only share more if people ask. So a friend asks, 'How are you doing?' and you say, 'Not so well. I'm really struggling with some questions about my faith, and it's kind of disturbing.' Or you say, 'I'm really enthusiastic about some new questions I've been grappling with. They're opening up some new ways of being a follower of Christ for me.' If your friend expresses interest in understanding what you're talking about, you might say, 'Well, now might not be the best time, but if you're still interested in a week or so, ask me again, OK?' The idea is to be the opposite of pushy and the opposite of unhelpful at the same time.[4] And if they show initial interest but then get nervous, just let them off the hook: 'You know, this really is something I need to grapple with, but it sounds like it's not necessary or helpful for you right now, so we don't need to go into it. Let's talk about something else.' At most, you might recommend a book that could give your friend a safe space to explore and think in private.

As important as books can be, though, those of us who have been on this quest for a while generally agree that you can read only so many books. It's been said that the first followers of

Jesus didn't think themselves into a new way of living, but they lived their way into a new way of thinking. Similarly, new ideas and understandings are worth little until they're translated into the ways we pray and worship and enjoy life in the Spirit, and into the ways we interact with other people – with our families and friends, with people of other classes, races and religions, and so on. New perspectives must also be interpreted, translated and incarnated into our work, our economics, our politics, our recreation . . . and even into our church lives. In this way, our quest will be translated into action that counts, and that translation process is a communal activity, not a solo sport.

Ironically, however, that's where the most difficulties often arise. Everywhere I speak on the emergence of a new kind of Christianity, I hear about these difficulties during Q&R sessions.

1. What should I do if my pastor or priest isn't interested in or open to any kind of quest for a new kind of Christianity?

I usually encourage people not to bother their spiritual leaders who are not interested. Just try to be a good member of the church. Serve with a positive attitude, learning and giving all you can for as long as you can. Don't force this quest on anyone, and don't hide it under a bushel either. Emphasise points of agreement. Stay on common ground as much as possible, and learn to love and accept people with whom you disagree; after all, that's when you get to practise a new kind of Christianity. Outside your church, you can find a local or online cohort for mutual support and encouragement, but, inside your church, just be a joyful presence as much as possible. A wise older friend once told me, 'Don't ever reject anybody. But if they reject you, be gracious and don't stay where you're not wanted. That's rude, and love isn't rude.' I've found that to be wise counsel.

2. But what if my thinking and values have changed so much that I'm no longer in basic agreement with the church's doctrinal statements or core ethos? Is it dishonest to stay under those circumstances?

If you have a crisis of conscience like this, then I think it's best to go to your pastor or priest and say something like this: 'I've been doing a lot of rethinking about my faith recently, and I realised I'm changing in some ways. I don't want to be a problem in any way to you or to the church, so I thought I'd share some of what's going on, and we can decide the best way forward. If you think it's best for me to find a different church, I'll be glad to leave without causing a problem, and if we can find a mutually satisfying way for me to stay, that would be even better.' This kind of approach relieves the pastor of having either to try to fix you or to reject you, and it saves you from causing damage to a precious group of people by leaving angry or staying and causing strife and division. It's a form of mature self-differentiation, and shows a humble willingness to 'lose'.[5]

3. Pastors often ask: What should I do if my congregation isn't interested in or open to this quest for a new kind of Christianity?

I always discourage pastors from forcing this quest on their parishioners. (Please, please, please don't announce an 'exciting new sermon series' on 'a new kind of Christianity' next Sunday!) Far better, in my experience, to invite a few interested people for conversation over a home-cooked meal than to subject a whole congregation (in yellow, green or blue stages) to a series of sermons on questions (appropriate to indigo or violet stages) for which they may not be ready. *Bless the people*, one of my mentors once said to me. *Don't try to lead them or challenge them until you have truly blessed them.* And, if you have patiently blessed them but they remain deeply resistant to your leading them into new territory (or a new zone, as we said in the previous chapter), then accept that reality: better to go elsewhere and join or start something different than to waste your time and theirs on something for which they simply aren't ready. This isn't a failure for you or for them: it's just reality. Remember, you weren't ready for this quest in the past; it's good to allow others that freedom too.

4. If our church isn't open to new ideas and some of us feel it's time for us to leave, should we start a new congregation? Or should we give up on church altogether and just create an informal circle of friends?

The truth is, we do need thousands of new churches – especially churches that take shape as companions on a faith quest instead of as institutions defending theological turf. I spent twenty-four years of my life planting and leading a local church, so I know both the hardships and rewards of this path, and I recommend it highly. If you feel a pull to explore church-planting – either as a pastor or a lay leader or an involved volunteer – you should. Not in a divisive spirit, of course, because that would simply serve to replicate some of the worst features of the conventional kinds of Christianity.

Around the world in recent years I've met many people who begin planting new churches, but in the process discover that the word 'church' just carries too much baggage. So, instead, they form what I call *faith communities*. Some are more formal and large and others are informal and small; some last a long time and others a few weeks, months or years; some have regular meetings and high commitment and others simply enjoy social interaction and the conversations that emerge spontaneously while eating, walking or working together. Opinions will differ as to whether these faith communities are in fact churches (I'm glad to have them 'count'), but, however they're categorised, I believe we also need thousands of them – both to sustain the faith of followers of Christ who can't survive in existing contexts, and to create space for seekers to be exposed to the way of Christ.[6] I think that in many cases established congregations and informal faith communities can learn to co-exist and in fact develop a real synergy together.

5. Our church or denomination is open, so how can we help it experience transformation and change through this quest?

Change-agency in churches and denominations is a huge subject about which many good books have already been written and many more need to be written.[7] When I'm asked this kind of question, I'll typically offer some very specific advice.

(a) *Get a consultant.* There is enormous power in having the guidance of a wise, gifted and experienced person who remains outside your congregational or denominational system. Good consultants are expensive, I know, but so are good heart surgeons, and the two have a lot in common.[8]

(b) *Try building a new para-structure to foster new approaches* to faith rather than trying to bend existing structures to that end. In the Roman Catholic Church, for example, renewal has often come through monastic and missional orders – Franciscans, Carmelites, Jesuits, Paulists, and so on. They have been described as *ecclesiolae in ecclesia*, little churches in the big church. By not challenging the existing structure, but rather creating a parallel structure to contain and convey their new ways and practices, they allow the *ecclesia* to tolerate their presence long enough for the influence of these *ecclesiolae* to spread widely.[9] The Methodist movement began this way in the Anglican Church, as a parallel structure sustaining and supporting new ways and practices (or *methods*) of Christian faith.[10] Para-church organisations had a similar effect in evangelical churches in the mid-twentieth century. More recently, the 'new monasticism' and 'emergent' cohorts, two inter-related and promising new *ecclesiolae*, are already having profound effects wherever their communities are welcomed.[11]

(c) *Expect to bring in a new day with new people.* I read these words from sage church consultant Lyle Schaller many years ago, and I've seen them prove true again and again. Schaller was echoing an observation of Thomas Kuhn: 'Almost always the [people] who achieve these fundamental inventions of a new paradigm have been either very young or very new to the field whose paradigm they change.' This is why 'spiritual immigrants' are so important in churches and denominations. It's the Mennonite-born pastor who can help a Pentecostal church change in ways that a lifetime Pentecostal can't. It's the person who grew up with no religious background who can help an Episcopal church change in ways that lifelong Episcopalians can't. It's the young leaders, often without normal/formal credentials, who can help established denominations change in ways the 'properly trained' can't. And it's the seekers who are welcomed into a faith community that often transform that community, just as a new infant or adopted child can transform a family.[12]

(d) *Add, don't subtract.* For example, imagine that a historic denomination begins to realise that its creeds and books of order, perhaps written in the sixteenth or nineteenth centuries, encode ways of thinking that were appropriate in those centuries but not our own. Then imagine the uproar if those foundational documents were put up for amendment or replacement. Then imagine an alternative approach: that some new creeds were written to supplement rather than replace the old, and that a new 'track' with a new book of order (albeit a very short one!) was developed for new churches to experiment with. That process would, no doubt, engender some opposition, but considerably less.[13]

(e) *Develop a theology of institutions.* When we dream of bringing change to institutions, we need to do so with appropriate wisdom and reflection. Thankfully, increasing numbers of theologians and scholars are helping us do so.[14] Without the help of these thinkers, a lot of us have foolishly identified institutions as the problem, something to be eradicated, not realising that our anti-institutionalism serves only to create new institutions by accident. The accidental institutions we create are all the more unhealthy for being reactive and invisible (to their founders, at least) rather than reflective and visible. From my perspective, *institutions* exist in a dynamic relationship with social *movements*: simply put, institutions preserve the gains of past social movements. And, with amazing consistency, they also oppose current social movements. With equal consistency, however, if a social movement survives being ignored, opposed or co-opted by the institution it seeks to change, that movement's gains will enrich the legacy of the institution, and the institution will conserve those gains.

So the Civil Rights movement was opposed by the institution of the US government, but through the Civil Rights Act and other legislation the US government slowly but surely began turning the movement's social dreams into social realities. Similarly, in the Bible, the prophets voiced the concerns of social movements, and the priests were guardians of religious institutions, and they both could equally claim to be part of God's work in God's world.[15] Guided by a maturing theology of institutions, wise leaders of 'priestly' institutions will always keep a listening ear open to the prophets of movements for change, who will similarly see the priestly leaders of institutions not as enemies, but as colleagues in a greater work. The goal is not to tear down institutions and replace them with movements, but rather for institutions and movements alike to express the kingdom of God in creative collaboration.[16]

(f) *Preach the Bible.* I've tried to show in these pages examples of how the Bible can be read to give birth to a new kind of Christianity, just as it has been read to defend an old kind. I'm convinced that the approach we're taking here is on the side of the Bible, wisely read and applied. As psychologist Jonathan Haidt has explained, there are five main lines of moral reasoning: fairness, compassion, tradition, in-group loyalty and purity. Liberals or progressives typically rely on the first two only, and conservatives on all five.[17] This helps to show why conservatives tend to think of progressives as less moral: they seem to run on two cylinders instead of five.[18]

If we are going to help more people embark on our quest, we need to use all five lines as we preach and teach from the Scriptures. Yes, we need to affirm that a new kind of Christianity is dedicated to fairness and compassion – themes that resonate on every page of the Bible. But we also need to show – as I hope I have done in these pages – that what we seek is more true, not less true, to our primal living tradition as found in Scripture. And, rooted in the Bible, we can proclaim that the group loyalty that is most God-like and Christ-like (and Pauline, recalling the Gospel Question) is loyalty to the wide come-on-in-group of all God's creation. And we can promote what Scripture presents as the highest kind of purity – purity of heart, motives, mind and soul, recalling Jesus' words, that the purity that counts depends not on what we take into our bodies, but on what comes out of our hearts.[19] We will find, at every turn, that in the light of our quest, the Bible comes alive in ways that it never did in the old paradigms.

(g) *Employ experiential learning.* Yes, preachers must preach towards the desired future drawing from Scripture, but many people won't 'get it' until they also go through an 'abductive experience', an experience that helps them see in a new way. Mission trips often create these experiences by exposing people to a world of great need and injustice, as do vision visits (where you visit another church to experience what they're doing). Reading groups (using books like this one) can be important, but the experience of well-facilitated interaction is at least as important as the content of the book being read, and the interaction must be followed by action. Especially powerful are listening teams – groups that form to listen to people to whom they would not normally listen. For example, your church's leadership team could take four evenings to which people who have dropped out of church would be invited – the young adult children of members and their friends are a good place to start. Your team's job would be to listen, to ask questions, to draw out deeper understandings of why people left – and to do so without judgement or defensiveness of any kind.[20] Then the team would reflect on their responses, leading to some sort of creative action. This kind of listening exercise could do more to help a congregation change than attending five conferences and reading twenty books.

(h) *Keep your short-term expectations low and your long-term hopes high.* The systemic institutional forces that oppose quests for change are strong, and they almost always win some of the time. In so doing, they test the ideas and characters of change-agents and weed out all but the strongest and most enduring. So we on this quest for a new way of being followers of Christ should expect setbacks and mistakes, opposition and misunderstanding, conflict and discouragement at every turn. At many points, we will be tempted to give up, certain that change is impossible, and pretty certain that we must be as nutty as others are telling us we are. We should never underestimate our own power to be wrong and to do or say something amazingly stupid at the worst possible moment. Every great endeavour in the biblical narrative goes like this, it seems, from Moses whacking a rock with his stick to Peter whacking off someone's ear with his sword. All this helps us not to take ourselves too seriously, and it reminds us that the old sage Gamaliel knew what he was talking about: this thing will survive and thrive only if God is in it. And God will be active in *it* only if God is active in *us*, and that reminds us, once again, that a new kind of Christianity must be embodied in both individuals and communities who practise it, and both in movements and institutions. Yes, that's messy. Yes, that's slow. But there's an old African proverb that says it well, I think: *If you want to go fast, go alone. If you want to go far, go together.*

A New Kind of Christianity

On my way through adolescence to adulthood, I caught something, and I haven't been able to shake it since. The symptoms
developed gradually, so I can't point to a single moment when
it began for me. I do clearly remember the people from whom
I caught it. First there was Tom, a shaggy and bearded recovering druggie. Then there was Dave, a clean-cut sporty type.
Then there was Rod, a clean-cut schoolteacher who, with his
wife, Judy, started taking in shaggy and bearded recovering drug-
gies. Then there was another Tom, a wild musician. And through
the years there were others too – two more Daves, a Larry, and
later a Doug, a Tony, a Chris, a Rob, a John, a Brad, a Jo-Ann,
a Kenzo, a Richard, a Peter, a Claude, a René, a Walter, a Phyllis,
a Diana. From each of them I got a little more infected, and
then we all started reinfecting each other with more complex
and incurable strains of the infection. The infection was a good
thing, a kind of anti-infection, really, because the worse case of
it you had, the better, healthier and more alive you became.

Tom, Dave, Rod, Judy and all the others were so different in so many ways, but so alike in their aliveness, in their passion, in their simple love for God and neighbour, and in their shared ambition to live life in a way that would make God proud and happy by making their neighbours better off. I didn't realise it at the time, but from each of them I was catching a good case of a new kind of Christianity. There are signs that the infection is spreading, and some fear (and others hope) that this could be the beginning of a major pandemic.

I do not expect, if this infection spreads, that it will lead to a sudden outbreak of mass agreement on the answers to these questions. I hope for something even better: that we could agree that these questions need to be asked, and that they invite us into reverent and respectful conversation and even friendship, whether or not we ultimately agree on the answers. And even better: I hope that this conversation and friendship would unite us in a quest to receive and participate in what Jesus called God's kingdom, life to the full. As we're moving forward in that quest together, I believe God's Spirit will continue guiding us into truth, as Jesus promised.[1] And as a result, while we continue grappling with these ten questions, other urgent questions will no doubt beckon us, and new light will be given to us.

What might the next round of questions include? I'd like to suggest a few by sharing a somewhat painful and embarrassing confession. In 2008 and 2009, some friends and I organised a speaking tour based on what I feel is one of my most important books, *Everything Must Change* (Thomas Nelson, 2007). In the book, I described four global emergencies that we face today:

1. The crisis of the planet (which I called the Prosperity Crisis, since our way of pursuing prosperity is unsustainable ecologically).

2. The crisis of poverty (which I called the Equity Crisis, since the gap between rich and poor is growing, leaving more and more people in a less and less equitable situation).

3. The crisis of peace (which I called the Security Crisis, involving a vicious cycle in which the widening gap between a rich minority and a poor majority causes both sides to become increasingly violent, arming themselves with more and more catastrophic weapons).

4. The crisis of religion (which I called the Spirituality Crisis, since all our world's religions are failing to inspire us to address the first three crises, and, in fact, too often they are inspiring us to behave in ways counterproductive to human survival).

Together, I said, these crises become like spinning gears in a suicide machine. Over those two years, as I spoke constantly about the relevance of Jesus' gospel of the kingdom of God to the suicide machine, I remember returning to my hotel room night after night with a strange uneasiness. As I tried unsuccessfully to drift off to sleep, I would realise that the same thing had happened once again: during the Q&R sessions (we called it 'Question and Response' since many questions aren't suited for a simple answer), most questioners simply ignored the four crises I had talked about. Instead, they focused on arguing fine points of theology with me – all within their conventional paradigms. It was as if they said, 'Oh yeah, yeah, a billion people live on less than a dollar a day. But you're decentralising our preferred theory of atonement!' Or, 'Yeah, yeah, yeah, we're in danger of environmental collapse and religiously inspired catastrophic war. But you seem to be questioning our conventional ways of reading the Bible about homosexuality!'

This frustrated me. And, frankly, it angered me. But gradually I realised that my conversation partners simply couldn't address life-and-death issues such as poverty, the planet and peace from within the conventional paradigms they inherited. Their inherited conventional paradigms – shaped, as we have seen, by the Greco-Roman narrative, founded on a constitutional reading of the Bible, and so on – rendered those life-and-death issues invisible, insubstantial and unaddressable. So there was no getting around it: those inherited paradigms couldn't simply be outflanked; they needed to be confronted, questioned and opened up, which then shaped the direction this book would take.

With that background in mind, it should be no surprise what directions I believe we should take in our next round of questions. We need to ask the same question Francis and Frank Schaeffer raised back in 1976: *How then shall we live?*

How shall we live in relation to the planet? How can we grow from a consumerist to a sustainable way of life, and from a sustainable to a regenerative way of life? What is our duty to the living and non-living creations among which we live and on which we depend? How has our faith been abused in the past in relation to these questions, and how can our faith provide healing, inspiration, formation and motivation for the way forward?

How shall we live in relation to poverty? Given that capitalism out-competed communism, what threats does capitalism in its current form pose for our world? How can capitalism be redeemed, retrained and redirected so that the minority of people don't continue to suffer the dehumanising meaninglessness of self-centred luxury while the majority suffer the dehumanising degradation of crushing poverty? How has our faith been abused in the past in this regard, and how can our faith provide motivation and wisdom for the way forward?

How shall we live in relation to people who are different from us – in respect of religion, region, race, class, caste, political party, sexual orientation, history, etc.? How has our faith been abused to increase alienation, fear and violence in the past, and how can it provoke understanding and reconciliation for the way ahead?

Maybe these questions make you feel overwhelmed. But ignoring them, I think, will make you feel something far worse: under-alive. The truth is, questions like these – worthwhile, significant, moral – will help us be more infected with profound aliveness, more alive as human beings and more alive as practitioners of a new kind of Christianity.

In some ways, I wish I didn't have to use those five words, *a new kind of Christianity*. For starters, I'm uncomfortable using *a new kind*, because really, this thing comes in many new kinds, not just one. The word *new* concerns me also because, as we've seen, this thing is not only new, it's also very ancient. I guess it's an ancient quest for newness, but just calling it *new* obscures that fact. I'm also ambivalent about the word *Christianity* since, as I've said, I don't believe Jesus came to start a new religion, nor do I believe Christianity (or any religion) is the answer. Of course, I believe it can be part of the answer, but only if it doesn't see itself as the answer.

Further, regarding the term *Christianity*, if I didn't believe that, with God, all things are redeemable, I'd be worried whether that term is redeemable. As we've seen, the term *Christianity* (like its cousin *orthodoxy*) has too often camouflaged something quite foreign to Christ and his message, something that is more the problem than the solution: a fusion of Greek philosophy and Roman power, alloyed or adorned with elements drawn from the Bible, which is interpreted and applied in ways that often betray Jesus' life and teaching. Its defenders have unofficially mandated that when people try to modify that Greco-Roman orthodoxy, they must wear an adjective that brands them as aberrant, like a scarlet 'A' sewn on their soul. For example, when theologians read the Bible through the lens of the Exodus narrative, they are called 'liberation theologians', but their counterparts who read it through the Greco-Roman narrative are never labelled 'domination theologians' or 'colonisation theologians'. Similarly, we have 'black theology' and 'feminist theology', but Greco-Roman orthodoxy is never called 'white theology' or 'male theology'. Having become utterly normative for most of us, it's just 'theology'. By modifying *Christianity* with *a new kind of*, I wonder, are we just playing into that same ongoing game whose rules aren't fair from the first move?

Are we just falling into the same patterns of the past, creating Protestant Christianity 2.0, or Reformed Christianity 2.0, or Catholic Non-Roman Christianity 3.0? Is what is trying to be born in and through us simply another spin on that familiar cycle? Or is it bigger than that?

It's true that what is trying to be born today echoes the Great Reformation in many ways. 'Out of love for the truth and desire to bring it to light', intrepid people of faith today continue to participate in dialogue about our contemporary issues and struggles. We may not nail theses to the door, but we post hypotheses on a website or publish questions and reflections in a book. We may not gather in secret around a table in a German castle, but we raise questions in conversations between sips of Kenyan coffee, Belgian beer or Australian, Chilean and South African wine. We may not argue about which propositions should serve as major and minor premises in formal debate, but we lovingly proposition people to consider secret liaisons with truths and dreams that 'the authorities' have outlawed.

Luther's posting in 1517 and the debate that ensued helped create the religious conditions in which we have lived for many generations. But now, nearly five centuries later, increasing numbers of us feel that we must again, 'out of love for the truth and the desire to bring it to light', raise new questions and open up new generative conversations – and these conversations will in turn raise many new questions and open up many, many more conversations. Just as Luther addressed urgent and emergent issues of corruption and confusion in the Church in Europe in the early sixteenth century, today's young Luthers raise questions about equally urgent and emergent issues in our time, seeking honest, open and charitable dialogue.

You will notice that I have not tried to answer these questions definitively, but only responded to them provisionally, seeking to open up conversation, not close it down. And you will no doubt feel that in many places, even acknowledging the limitations of one book of so-many pages, I have not responded nearly as well as you could, which gives you a choice. You can either criticise my responses from a distance (in a yellow, green, blue or indigo way, recalling the previous chapter), or you can come to the table and join the conversation and make your own contribution. Be assured, if you come in that spirit of collegial contribution and creative collaboration, many of us will be eager to hear what you have to offer as we journey forward together.

As we near the five-hundredth anniversary of the day when Martin Luther came out of the closet so that all would know what he had been thinking in secret, it is time, I propose, to reinvigorate the dialogue by having many of us come out of our closets and admit we have been asking these and other important questions in secret. We must stop being ashamed of our questions, and we must stop pretending to be content with unsatisfying answers. Instead, we must let our questions and our fresh readings of Scripture become passageways out of the thought-boxes and mental stages and cages that can confine us. We must let our questions be the picks and shovels of a Spirit-inspired jailbreak. Once free, we can launch an exodus and continue our adventure, our quest for truth in the wild, unmapped places, as the biblical story beckons us to do.

Doing so is scary. We don't want to betray our heritage. We don't want to prove unfaithful to the faith that has nourished our souls and formed the communities to which we belong. Yet we must realise what being faithful and true to our spiritual forebears really requires. It's not simply a matter of repeating again and again what Luther and the other Reformers said (or, going back further, what the scholastics or eremetics or patristics said). Rather, true fidelity means we must do what they did. Like them, out of love for the truth, we must dare to precipitate a change, to foment a kind of gentle and hopeful revolution, to give birth to a new generation of Christian faith. By transcending and including, we must now rise to a new zone on the spectrum – to turn a page and open a new chapter by vulnerably exposing our previously secret thoughts, and by tenderly, reverently listening to one another as we do so.

Yes, we have a past, to be sure, to which we must show proper honour and with which we must maintain proper continuity. That past should always have a vote, as G. K. Chesterton famously said when he defined tradition as 'the democracy of the dead'. But I would add that the dead should not be given excessive veto power. As part of our inheritance from the past, we have been entrusted with an ongoing mission, and that mission requires us to be loyal, yes, to beloved tradition, but no less to the beloved present world in which we serve. And perhaps our greatest loyalty should be directed forward, to a beloved future which we are co-creating with the Spirit of the living God. To be loyal to *the God who was* without being loyal to *the God who is* and to *the God who is to come* would be, it seems to me, only a 33 per cent infection with a new kind of Christianity. When I started this quest, I think I started catching the other two-thirds as well.

Recall once more Luther's introduction and Thesis 1 of his 95 Theses:

> Out of love for the truth and the desire to bring it to light, the following propositions will be discussed . . . Our Lord and Master Jesus Christ, when He said *Poenitentiam agite*, willed that the whole life of believers should be repentance.

To put it in a slightly different way, but one I'm sure is in line with Luther's original intention, we could say that repentance or radical rethinking and change was necessary at the birth of the Christian community. And it was no less essential in its early childhood, and then in its middle childhood, and then in its early adolescence, and now as it stands poised on the brink of late adolescence or perhaps early adulthood:

> Out of love for the truth and the desire to bring it to light, the following proposal is offered . . . Our Lord and Master Jesus Christ, when He said *Poenitentiam agite*, willed that the whole history of Christianity should be repentance, rethinking and quest.

And so, wherever that willingness to rethink has been squelched, wherever that sense of quest has been buried under convention and complacency, the Christian faith in all its forms is in trouble. But, even there, something is trying to be born. Even now, right here, among us, inside you, inside me. You may feel it as a curiosity, a desire for better answers than you have inherited so far. You may experience it as frustration, knowing that there must be more to faith than you currently know. You may know it as hope – hope that God is seeking humble people whose hearts and lives can be the womb of a better future. You may be carrying this pregnancy now, with symptoms beginning to show – increasing love, joy and peace, growing patience, kindness and goodness, strengthening faithfulness, gentleness and self-control. In you, in your family, in your faith community and circles of friends, among people of peace and faith everywhere, something is trying to be born, indeed, indeed.

Notes

Chapter 1

1. Jim Peterson, *Evangelism as a Lifestyle* (NavPress, 1985).
2. GED is the General Educational Development test taken by American high-school pupils who do not attain a high-school diploma.
3. My book *Finding Faith*, later released as two short books (*A Search for What is Real* and *A Search for What Makes Sense*), attempts to articulate some of what I learned on this quest (Zondervan, 2007).
4. Kinnaman.
5. Len's pioneering book *Quantum Spirituality* (United Theological Seminary, 1991) and Sally's book *Worship Evangelism* (Zondervan, 1995) were especially helpful in my thinking.
6. Later, I became acquainted with the Asian network launched by Sivin Kit and friends (http://rohmalaysia.wordpress.com/) and the African network led by Claude Nikondeha and his wife Kelley Johnson (amahoro-africa.org). Now hardly a month goes by when I don't hear about new networks forming around the world.

7. Most recently, Dave Kinnaman and Gabe Lyon's *UnChristian* (Baker, 2007) and Robert Wuthnow's *After the Baby Boomers* (Princeton, 2007) have been especially helpful.
8. See Michael Gerson's article, 'A Faith for the Nones', available at http://www.washingtonpost.com/wp-dyn/content/article/2009/05/07/AR2009050703056.html.
9. Dan Kimball, a church-planter and pastor, reported what many church-planters were beginning to see in *They Like Jesus But Not the Church* (Zondervan, 2007).

Chapter 2

1. I believe I originally heard this contrast from Dr Leonard Sweet in one of his brilliant lectures.
2. Note that I do not say our quest is for new *things* to believe in contrast to old things, but rather new *ways* to believe. In *How (Not) to Speak of God*, Peter Rollins expands on this distinction: 'Instead of following the Greek-influenced idea of orthodoxy as right belief . . . the emerging community is helping us to rediscover the more Hebraic and mystical notion of the orthodox Christian as one who believes in the right way – that is, believing in a loving, sacrificial, and Christ-like manner. The reversal from "right belief" to "believing in the right way" is in no way a move to some binary opposite of the first (for the opposite of right belief is simply wrong belief); rather, it is a way of transcending the binary altogether. Thus orthodoxy is no longer (mis)understood as the opposite of heresy but rather is understood as a term that signals a way of being in the world rather than a means of believing things about the world' (SPCK, 2006, pp. 2–3). Peter Rollins adds that this approach 'emphasizes the priority of love: not as something which stands opposed to knowledge of God, or even as simply more important than knowledge of God, but more radically still, *as* knowledge of God'.

3. Thanks to Peter Rollins for this language of faithful betrayal, from his book *The Fidelity of Betrayal* (Paraclete, 2008).

4. My evangelical friends would probably prefer me to deal with the Bible question first, and originally I did. But, after some conversations with early readers of this manuscript, I felt it was better to start with our pre-critical assumptions about the shape of the biblical narrative, assumptions that predispose us to read the Bible in certain ways. Then we will move to the question of how the Bible is read and what kind of authority it is given. These two questions together open up space to explore all the others.

Chapter 3

1. Our denominations and local congregations face the daunting but also exciting and creative challenge of discovering new forms of affinity. In many cases, this means trading in old unifiers such as loyalty to institutions, assent to beliefs and appreciation for styles of music for new ones such as a common mission, shared practices and a unifying dream. These new centres of affinity will, I imagine, create a radically different social shape and require new approaches to polity, a subject to which we shall return in chapter 16.

Chapter 4

1. An important admission must be made here. My invention and use of an abstraction called *Greco-Romanism* is fraught with vulnerabilities and temptations, among them exactly the kind of dualistic reductionism that I will suggest is characteristic of Greco-Romanism! What I will say about Greek thought could mislead uncareful readers into thinking there was one monolithic system within Greek thought, but, as we will see shortly, inherent in Greek thought were many different theological schools. Even a

term like *Platonism* can hide the fact that Plato's thought was so highly nuanced and richly layered that scholars who have devoted their lives to his work interpret it in strikingly different ways. Similarly, in contrasting what we will call Greco-Roman thought with Hebrew thought, we can convey the false impression that there was such a thing as unified Hebrew thought. As the highly varied perspectives of Pharisees, Sadducees, Zealots, Essenes and the Qumran community make clear, within Judaism there was profound disagreement, not a single shared, coherent 'worldview'. We will be sliding into a common trap if we excessively vilify Greco-Romanism (which, in chapter 20, we will locate within an early zone in our quest) or if we excessively idealise Judaism (which, like all faiths, is always a composite of many competing and conflicting communities). In addition, some will argue that what I'm calling the Greco-Roman narrative is simply the Christian narrative. Obviously, I do not want to capitulate to that conclusion for even an instant; I believe that however predominant this narrative has been in Western Christian history for 1,700 years, there have always been minority reports – among the desert fathers and mothers, the Celts, the Franciscans, the Anabaptists, the Catholic and Protestant mystics – not to mention the other main wing of the faith known as Eastern Orthodoxy. These persistent voices encourage us that the future of the Christian tradition can be different from – and better than – its Western, Greco-Romanised past. Mindful of all these provisos, we can use the term profitably. For a helpful overview of the concept, see the first few chapters of Thomas Cahill's *How the Irish Saved Civilization* (Anchor, 1996).

2. In emphasising the reframing of the biblical narrative by Greek philosophy in this chapter, I feel I have underemphasised the role of Roman power. The two are profoundly related. Plato, for example, didn't believe in the Olympian gods of Greek religion, but he felt that certain beliefs were necessary for social stability

– namely belief in a Supreme Being and in the threat of eternal punishment for wrongdoing in the afterlife. Plato considered these beliefs so important to the social order that he recommended (*Laws*, Book 10) that people be punished by the state with five years of banishment for the first offence against them and death for the second. Roman imperial powers, preoccupied with regime continuation, would obviously share Plato's affection for politically useful beliefs – beliefs that unify and pacify, we might say. It's interesting in this light, and probably not accidental, that these became the very preoccupations of the version of Christianity that the Roman Empire sanctioned in the fourth century. By the fifth century the Church and state together routinely imposed banishment and the death penalty for misbelief, exactly as Plato had recommended centuries before. See Harvey Cox, *The Future of Faith* (HarperOne, 2009), p. 219.

3. Although I'm highly critical of the unintended consequences of the embrace of the Greco-Roman narrative by early Christian theologians, I must acknowledge the absolute brilliance of their move. By retelling their story in the terms of Greek philosophy, they integrated Plato and Aristotle into their own larger whole – something Greek philosophers hadn't been able to do on their own. As a result, they 'saved' Aristotle and gave him an honoured role as philosopher of time, and they 'saved' Plato and gave him the honoured place as philosopher of eternity. Their instinct – to save and embrace the great philosophers rather than condemn and exclude them – was, I judge, a Christ-like one. The way it was done, however, created a lasting Greco-Roman syncretism under the guise of orthodoxy and, as a result, the 'frontwards' storyline of the Bible in which Jesus emerged was largely lost. (This story is complicated by the fact that Aristotle's works were lost to the West for several centuries, due to the plundering and burning of libraries by invading tribes from the north. Aristotle's

works had, however, been preserved by Muslim scholars to the south, who later shared them with Christian scholars. In the absence of Aristotle's influence, Western Christianity had become increasingly Neo-Platonic, and when his influence returned, that state of intellectual affairs was destabilised.)

4. If this play on words helps you (it may not), for Platonists (in the tradition of Plotinus) the material (composed of matter) is immaterial (unimportant, insubstantial) and the non-material (not composed of matter) is material (substantial, important).

5. Again, Aristotle's thought was deliciously more complex than this simplification, but this simplification accurately reflects the general impression commonly and popularly associated with his thought.

6. This imaginary conversation has been immortalised in Raphael's iconic painting of 1510/11, 'The School of Athens'. For more on the painting, including an image, see http://en.wikipedia.org/wiki/The_School_of_Athens.

7. Jeffrey L. Bineham attributes the superiority complex of the modern Western mind to other related causes. Dependence on written over oral communication, he says, creates this superior attitude. Drawing from the work of Sally McFague, James Chesebro and Walter Ong, Bineham says that dependence on the written medium 'blinds many to the relativity of interpretive contexts' and privileges the writing-based perspective as 'absolute truth' in the minds of writing-based people. This writing-based 'pattern of understanding' renders writing-based people (in Ong's words) 'abject prisoners of the literate culture'. By marginalising or rejecting oral-based perspectives, writing-based people lose an appreciation for 'the metaphorical, open-ended, and tentative nature of language'. The Protestant Reformation's characteristic focus on the printed Scriptures as their primary authority thus tends to blind Protestants to 'the

notion of scripture as a living testimony', and then binds them to 'an absolutist literalism'. See 'Parables and the Oral Medium: A Metaphorical Approach to Religious Language', in *The Journal of Communication and Religion*, March 1991, pp. 1–8.

8. I believe this is the best sense in which the highly nuanced term 'metanarrative' should be understood. A metanarrative is not just a big story; it's a big story that marginalises, discredits, assimilates, domesticates, invalidates, or in some other way annihilates all other stories. In this sense, I do not believe the real biblical narrative is a metanarrative, but I do believe the Greco-Romanised Christian narrative is.

9. The fact that for many of us this multicultural view of history seems messy and therefore hard to imagine or accept suggests how deeply we have imbibed the elitist Greco-Roman spirit.

10. Of course, one might ask why we need to reduce history to a single line at all, and we will explore exactly this point in our eighth question on this quest.

11. This desire for stasis is described accessibly by Thomas Cahill in *How the Irish Saved Civilization*.

12. See the brilliant work of African theologian Kwame Bediako, *Theology and Identity* (Authentic Books, 2000), pp. 38ff. and 174ff.

13. For some other factors in this loss of the Jewish storyline, see the Appendix to *The Secret Message of Jesus* (Nashville: Thomas Nelson, 2007).

14. There's a lot of argument afoot about whom to blame for this profound embrace of Greco-Roman categories. Prime suspects include Emperors Constantine and Theodotius and the bishops who willingly subordinated the Church to their imperial regimes. St Augustine, for all his brilliance, is also implicated. Regardless of who is blamed, Harvey Cox sums up the matter well: 'In entering the Greek world, Plato's turf, the early

Christians mixed biblical ideas into a Greek framework that gravely distorted their original meaning . . . The triumph of the clerical elite under Constantine cemented this distortion into the structure of the church' (*The Future of Faith*, p. 221). Far better than merely blaming, to my mind, would be understanding more deeply how the story of Jesus and the reign of God became Greco-Romanised, and what the effects of that conversion have been. With that understanding, we can be de-converted and liberated in the present so as to help create a better future.

15. This is not to reject the reality of sin's horror and universality. It's just to say that terms such as *the fall* and *original sin* and *total depravity* frequently derive their meaning from a story that is, I believe, inherently un-Jewish and unbiblical, and so when they are read into the biblical story, they distort and pollute it. For more on this subject, see J. Philip Newell, *Christ of the Celts* (San Francisco: Jossey-Bass, 2008).

16. This Greco-Roman framing story may help explain why Christian pastors and counsellors have such a hard time convincing Christians that God actually loves them. Instinctively they know that Theos *can't*.

17. We see the tension between more and less Platonic views of God playing out among the early church fathers, such as Origen (more Platonist) and Gregory of Nyssa (less so). As Jean Daniélou writes, 'For the Platonist, change is a defect . . . Even the Christian Platonism of Origen cannot avoid this difficulty. Change is always thought of as a degeneration from a state of initial perfection; and the transformation wrought by Christ has for its sole purpose to destroy change and restore immutability . . . Now to overcome this difficulty Gregory had to destroy the equation: good = immutability, and evil = change. And consequently he had to show the possibility of a type of

change which would not merely be a return to immobility.'
Daniélou described Gregory's un-Platonic notion of change as
'the soul's perpetual progress in sanctity . . . a process of
infinite growth' (*From Glory to Glory*, Crestwood, NY: St
Vladimir's Seminary Press, 1995, pp. 47, 46). Thanks to Heidi
Miller Yoder for this reference.

18. In other words, they receive, recalling an earlier note, exactly
the imperial punishment for misbelief that Plato had
recommended: the death penalty and banishment.

19. You can learn more about Michael and hear the song at
http://www.michaelkellyblanchard.com. 'The god of the
philosophers' was a term Blaise Pascal used to describe a
spiritual experience I recounted briefly in chapter 18 of
Finding Our Way Again (Thomas Nelson, 2008) and chapter
19 of *A Generous Orthodoxy* (Zondervan, 2004).

Chapter 5

1. An apology is due here, a profound and heart-rending apology,
an apology to the Jewish people for the ways we Christians
have colonised their story and then – this can hardly be said
without a feeling of acute nausea – turned it against them
through anti-Semitism and other forms of religious supremacy.
And I must also apologise because I have not been careful
enough in the past to avoid recolonising their story, and I may
inadvertently fail again in these pages. But I hope my Jewish
readers will see that many of us are trying to fix something
that we now realise is terribly broken, and sometimes fixing
can only be done in steps and stages, and these pages are, I
hope they will agree, at least small and faltering steps in the
right direction.

2. I explore this theme in more detail in *The Story We Find
Ourselves In* (Jossey-Bass, 2005).

3. The term *perfect* as often used in the New Testament – and as used within the Wesleyan tradition – does not necessarily mean technical Greco-Roman perfection, contrary to popular opinion; it is not 'a perfect 10 in the ontological beauty pageant'. Instead it means 'mature', 'fully formed', 'complete' or 'whole'.

4. *Evolving* is a blasphemy in the world of Theos, which helps explain why some strains of Western Christianity have resisted it so viscerally, against all evidence. Evolution fits beautifully in the good world of Elohim.

5. It's interesting, in this context, to reflect on the use of the word *development* in economics today, contrasting the 'developed world' with the 'developing world'. We might replace the former with 'the Greco-Roman world' or 'the colonised world', and the latter with 'the world being colonised and brought into the empire of Western (Greco-Roman) civilisation'. In the light of the ecological crisis, this is all terribly ironic and tragic, because 'developers' typically destroy or undevelop a sustainable, beautiful and regenerative ecosystem, turning it into something profitable for an elite few, plundering it and rendering it unsustainable, ugly and spent for everyone else. Mountain-top removal in Appalachia provides an icon of this tragic and ironic kind of 'development'.

6. You feel how powerful and fresh this vision is when you contrast it with, say, an Egyptian creation narrative, where the earth is created fully formed, the irrigation channels dug and the shadoofs in place. Then humans are created to maintain it all. Quite a convenient myth to keep the masses in their 'god-given' place, for the benefit of the elite!

7. Again, this is not to discredit the brilliance of either Plato or Plotinus (or Boethius, who later did much to bring their brilliance into the Christian tradition, and did so beautifully and with much good effect). Nor do I intend to sanctify Aristotle

and replace a Platonist framing of the biblical narrative with an Aristotelian one. Instead, I'm seeking to discern a healing narrative in the biblical text that itself can better prepare us to live responsibly, ethically and wisely before God in our present and future.

8. One fascinating dimension of the 'new' or 'social' trinitarianism is the idea that the Father, Son and Holy Spirit live as a dynamic (as opposed to static) society, that within God there is an unending story of relationship (in which things happen) and that, in a real sense, the living God 'has a life', a history, a story. This dynamic vision, it seems to me, is fundamentally irreconcilable with a static, unmoved and immovable Theos. Theos may be a Supreme Being, but the triune God is a Supreme Living and a Supreme Loving.

9. The tree, field, water and tower in the story are intentionally and playfully chosen for reasons I hope are clear, or will be clear soon.

10. My friend Don Golden, co-author with Rob Bell of *Jesus Wants to Save Christians* (Zondervan, 2008), puts it like this, reflecting on the story of Hosea: 'When God encounters evil, God doesn't destroy it – God marries it' (from a personal conversation). By uniting with a people gone astray – loving, entering, incarnating and remaining faithful to them in spite of their unfaithfulness – God absorbs their evil in his greater good, and evil is thus overcome. This insight resonates with a chapter on atonement theory I contributed to *Proclaiming the Scandal of the Cross* (Baker Academic, 2006), edited by Mark Baker.

11. As we will see again when we read the story of Job in response to 'the authority question', it may help us here to see 'God' not simply as the real God, but as a character in a story, seen and described unapologetically from a human point of view. This

character is thus rendered in starkly human terms, which excuses the character for displaying less emotional maturity than we might expect in an actual deity. This character seems, if we're honest, rather limited in foresight (threatening and then not imposing the death penalty with Adam and Eve, not anticipating Cain's violence to Abel), and somewhat insecure and threatened by human potential, worrying first that humans 'will become like us', and later that 'nothing will be impossible for them'.

12. Biblical scholars often use the word 'chiastic' (or X-like) to describe the shape of narratives in the Hebrew Bible. Like Plato's narrative (but without the philosophical dualism), there is descent through the stories of Adam, Cain, Noah and Babel. Then there is ascent through the stories of Abraham, Isaac, Jacob and Joseph.

13. It should be noted that Joseph himself ends up selling the entire nation of Egypt into slavery to Pharaoh (Gen. 47:13ff.), consolidating power and wealth for a dynasty that will eventually enslave his descendants. The complex entanglements of good and evil don't disappear even in this otherwise happy ending.

14. The difference here – between simply 'knowing' the difference between good and evil and actually overcoming evil with good – is more significant than it may first appear, and more inherent to the structure of the Genesis story than many realise. As further evidence of the book's chiastic structure (see note 12 above), Joseph serves as a kind of mirror to Adam: for example, he refuses to yield to the temptation of a woman (Potiphar's wife) as Adam did, and he refuses to blame her for his plight as Adam did.

Chapter 6

1. *Natural* and *supernatural*, we should remember, are also terms alien to the biblical narrative, reflecting assumptions, dualisms, concerns and constructions of the modern era.

2. The dream of a peaceable kingdom takes a tragic turn in David's son Solomon, which is described powerfully by Don Golden and Rob Bell in their book *Jesus Wants to Save Christians* (Grand Rapids: Zondervan, 2008).

3. Many thanks to Tom and Christine Sine (www.msainfo.org) who were the first teachers to sensitise me to the power of these prophetic images at a seminar in Three Hills, Alberta some years ago. For more on this subject, see Walter Brueggemann, *The Prophetic Imagination* (Fortress, 2001).

4. Note this pattern of expansion: from one chosen people in one promised land to all people across the whole earth. We'll see this pattern of expansion recur again and again in the Bible, for example in Matt. 28:18–20 or Acts 1:8.

Chapter 7

1. For a scathing indictment of violence in monotheistic texts and traditions, see Jack Nelson-Pallmeyer, *Is Religion Killing Us? Violence in the Bible and the Quran* (Harrisburg: Continuum, 2005).

2. A startling slave trade exists today in new forms. For more information, see the work of International Justice Mission (www.ijm.org) and David Batstone's Not for Sale Campaign (www.notforsalecampaign.org).

3. From *Slavery Defended: The Views of the Old South* (New York: Prentice-Hall, 1963). This book is out of print, but it is widely referenced in relevant articles easily accessible on the internet, especially 'Roots of Racism', from which much of the material in this chapter is derived. The original article was published in *Flagpole Magazine* (17 November 1999) and is available online at http://www.lawsch.uga.edu/academics/profiles/dwilkes_more/his29_racism.html.

4. Cornell University Library makes available a digital reproduction

of the original 1864 edition. For information, see
http://www.amazon.com/Nellie-Norton-scriptural-abolitionists-
vindication/dp/142971770X/ref=sr_1_1?ie=UTF8&s=books&qid
=1238786478&sr=1–1.

5. Many of us routinely hear or read identical rhetoric in response
to our positions today.

6. Note the similarity between these words and the words of a
widely respected evangelical Bible teacher and radio preacher who
is quoted in chapter 13. Also note that the character avoids Paul's
letter to Philemon on I Timothy 1:10, the former urging the
release of a slave and the latter condemning the trade in slaves.

Chapter 8

1. I hope that readers from the UK and other nations that don't have
constitutions will be able to make sense of this metaphor. I could
also speak of the Bible as the key element in a social contract: we
agree to associate with one another as long as we affirm a set of
interpretations (some written, some unwritten) of it.

2. We generally avoid quoting Mark 2:27, where Jesus says, 'The
Sabbath was made for people, not people for the Sabbath.' This
statement radically undermines a constitutional approach to
Scripture, since it subordinates the requirements even of 'the Law'
to the well-being of human beings.

3. Constitutions generally have provisions for their own amendment
so they can be updated to deal with new situations. However, since
the Bible was never designed as a constitution, it has no such
provisions, rendering it more inflexible than, and therefore in at
least one way inferior to, any actual constitution.

4. His opponents – religious lawyer-types – were about to use 'the
Law' to *stone* a woman for committing adultery. The Law had
ostensibly been written by the finger of God on *stone*. Now Jesus,
who had said elsewhere that the law was made for humanity and

not humanity for the law, writes with his finger in *dust* – ostensibly the substance from which humanity was formed by the hand of God. It is an amazingly evocative symbolic action, isn't it?

5. We might also suggest that the ability to maintain multiple perspectives energizes a community and equips it with a kind of intellectual flexibility that enhances its health and vigor, like diversity in a gene pool. A community that resolves tensions and reduces viable perspectives to one agreed-upon ideology would be correspondingly weakened and its vision flattened and narrowed.

6. In previous chapters, we considered the profound argument between Plato and Aristotle. Western culture has preserved that tension, not sought to resolve it. We haven't decided Plato was right, so Aristotle should no longer be taught, nor have we done the reverse. We have realised that each is more interesting and provocative in the light of the other, and that we are better off for having both voices than for sanctioning one and silencing the other. When we see the Bible as a library, we can see similar tensions between priest and prophet, Paul and James, Jesus and Moses, and so on.

7. I'm aware that I'm bypassing arguments about *canonicity*, the process by which certain documents were included and others rejected by the Church for inclusion in the biblical library. Those arguments are important and fascinating, but peripheral to our line of thinking here, apart from two brief observations. First, the process of including or rejecting articles in a constitution is very different from the selection of documents in a library. The former requires that uniformity and consistency be maintained, and the latter that an adequate range of voices and perspectives be maintained. Second, to understand the canonised texts in a small library such as the Bible still requires reference to thousands of other texts not included, because the words and imagery used in the canonised texts can be fully understood and appreciated only

by consulting their use in other texts outside the canon. A canon (or standardised list) of texts, then, is not a hermetically sealed universe: it is more like a city defined by prescribed city limits. The city is not independent of the surrounding suburbs and countryside, but, rather, they have an interdependent relationship.

8. For a ground breaking book that addresses this issue brilliantly, see John Franke's *Manifold Witness: The Plurality of Truth* (Abingdon, 2009).

9. For highly accessible treatments of these important matters, I again recommend John Franke's *Manifold Witness*, and his *Beyond Foundationalism* (WJK, 2001), with Stanley Grenz.

10. For convinced Bible-as-constitution folks, I offer this question: *If the abolitionists read the Bible correctly and pro-slavers didn't, what can we learn from the abolitionist way of reading?* An informed reply would include these four guidelines. First, they valued the general over the specific: 'Do unto others . . .' carried more weight than the verses typically quoted by pro-slavers. Second, they read the Bible narratively, as an unfolding story. This led them to expect a rising ethical standard over time. Third, they read the Bible Christocentrically, which means they gave the words of Christ more weight than, say, the words of Leviticus. Fourth, they read the Bible relationally as a book about love, rather than analytically as a book about law. This led them to ask not simply whether slavery was permissible to a law-giving God, but whether it was desirable to a slave-loving God – considering that the slave is also God's child, and so (in the words of the revolutionary Christmas hymn 'O Holy Night') 'the slave is our brother'. For more on guidelines for reading the Bible, see my website, www.brianmclaren.net.

Chapter 9

1. For more on the use of torture by Christians, see Bruxy Cavey, *The End of Religion* (Navpress, 2004), chapter 4. Also see Spencer Burke's four Interludes in *A Heretic's Guide to Eternity* (Jossey-Bass, 2006), and Harvey Conn's *The Future of Faith* (HarperOne, 2009). For more detailed treatments, see James Haught, *Holy Horrors* (Prometheus, 1999) and Helen Ellerbe, *The Dark Side of Christian History* (Morningstar Books, 1995).

2. For more on this subject, see T. J. Wray and Gregory Mobley, *The Birth of Satan* (Palgrave MacMillan, 2005), or John Anderson's self-published *Satan: An Authorized Autobiography* (Voice of Reason, 2007).

3. From 'Tell All the Truth but Tell It Slant', by Emily Dickinson. Thanks to Jodi McLaren for her insights into this poem.

4. John Franke's work in this regard is extremely helpful. See *The Character of Theology* (Baker Academic, 2005) and *Manifold Witness*.

5. Peter Rollins explores this theme beautifully in *How (Not) to Speak of God* (Paraclete, 2006).

6. Perhaps when our conservative friends ask those of us on this quest if we believe in the inerrancy of Scripture, our reply should be, 'No, I believe that Scripture is better than inerrant. I believe it's beautiful.' If they ask us what we mean by 'beautiful', we can explain, 'It's beautiful for creating a community that extends across generations and cultures to engage with God so they can experience, in that engagement, the gift of revelation.' They probably won't be satisfied, but we might help them think a bit.

7. It's worth noting again how long in the story God remains completely silent. That silence says a lot, I believe, about God's desire for us to have time and space to think out loud.

8. I'm aware of the fact that some of my wonderful conservative

evangelical friends will find this terribly unsatisfying in comparison to the gains they accrue through a constitutional reading. That's why I don't expect many, if any, of them to be convinced by this chapter. But I'm thinking about thousands of their children, grandchildren and outside-the-church friends for whom their approach simply feels intellectually dishonest and morally unacceptable. I suspect that this approach could be as exciting and promising to the latter as it is disappointing and unconvincing to the former.

Chapter 10

1. For this reason, I would grimly prefer atheism to be true than for the Greco-Roman-Theos narrative to be true. And for this reason, I joyfully celebrate the narrative centred in Jesus as a better alternative to both. For more on the subject of hell, see my *The Last Word and the Word After That* (Jossey-Bass, 2005), and an extremely helpful and concise article by Nik Ansell, 'Hell: The Nemesis of Hope' (available online at http://www.theotherjournal.com/article.php?id=746). There he quotes evangelical patriarch John Stott saying of the conventional view of hell, '[E]motionally, I find the concept intolerable and do not understand how people can live with it without either cauterizing their feelings or cracking under the strain'.

2. I suppose this evolutionary understanding could actually be incorporated within the Bible-as-constitution approach; later views could be seen as amendments to the constitution.

3. See, for example, the ability of the Egyptian magicians (Exod. 7ff.) to perform miracles through the power of their gods, which – with delicious irony, by the way – just makes things worse, as if Egypt needed even more frogs! Or consider the 'gods' of 1 Chr. 16:25 and Pss. 86:8; 95:3; 96:4; or 97:9.

4. See, for example, Isa. 1:11ff.

5. Michael Gerson, quoting research by Andrew Newberg and Mark Robert Waldman about religion and brain activity, explains, 'But Newberg's research offers warnings for the religious as well. Contemplating a loving God strengthens portions of our brain – particularly the frontal lobes and the anterior cingulate – where empathy and reason reside. Contemplating a wrathful God empowers the limbic system, which is "filled with aggression and fear". It is a sobering concept: The God we choose to love changes us into his image, whether he exists or not' (http://www.washingtonpost.com/wp-dyn/content/article/2009/04/14/AR2009041401879.html).

6. If we believe that the same God who created an evolving universe is revealed in an evolving Bible, we can derive some fascinating insights from contemporary studies of genetics. Today's chickens, it turns out, still have the genetic information in their DNA that was used to produce long tails, scales and teeth in their ancestors the dinosaurs. During embryonic development, some of those primitive dinosaur characteristics still manifest themselves in chickens. (Human embryos similarly have stages where they sport gills and tails, so it is said that our ontogeny recapitulates our phylogeny.) We might say that the Bible similarly retains a record of its own evolution, and in our individual spiritual development we may personally recapitulate earlier stages. This is a theme to which we will return in our last few chapters.

7. Words such as 'best', 'must' and 'only' suggest that all this was according to a predetermined plan, but that's not the only way to see it. You could say that the learning process works like a seedling that always moves towards warmth and light. If a rock or log accidentally falls on the ground directly above it before it germinates, it will eventually curve around the obstacle, drawn

towards warmth and light. Similarly, our religious histories may move not according to a plan determined in the past, but according to a purpose that draws them towards a future in full sun.

8. The idea of stages in our growth is suggested in 1 John 2:12ff. The idea that we love and know God in the other is reflected throughout the epistle: see 2:3–6, 9–11; 3:11–19; 4:7–12, 16–21; 5:1.

9. Several writers have helped me think in these developmental terms, notably developmental psychologist William Perry, Christian theologians Walter Brueggemann and N. T. Wright, Jewish lawyer Alan Dershowitz (*The Genesis of Justice*, Grand Central Publishing, 2001), philosopher Ken Wilber, pastors and authors Bruce Sanguin (*The Emerging Church*, Copperhouse, 2008) and Richard Vincent (*Integral Christianity*, available through http://christianfutures.com/books8.shtml). Thanks to Dr. Jay Gary for his many contributions to my own thinking about the future.

Chapter 11

1. See Sarah Dylan Breuer's helpful chapter in a book I co-edited called *The Justice Project* (Baker, 2009).

2. See *Everything Must Change* (Thomas Nelson, 2007), chapter 19.

3. We might say that this willingness to learn, grow, transcend and 'trade up' distinguishes 'believe' from 'make-believe', or 'good faith' from 'bad faith'.

4. Let's keep in mind the Greco-Roman tendency to eliminate complexity and diversity and reduce everything to the one 'right' line, and let's also remember that we're working in only two dimensions in this diagram. In Question 8, we'll consider a more three-dimensional way to conceive of the biblical narrative.

5. To fine-tune the point, we would also need to say that Jesus must first and foremost be understood in terms of the history in which he was raised and the times in which he lived – rather than in terms of controversies or issues of the fourth, fifth, sixteenth or twenty-first centuries.

6. This flat reading was expressed quite clearly in an online debate about gay marriage in late 2008, hosted by *Newsweek*. The conservative spokesperson argued, 'When one puts the teachings of Paul on the same authoritative ground as the teachings of Jesus, one must conclude that God does not condone homosexual behavior. The Bible does not suggest that there are two levels of spiritual authority in the Bible – the more authoritative teachings of Jesus and the teachings of Paul and the other New Testament writers. They are all equally authoritative. Consequently, I cannot see any biblical justification for condoning homosexual behavior' (http://www.newsweek.com/id/175223/page/2, accessed 17 December 2008). His transparent willingness to accord Jesus no more authority than Paul renders me . . . speechless.

Chapter 12

1. See, for example, *A Search for What is Real: Finding Faith* (Zondervan, 1999, 2007), chapter 8; *A Generous Orthodoxy* (Zondervan, 2004), chapter 1; *Everything Must Change* (Thomas Nelson, 2007), chapter 18; *The Secret Message of Jesus* (Thomas Nelson, 2006).

2. The clip can be viewed here: http://www.youtube.com/watch?v=zKDC2iBQTYg.

3. See *The Secret Message of Jesus* and *Everything Must Change*.

4. One of the greatest comedic movies since the big bang (in my humble opinion) is Weird Al Yankovic's *UHF*. In it, there is a fake ad for a new movie called *Gandhi II*. 'He's back,' the deep

voice on the trailer begins, 'and this time he's mad. No more Mr Passive-Resistance this time. He's out to kick some butt.' The 'second-coming Gandhi' wields a mean machine gun and likes to party with beautiful women (one on each arm) to boot. You can watch the clip here: http://video.google.com/videoplay?docid=3913203940475670642.

Chapter 13

1. The interview can be found here: www.youtube.com/watch?=OH1yOmij7Q4.

2. One recalls the words from the novel *Nellie Norton*, quoted in chapter 7: 'in the catalogue of sins denounced by the Savior and His Apostles, slavery is not once mentioned . . . not one word is said by the prophets, apostles, or the holy Redeemer against slavery . . . the Apostles admitted slaveholders and their slaves to church membership, without requiring a dissolution of the relation'. One imagines that it would be far easier for a slave-owner or radio broadcaster to say these words than it would be for a slave or a slum dweller.

3. Thanks to Dr John York of Lipscomb University for stimulating my thinking on the resonances between Jesus and Moses in John's Gospel.

4. Since we aren't pre-assuming the six-line narrative, it would be an unwarranted conclusion to equate words found in John such as 'condemnation', 'death' and 'perish' with the word 'hell', which is never found in John.

Chapter 14

1. In a personal communication.

2. *The Secret Message of Jesus* and *Everything Must Change* (Thomas Nelson, 2006, 2007).

3. Although they differ in some assumptions and conclusions, the

following authors have all helped me to understand better the message of the kingdom of God: Martin Luther King, Jr, Steve Chalke, N. T. Wright, Dallas Willard, John Dominic Crossan, Marcus Borg, John Howard Yoder, Ched Myers, Jacques Ellul and William Herzog.

4. Anglican bishop N. T. Wright has explored this theme powerfully in his work, as have Dominic Crossan and Marcus Borg.

5. Even more ludicrous: imagine him saying, 'And we're going to eternally torture anyone who doesn't accept this new religion named after me.'

6. This recalls what I said earlier about there being many *Christianities*, and it has many other implications as well, as we will explore under Question 9.

7. I should add that I had just read N. T. Wright's *What St Paul Really Said* (Eerdmans, 1997), and I felt as many readers may feel reading this book: I found his ideas intriguing but disturbing, and I half-hoped to prove him wrong. Happily, I failed to do so.

8. See Matt. 8:9–11.

9. Dr Ray Anderson, one of the unsung theological heroes of our time who passed away as I was editing this book, described this process beautifully in his delightful book *An Emergent Theology for Emerging Churches* (IVP, 2006).

10. Of course, we have had to deal with these kinds of issues ever since – right down to the present day, as we struggle with how to experience true racial reconciliation, true ethnic, class and caste reconciliation, even true acceptance of homosexuals, hermaphrodites and (in some settings) Democrats or Republicans.

11. It's worth mentioning that the words *salvation* and *save* have acquired a certain definition within the six-line Greco-Roman narrative, and that this definition must be reconsidered when resituated in the three-dimensional biblical narrative. Try

reading *liberation* for *salvation*. Similarly, for the key term *righteousness of God*, try substituting *restorative justice of God*. Thanks to Brian Walsh and Sylvia Keesmaat for the latter rendering of the Greek term *dikiasoune theou*. See Sylvia's chapter in *The Justice Project* (Baker, 2009), and watch for their upcoming book *Romans Disarmed*, a sequel to their brilliant *Colossians Remixed* (IVP, 2004.)

Chapter 15

1. Much is made of Paul's reference to homosexuality in this passage, but Paul doesn't refer to people who are born with an inborn orientation to the same sex. The whole idea of sexual orientation would probably have been inconceivable to Paul as a man of his times. He explicitly refers to people who are born with inborn attraction to the opposite sex and then choose to engage in homosexual behaviour, probably as part of orgies or as expressions of domination, both of which were common in Roman culture. I should add that the wrath of God of which Paul speaks here (1:18) does not dangle sinners over the flames of hell as so many preachers have done. Hell is never mentioned in Romans. In fact, in this passage, the consequence of sin is to be 'given over to it'. In this way, God's wrath is revealed by letting people reap the consequences of their foolish or evil behaviours.

2. Repeatedly in Romans, just when Paul feels he succeeds in making a point, he then seems to anticipate how he will be misread by people who want to caricature what he has said and render it more extreme than he intends. So we see a repeating pattern like this: statement (via illustration), possible objection, qualification and clarification (sometimes via illustration); statement (via illustration), possible objection, qualification and clarification (sometimes via illustration).

Notes

3. Thousands of pages have been written trying to derive from the details of this passage coherent doctrines of sin and sanctification and perhaps anthropology too, oblivious to the larger rhetorical structure and aim we have been tracing. Again, too often we treat a personal letter – dictated to a scribe, full of semi-successful metaphors and needed qualifications, fertile imaginatively though frustrating at times logically – as if it were a technical dissertation written by a mechanical engineer, a material finding written by an accountant, a work of scholarship written by a senior theologian at a top Bible college, or (recalling our second question in this quest) a legal opinion written by a constitutional lawyer.

4. If 'Christ' means 'God's anointed liberating king', then to be 'in Christ' means to be 'in the liberating king', which, it seems to me, is another way of saying 'in the kingdom of God'. If readers keep that in mind whenever they read Paul, I believe they will see more deeply how Paul's gospel is the same as Jesus' gospel. (If readers aren't careful, they will work with the disastrous assumption – to me, at least – that 'in Christ' means 'in the religion called Christianity'.)

5. Paul's phrase 'have mercy on them all' recalls Jesus' teaching in his 'kingdom manifesto' (the Sermon on the Mount, Matt. 5:43ff.) that God causes his sun to rise on the evil and the good, and sends rain on the just and the unjust. Luke's version resonates even more strongly with Paul's word 'mercy': '[God] is kind to the ungrateful and wicked. Be merciful, just as your Father is merciful' (Luke 6:35–6).

6. We should remember that Paul wrote his letters before Matthew, Mark, Luke and John were written down. In Paul's day, the stories and sayings of Jesus would have been preserved through oral tradition, which would later be chronicled by the four Evangelists. In this way, Paul's moral teaching, which at every

turn parallels or paraphrases Jesus' teaching, is not simply a practical add-on at the end of his 'doctrinal' letters: it is a fulfilment of Jesus' mission for apostles, namely, to teach others to practise the way of life Jesus taught the original disciples by word and example (Matt. 28:18–20). We could say that Paul's doctrinal reflections set the stage for his primary work of spiritual formation or disciple-making.

7. In two of my earlier books, I have proposed that Jesus would almost certainly not use the term 'kingdom of God' if he were here today. Today the term is an anachronism; in his day it named the dominant social, political, cultural and economic reality. I propose a variety of possible 'translations' into our context, including peace revolution, new love economy, sacred ecosystem, beloved community or society, dream, dance and movement. See *Secret Message of Jesus* and *Everything Must Change* (Thomas Nelson, 2006 and 2007, chapter 16 in both books).

Book 2 introduction

1. Just yesterday I received a phone call from a man who described himself as an ex-Christian and non-theist. But after reading my book *Secret Message of Jesus* and getting a glimpse of the gospel we considered in the previous chapters, he said, 'I don't know how to explain this, but even though I'm not sure about God, now I know I love Jesus – even more than I did when I was a Christian!'

2. Thanks to Rod Washington, in a personal communication, for that term *be-ology*.

Chapter 16

1. Respectively: Alan Jamieson (SPCK, 2002); David Kinnaman and Gabe Lyons (Baker, 2007); Dan Kimball (Zondervan, 2007); Julia Duin (Baker, 2008).

2. Two beautifully written examples in this regard would be Diana Butler Bass, *Strength for the Journey* (Jossey-Bass, 2004), and Sara Miles, *Take This Bread* (Ballantine, 2008).

3. According to a study by the Pew Forum on Religion and Public Life, most who leave churches do so by drifting away. See http://www.washingtonpost.com/wp-dyn/content/article/2009/04/27/AR2009042701460.html?hpid—topnews. Many of their reasons for doing so, I believe, are related to the issues we have addressed so far. First, the Greco-Roman six-line narrative is standard orthodoxy in many churches, and many people want God without Greco-Romanism. Second, most churches read the Bible as a constitution rather than as a story and conversation, leading the church to take legally binding stands that more and more people find morally indefensible. Third, many churches unwittingly preach, sing and celebrate a tribal, nationalistic and violent Theos rather than the just, holy and compassionate God and Father of our Lord Jesus Christ. Fourth, people often can't figure out which Jesus (of the many we considered earlier) their churches stand for, and too seldom do they feel that the church is actually helping its members become Christ-like in the best sense of the word. Fifth, most churches are preaching a gospel that lacks the reconciling dynamic of Jesus' good news of the kingdom of God. In this light, it's a wonder more of us haven't drifted away already, until we recall Peter's reply to Jesus (John 6:68): *where else would we go?*

4. I don't believe the old saw that hierarchical organisations are like ocean liners and you can't turn them around quickly; I think hierarchical organisations are frequently the only ones that can be turned quickly. If you doubt that, imagine turning around a convoy of 10,000 motorboats, all of whom are using their radios for broadcasting, not listening!

5. About the relative difficulty of starting new churches in comparison to renewing existing ones, people often quip, 'It's easier to give birth than raise the dead'. I have never heard a mother say this; for those experienced in either church-planting or childbirth, the words 'birth' and 'easy' don't generally appear in the same sentence. Even if it were relatively easy to plant new churches that simply compete within conventional paradigms for market share, it is far more challenging to start new churches that seek to participate in this quest for a new kind of Christian faith and life.

6. The Fresh Expressions movement among the Church of England, British Methodists and others is an encouraging example of this kind of 'R&D department', as are the various emergent networks in US denominations. (For links, see www.freshexpressions.org.uk/index.asp?id=1, and www.emergentvillage.com.)

7. In *The Future of Faith*, Harvey Cox paraphrases Charles S. Maier: '[E]mpires . . . use similar methods to control their subjects. That method is a combination of military might, either used or threatened, and cultural hegemony, through education, religion, language, and . . . popular culture . . . [E]mpires all tend to spread their pyramidal-hierarchical pattern into all institutions within their orbit. People not only live within empires; the empires live within them . . . [E]mpires by nature tend to transform grassroots institutions into their own top-down image . . . They replicate their hierarchical structures and their divisions at all spatial levels, macro and micro . . . All recapitulate the structure of the whole.' Cox then adds, 'This tendency to replicate the structure of empire helps explain why so much of the Christian movement, which began as a persecuted victim of the Roman empire and provided an alternative to it, then became a sycophantic mimic of that

empire and finally its obsequious acolyte' (HarperOne, 2009, pp. 71–2).

8. This discussion brings me back to the first chapters of the first book I wrote over a decade ago. In the second edition of *The Church on the Other Side*, I explained my own pilgrimage in thinking about the essential mission of the Church, which I articulated as 'being and making disciples, in authentic community, for the good of the world'.

9. This unifying vision challenges us to name what are the actual, though often covert, missions around which we are currently gathered. They may include: (1) the defence of a list of dogmatic pronouncements by some group of the revered dead, recently or long deceased; (2) the perpetuation and support of a clergy and/or scholarly class; (3) the maintenance of real estate – from the humble cemetery behind an old country church to the sparkling headquarters of historic denominations; (4) the sustenance of an ethnic or tribal identity or a political or economic ideology; (5) the shared enjoyment of a beloved living leader, or the memory of one dead; (6) the continuation of a liturgical form deemed beautiful by some, living or dead; (7) the continued opposition to an enemy, existent or extinct; (8) the obligation to fulfil a debt to one's parents, grandparents and other ancestors by preserving something they loved. A list like this (expanded as necessary) could be a useful tool of self-examination for congregations and denominational bodies.

10. The New Catholic Catechism (http://www.christusrex.org/ www1/CDHN/ccc.html) captures this grand vision beautifully in Article 294, also quoting Irenaeus: 'The glory of God consists in the realisation of this manifestation and communication of His goodness, for which the world was created. God made us "to be His sons through Jesus Christ, according to the purpose of His will, to the praise of His glorious grace" (Eph. 1:5–6)

for as St Irenaeus states, "the glory of God is man fully alive; moreover man's life is the vision of God: if God's revelation through creation has already obtained life for all the beings that dwell on earth, how much more will the Word's manifestation of the Father obtain life for those who see God." The ultimate purpose of creation is that God "who is the creator of all things may at last be all in all, thus simultaneously assuring His own glory and our beatitude" (1 Cor. 15:28).'

11. I've written about the spiritual life in *Finding Our Way Again* (Thomas Nelson, 2008), and plan to return to this subject in the near future.

12. In speaking of *knowing as I am fully known*, Paul may be alluding to sexual intercourse, which was often referred to as *knowing* in Hebrew literature. Maturity, he may be suggesting, is not simply subject–object knowing, any more than making love is a subject–object affair. If it isn't relational, one-anotherly, mutual, it is neither true love nor true knowledge.

13. N. T. Wright calls this *an epistemology of love*: 'We dare not, as Christians, remain content with an epistemology wished upon us from one philosophical and cultural movement, part of which was conceived in explicit opposition to Christianity . . . we should allow our knowledge of [Jesus], and still more his knowledge of us, to inform us about what true knowing really is . . . I believe that a biblical account of "knowing" should take love as the basic mode of knowing, with the love of God as the highest and fullest sort of knowing that there is, and should work, so to speak, down from there . . . When I love, I affirm the differentness of the beloved; not to do so is of course not love at all but lust. But at the same time when I love, I am not a detached observer, the fly on the wall of objectivist epistemology. I am passionately and compassionately

involved with the life and being of that . . . which I am loving
. . . I believe that we can and must as Christians within a
postmodern world give an account of human knowing that
will apply to music and mathematics, to biology and to history,
to theology and to chemistry. We need to articulate, for the
post-postmodern world, what we might call *an epistemology
of love* (italics mine, from *The Challenge of Jesus*, IVP, 1999,
pp. 197–8).

14. *Dojo* is Japanese for a 'place of the way'.
15. See Mark's wonderful book *Soul Graffiti* (Jossey-Bass, 2008),
    for more on this idea of a Jesus dojo.
16. Some may wonder why I don't identify worship as the one
    primary calling. Worship, as I see it, is a practice profoundly
    inherent to the life of a disciple. In that light, forming Christ-
    like disciples means forming worshippers – people who love
    God and express that love with joy and reverence. Trying to
    facilitate worship as a public spectacle without forming disci-
    ples in the way of love seems to me to be an adventure in frus-
    tration. So you can make worship your mission without
    forming Christ-like agents of love, but you can't do the latter
    without also forming people who worship.
17. By heuristics, I mean creative, practice-based approaches to
    learning that focus on desired outcomes. These approaches
    would include experiential learning, rites of passage, learning
    journeys or pilgrimages, spiritual direction and action–reflection.
18. By space, I mean creative, social, spiritual space – not merely
    architectural space, although, again, architecture isn't a bad
    thing if it serves this purpose.

Chapter 17

1. A version of this introduction appeared as a foreword to
   Andrew Marin's *Love is an Orientation* (IVP, 2008).

2. On this important revolution in Christian anthropology, see Joel Green's work, beginning with *What About the Soul: Neuroscience and Christian Anthropology* (Abingdon, 2004). See also Nancey Murphy's work, including *Bodies and Souls, or Spirited Bodies?* (Cambridge University Press, 2006) and Kevin Corcoran, *Rethinking Human Nature: A Christian Materialist Alternative to the Soul* (Baker, 2006).

3. See, for example, Levirate marriage in Deut. 25:5–10. Polygyny here refers to having multiple wives.

4. See Mark 2:27, and also 1 Cor. 7:8–9, where Paul relativises marriage and subordinates it to higher goals.

5. Jonathan Merritt, arguably the most courageous Southern Baptist in America, wrote, 'According to Public Religion Research, 37% of evangelicals ages 18–34 have a close friend or relative who is gay. Only 16% of evangelicals 35 and older can say the same' (http://blogs.usatoday.com/oped/2009/04/an-evangelicals-plea-love-the-sinner.html#more). That difference goes far in explaining why younger evangelicals are changing their opinion on sexuality. Knowing a gay person is like observing the retrograde motion of the planets.

6. Among social activists, there is a famous saying attributed to Mahatma Gandhi that roughly parallels this process: 'First they ignore us, then they laugh at us, then they fight us, and then we win.'

7. As noted in chapter 11, many are happy to put 'the teachings of Paul on the same authoritative ground as the teachings of Jesus', because they believe that 'the Bible does not suggest that there are two levels of spiritual authority in the Bible – the more authoritative teachings of Jesus and the teachings of Paul and the other New Testament writers. They are all equally authoritative.' (http://www.newsweek.com/id/175223/page/2) Accessed 17 December 2008).

8. See my discussion of the so-called Canaanite woman in
   Everything Must Change (Thomas Nelson, 2007), chapter 19.
9. See, for example, 2 Kgs 20:18; Isa. 39:7; and Esth. 1:10; 2:3–15.
10. Ethiopia and Israel had strong connections going back to the
    liaison between King Solomon and the Ethiopian queen.
11. 'No man who has any defect may come near: no man who is
    blind or lame, disfigured or deformed; no man with a crippled
    foot or hand, or who is a hunchback or a dwarf, or who has
    any eye defect, or who has festering or running sores or
    damaged testicles' (Lev. 21:16ff.).
12. Speaking of the 'Jesus movement', a documentary about the
    Jesus Movement in the US tells a sad story, almost the mirror
    image of this one: David DiSabatino's *Frisbee: The Life and
    Death of a Hippie Preacher* (2008).
13. Margaret Talbot summarised an important 2007 study like this:
    'Last year, Mark Regnerus, a sociologist at the University of
    Texas at Austin, published a startling book called *Forbidden
    Fruit: Sex and Religion in the Lives of American Teenagers*,
    and he is working on a follow-up that includes a section titled
    "Red Sex, Blue Sex." His findings are drawn from a national
    survey that Regnerus and his colleagues conducted of some
    thirty-four hundred thirteen-to-seventeen-year-olds, and from a
    comprehensive government study of adolescent health known as
    Add Health. Regnerus argues that religion is a good indicator
    of attitudes toward sex, but a poor one of sexual behavior, and
    that this gap is especially wide among teen-agers who identify
    themselves as evangelical. The vast majority of white evangelical
    adolescents – seventy-four per cent – say that they believe in
    abstaining from sex before marriage. (Only half of mainline
    Protestants, and a quarter of Jews, say that they believe in
    abstinence.) Moreover, among the major religious groups,
    evangelical virgins are the least likely to anticipate that sex

will be pleasurable, and the most likely to believe that having sex will cause their partners to lose respect for them. (Jews most often cite pleasure as a reason to have sex, and say that an unplanned pregnancy would be an embarrassment.) But, according to Add Health data, evangelical teen-agers are more sexually active than Mormons, mainline Protestants, and Jews. On average, white evangelical Protestants make their "sexual début" – to use the festive term of social-science researchers – shortly after turning sixteen. Among major religious groups, only black Protestants begin having sex earlier' (http://www.newyorker.com/reporting/2008/11/03/081103fa_fact_talbot?currentPage=all).

14. I'm not aware of any global data on this subject, but the positive correlation between Christian (as opposed to Muslim) affiliation and HIV/AIDS rates in Africa suggest that we may be dealing with a global Christian (and human and urban) problem, not just a Western Christian one.

15. African-American Christians in the US, for example, have some of the highest divorce rates and highest levels of opposition to homosexuality (http://www.wanderingheretic.com/2007/08/22/evangelical-divorcepremarital-sex-revisited/).

16. See Wendell Berry, *Sex, Economy, Freedom and Community* (Pantheon, 1994).

17. Thanks to Gareth Higgins, author of *How Movies Helped Save My Soul* (Relevant, 2003), for this important insight.

18. Baptist theologian Miguel A. De La Torre says it well in his ground breaking new book, *A Lily Among the Thorns*: 'Neither the conservative nor the liberal view toward sex in the United States is adequate. Both are rooted in the hyperindividualist U.S. culture . . . We need a new way of approaching Christian sexuality' (San Francisco: Jossey-Bass, 2007, p. xii).

19. Many Catholics would be surprised to learn that St Thomas

Aquinas actually defended the legalisation of prostitution in his day. His line of reasoning is also fascinating: 'Rid society of prostitutes and licentiousness will run riot throughout. Prostitutes in a city are like a sewer in a palace. If you get rid of the sewer, the whole place becomes filthy and foul' (quoted in De La Torre, *A Lily Among the Thorns*, p. 158, from *Summa Theologica* II:2).

Chapter 18

1. Not to be confused with *scatology*, the study of scat, or faeces.
2. In a rather sad irony, left-behind theology has interpreted the phrase 'left behind' (from Matt. 24 and Luke 17) about 180° off course. For Jesus, to be *taken* meant to be taken by invading enemies, to be victims of a violent conquest. The *fortunate* ones were those *left behind*!
3. In the days during which I've been writing and revising this chapter, there have been two murders by people obsessed with apocalyptic theories, so perhaps the word 'harmless' isn't appropriate.
4. Beyond the US, several Latin American countries also have sizeable political constituencies with similar eschatological leanings. And, of course, dispensationalists have their Jewish and Muslim counterparts, including (at the time of writing) Iranian president Mahmoud Ahmadinejad, whose readings of their sacred texts could lead to similar policies of cosmic war.
5. For additional critique of popular conventional eschatologies, see Barbara Rossing, *The Rapture Exposed* (Basic, 2005); Craig Hill, *In God's Time* (Eerdmans, 2002); and Tony Campolo's chapter on the end times in our co-authored book *Adventures in Missing the Point* (Zondervan, 2003, pp. 54ff.).
6. It's odd, though: tell some people about this three-dimensional view, and they recoil in fear. They seem to prefer their linear

world. Why would people prefer a flat, determined world? Primarily, I suspect, because their religious authority figures have taught them to fear life in three dimensions. Why would their authority figures do so? First, because they themselves, schooled in the Greco-Roman mindset, believe that the Bible mandates this flat universe for believers to inhabit. They're being faithful to what they understand to be true. But I think there is a second reason, too, a more social one: when you're an authority figure seeking to keep people 'in line', it helps to keep them in lines. And when you want to belong and be accepted by a group supervised by a linear authority figure, then you want to keep yourself in line as well.

7. Kung said, 'A church which pitches its tents, without constantly looking for new horizons, which does not continually strike camp, is being untrue to its calling . . . We must play down our longing for certainty, accept what is risky, live by improvisation and experiment.' (The quote is widely attributed to Kung, without noting the source. See, for example, http://www.the-next-wave.org/missionalspirituality.) Similarly, Kevin Van Hoozer frequently talks about biblical history as a drama in which we improvise, and N. T. Wright employs similar language. My friend Ron Martoia will explore this theme in an important upcoming book called *The Bible as Improv* (Zondervan, 2010).

8. Several of us have begun using this term quite independently of one another, including Marcus Borg, Thomas Oord and Tim King.

9. We've already seen how the warrior-and-white-horse language of Revelation 21 wasn't actually about Jesus repudiating peace and reverting to violence. It was a way of saying that the *Pax Christi*, where Christ rules by a reconciling word, is more powerful than the *Pax Romana*, where Caesar rules by the dominating sword.

10. The work of N. T. Wright is a good place to begin. See *Surprised by Hope* (HarperOne, 2008). An amazing array of his lectures and articles are available at http://www.ntwrightpage.com/.

11. For a number of reasons, I am putting aside the kinds of questions raised in 'higher' biblical criticism and the Jesus Seminar about both Pauline authorship and the authenticity of the Gospels. So far, I've noticed that when disputed statements and texts are taken out of the Greco-Roman, constitutional, tribal and related paradigms we are questioning in this quest, they lose much, if not all, of their perceived dissonance with the undisputed texts.

12. To be clear: I'm not denying the *parousia* in any way; I'm simply suggesting that what *parousia* meant to the early Christians may have been very different from what Christians today mean by *the second coming of Christ*.

13. See *Jesus and the Victory of God* (Fortress, 1996), pp. 360ff.

14. This understanding – *parousia* as the beginning of a new beginning – corresponds with the original political image of a king arriving after a victory. His arrival marks the beginning of a new reign, a new kingdom.

15. To me, the phrase *new generation of humanity* aptly captures the gist of *son of man*, so important in the Gospels. The phrase evokes Dan. 7, where the son of man appears singularly as an individual (7:13ff.) and socially as a people, 'the holy people [or saints] of the Most High (7:18, 22, 27). In this way, when Jesus speaks of 'the coming of the son of man', he can be referring both singularly to himself having already come (as the 'firstborn' of this new generation – see Paul's use of the term in Rom. 8:29 and Col. 1:15, 18; also Heb. 1:6; 12:23) and socially to the 'holy people/saints' to come (such an important term to Paul, appearing constantly in his letters). Just as the singular new generation of humanity came in Jesus (explaining

his use of the term *has come* or *came* to describe himself, as in Matt. 11:19 or Mark 10:45), the social new generation of humanity was coming soon, and Paul would call it 'new creation' or 'new humanity' (2 Cor. 5:17; Eph. 2:15; 4:20–24; Col. 3:9). For a highly nuanced and closely researched exploration of this term and its implications today, see Andrew Perriman's *The Coming of the Son of Man* (Paternoster, 2006) and *Re:Mission* (Paternoster, 2008). See also the work of Tim King and friends at www.presence.tv.

16. The already/not yet language is often applied to the present, but I'm suggesting that it more accurately applies to the period between Christ's resurrection and the temple's destruction.

17. For more, see *Everything Must Change* (Thomas Nelson, 2007, chapter 18) and *Secret Message of Jesus* (Thomas Nelson, 2006, chapters 19–20).

18. Thanks to Diana Butler Bass, in a personal communication, for this term *anticipatory ethic*. See her *A People's History of Christianity* (HarperOne, 2009) for a masterful overview of Church history from this perspective.

19. Songwriter Bruce Cockburn captured the laughability of human effort achieving the peaceable kingdom in a 1976 song, 'Laughter': 'Let's hear a laugh for the man of the world/Who thinks he can make things work/Tried to build the New Jerusalem/And ended up with New York/Ha Ha Ha . . .'

20. Jesus' mother also provides a model for the participatory way God's good future comes into history. Mary was not impregnated against her will, nor did Jesus suddenly appear adult and motherless, as if 'beamed down' by magic from heaven. Instead, God participated with Mary, and Mary with God, in the bringing of Jesus into the world. Like Mary, even if we deem ourselves small and insignificant, we receive a tender proposal to be participants and protagonists in history rather than mere

observers or victims of it. Like Mary, we accept and participate by saying, 'Let it be to me . . .' We let our lives be taken up into God's unfolding drama as the Holy Spirit 'comes upon' us and the gentle power of God 'overshadows' us (Luke 1).

21. See Michael Gorman's *Cruciformity: Paul's Narrative Spirituality of the Cross* (Eerdmans, 2001).

22. This is the umbrella term that includes dispensationalism.

23. An older conventional view associated in the US with Manifest Destiny and Christian reconstructionism, post-millennialism was used to justify Christians seizing political power and even using violence (against Native peoples, for example) to 'bring God's kingdom' to earth. Post-millennialism experienced a resurgence in the reconstructionist movement of the 1970s and 1980s that so inspired and influenced the American religious right in the late twentieth century.

24. This is an appalling command in one sense: Jonah was a citizen of a small, vulnerable country, being sent to the capital city of the restless empire to the north and east, threatening to conquer and assimilate Jonah's homeland at any moment.

25. The open ending most similar to this one, I think, is the Apocalypse, which concludes with a haunting invitation, an echoing *Come!* that simultaneously invites Christ into our present and beckons us into God's future: *Come!*

26. For all the openness, the main theological point is quite obvious, even though it's bound to be unpopular and hard to swallow to practitioners of tribal religion: God stubbornly refuses to be shrunk to the convenient tribal or nationalistic size that religious people typically prefer. God's scope of compassion is bigger than our religious systems and tribal or nationalistic identities can handle, and God's concern extends to all nations, even our enemies. What would it mean to anticipate ethically that scope of concern in our lives as individuals, churches, nations and

civilisations? Obviously, there are powerful connections between these considerations and our next chapter on religious diversity.

27. That same open non-ending comes to us in the Bible's final book, which is so often misinterpreted within the narrow Greco-Roman timeline. There, the New Jerusalem is pictured as a cube descending to the earth (almost certainly evoking the cubicle Holy of Holies in the temple). But it is not a closed box: it is full of gates and doors on all sides, and those doors remain perpetually open (Rev. 21:25) to welcome in every good thing. The river of life is not fenced off (22:1–3) and closed to the public: it flows and nourishes the tree of life whose branches offer healing to every nation on earth. The last word of the Bible's last book is an echoed invitation – an open invitation. First, God invites us, 'Come! Come! Come! Whoever is thirsty, whoever desires it, take the water of life for free!' And then we echo the invitation: 'Amen. Come, Lord Jesus.' The vision is of a profound openness of God to us, and of us to God.

28. For more on this subject, see Rom. 14:9–13; Heb. 4:12–13.

29. I think this is what Peter is saying in Acts 10:42ff. Jesus is appointed by God to be both the judge of the living and the dead, and the source of forgiveness. Judgment and forgiveness are not mutually exclusive.

30. Paul envisions this scenario in 1 Cor. 3:10ff.

31. Heb. 9:27.

32. Once the selfish and unjust parts of some people and groups have been burned away as worthless, there may be little substance left to be associated with their name and story. This is the warning inherent in the message of judgement. For more on the personal dimensions of eschatology – around the question, 'What happens after I die?' – see the article 'Making Eschatology Personal' on my website, brianmclaren.net.

33. From 1 Cor. 15:24–8, with a nod to Julian of Norwich.

34. From 'A Christmas Sermon on Peace', 24 December 1967. Widely available online, including http://portland.indymedia. org/en/2003/12/276406.shtml.

35. *The Crucified God* (London: SCM, 1974), p. 178. See also his 'The Final Judgment: Sunrise of Christ's Liberating Justice', *Anglican Theological Review* (89/4), pp. 569–70. There he says, '[W]e live in an unjust, hostile, and divided world. We live and suffer in an ongoing struggle for power. We must therefore take sides with the poor, the weak, and the victims of violence, if we want to work for a universal redemption and anticipate the coming liberating and healing justice of God. God's justice is first of all for the victims of sin, and then thereby also for the slaves of sin, to overcome sin on both sides. The liberation of the oppressed is the first option and includes as the second option also the healing of the oppressors. For overcoming the power of sin and evil we need liberation on both sides. It is God's own action in history to take sides of the victims and to redeem the perpetrators from their violence through this partisanship.' Thanks to Jonathan D. Stanley for his insights into Moltmann in his unpublished paper, 'The Trouble with Judgment: Re-imagining the Final Judgment for Our Time'.

Chapter 19

1. In 1932, at the dawning of a decade of terror in Germany, Karl Barth wrote in *Church Dogmatics* (Vol. 1, Book 1, pp. 76–7), 'How disastrously the Church must misunderstand itself if it can imagine that theology is the business of a few theoreticians who are specially appointed for the task . . . Again, how disastrously the Church must misunderstand itself if it can imagine that theological reflection is a matter for quiet situations and periods that suit and invite contemplation, a kind of peace-time luxury . . . As though the venture of proclamation did not mean that the

Church permanently finds itself in an emergency! As though theology could be done properly without reference to this constant emergency! Let there be no mistake. Because of these distorted ideas about theology, and dogmatics in particular, there arises and persists in the life of the Church a lasting and growing deficit for which we cannot expect those particularly active in this function to supply the needed balance. The whole Church must seriously want a serious theology if it is to have a serious theology.'

2. If you ask Jews about Christianity's track record with 'the other', they know. (See James Caroll's *Constantine's Sword*, Mariner, 2001, if you would like a primer in Christian anti-Semitism.) If you ask Native peoples, they know. (See the work of Richard Twiss if you would like a gentle introduction, and read Randy Woodley's work, including his contribution to *The Justice Project*, Baker, 2009, if you're ready for a more bracing introduction.) If you ask the descendants of slaves, they know. If you ask Muslims, Hindus, Buddhists and New Agers, they know. If you ask atheists, they know. If you ask feminists and gay people, they know too. (See the work of Mel White, Peggy Campolo, Wendy Gritter and Andrew Marin – in print and online – to gain an education in this regard.) For an American history that tells the truth on these matters, see the excellent work of Richard Hughes, *Myths America Lives By* and *Christian America and the Kingdom of God* (University of Illinois, 2004, 2009).

3. I've spent a lot of my life equally clueless and in denial. But I received help in coming out of my denial from some of my loyal critics. When some of us began raising the questions in this book, we expected and welcomed critical evaluation: new ideas deserve nothing less. But a vocal cadre of our fellow Christians treated us to even more than we expected: damnation, mockery, insult and the accusation of bearing false witness. So we've had a front-row seat to watch how easily we Christians, in the name

of truth, write falsehoods; in the name of love, attempt to harm; and in the name of Jesus, accuse like the devil. But I'm not complaining: all of this has been a great gift to me and my friends, because it has given us a clue as to how it feels to be identified as an enemy, threat or outsider to the Greco-Roman version of Christianity. (Fortunately, there have been many who, I imagine, disagreed with us no less, but who sought to display a more Christ-like attitude in their critique.)

4. John 12:32 is especially helpful in showing that *judgement* doesn't simply mean punishment, hell or condemnation for John, as so many readers assume. Here, it means that evil will be driven out and all people will be drawn to Jesus. It means that God will restore justice.

5. In Rom. 3, Paul will make it clear that, in an ultimate sense, nobody does only good all the time, and all are ultimately forgiven by grace, not by works. But that in no way nullifies what he says here.

6. See, for example, Exod. 23:3; Lev. 19:15; Acts 10:34; Rom. 2:11; Gal. 2:6; Col. 3:25; Jas 2:1.

7. To sharpen the irony, the response implies that to believe Jesus is the only Saviour means we cannot obey him as Lord or follow him as Teacher when it comes to our relationship with our neighbours of other religions.

8. Speaking of 'the mind of Christ', imagine if, whenever the issue of pluralism came up, we habitually referred to Phil. 2:1–11, instead of John 14:6. Imagine what would happen if we Christians humbly treated Muslims and Hindus as better than ourselves (2:3), if we considered the interests of Buddhists, atheists and Jews and not only our own (2:4), and if we did not try to grasp superior spiritual status (2:6), but instead acknowledged our common humanity (2:8) and acted as servants to people of other religions (2:7), even to the point of suffering,

Notes

humiliation and death in solidarity with them (2:9). My suspicion is that people would be far more ready 'to bow the knee' to glorify God and honour Jesus as God's anointed leader, teacher and liberator. (Note: the text never suggests that all people will 'bow the knee to Christianity' or 'join the Christian religion' or 'renounce the traditions in which they were born and submit to the Greco-Roman Christian tradition'. Interpreting the text that way surely indicates a Greco-Roman habit of mind.)

9. This is Jesus' diagnosis of the problem of 'the Gentiles' – meaning the Greco-Romans – in Matt. 6:25–34.

10. It's obvious how this mindset needs and loves the conventional doctrine of hell, which I attempted to deconstruct in my book *The Last Word and the Word After That* (San Francisco: Jossey-Bass, 2005). Jürgen Moltmann offers a powerful reconstruction of what I attempted to deconstruct in his article 'The Final Judgment: Sunrise of Christ's Liberating Justice', *Anglican Theological Review* (89/4), pp. 565ff. Evil, Moltmann believes, will not merely be punished: God is greater than that. Evil will ultimately be healed, as God brings restorative justice to victims of evil and sets right the perpetrators of evil. God's justice is redemptive, not merely retributive, and just as there is no redemption without judgement, there is no judgement without redemption: 'It is God's own action in history to take sides of the victims and to redeem the perpetrators from their violence through this partisanship' (p. 576). In this light, Jesus can never be seen as 'an enemy of unbelievers', nor is he 'an executioner of the godless' (p. 574). Moltmann concludes, 'Whoever thinks there are lost people Christ has not found is declaring him ineffective and rather unsuccessful' (p. 570). Thanks to Jonathan D. Stanley and his unpublished paper, 'The Trouble with Judgment', for these insights into Moltmann.

11. This warrior mindset will be explored beautifully and simply

by my friend Cassidy Dale in his upcoming book *The Knight and the Gardener*. I talk about this mindset in some detail in *Everything Must Change* (Thomas Nelson, 2007), and plan to explore it more deeply in an upcoming book.

12. Quoted in Gregory Boyd, *The Myth of a Christian Religion* (Zondervan, 2009).

13. We might also hypothesise that Constantine made Christian leaders a series of offers they couldn't refuse, and they sold out. Or that Christian leaders made a series of seemingly logical compromises that ended up having disastrous unintended consequences. Or all of the above.

14. In this regard, Dorothy Day frequently quoted Catholic theologian Romano Guardini (1885–1968), who said, 'The Church is the Cross on which Christ is always crucified. One cannot separate Christ from his bloody, painful church. One must live in a state of permanent dissatisfaction with the church.' From Robert Coles, *Dorothy Day: A Radical Devotion* (Da Capo, 1989), p. 66.

15. For more on the torture study, see http://www.brianmclaren.net/archives/blog/what-do-white-evangelicals-stand.html. For more on the racism study, see http://findarticles.com/p/articles/mi_m1058/is_21_124/ai_n27416 742/pg_3/.

16. Even if the worst happens, God will surely graft some other new branches into the ancient tree of peace, justice, healing, reverence and life that has been growing on earth since long before the term 'Christianity' was ever invented. God doesn't depend on any single religious institution or movement to accomplish his good pleasure. (Here I'm recalling Paul's warning in Rom. 11:18ff., a seldom-discussed passage which I think is strangely relevant to many branches of the Christian religion today.)

17. My favourite book on this subject is by Samir Selmanovic, *It's Really All About God: Reflections of a Muslim Atheist Jewish Christian* (Jossey-Bass, 2009).

18. Not electro-convulsive therapy, but eternal conscious torment.

19. By art, I am referring to Jesus' use of creative short fiction (parables), poetry (the beatitudes), guerilla theatre (cleansing of the temple, triumphal entry) and beautiful performance art (healings, feedings, etc.).

20. In applying Jesus' teaching of neighbour-love only to fellow Christians, we perfectly fit into Jesus' critique in the Sermon on the Mount/Plain (Matt. 5:43ff.; Luke 6:27ff.), where he deconstructs the us–them, insider–outsider, political–religious identity: 'If you love those who love you, what credit is that to you? Even sinners love those who love them!'

21. These questions, remember, make perfect sense within the six-line, Greco-Roman soul-sort narrative, but are hard to imagine outside it.

22. Jesus mysteriously says he is going somewhere others cannot come no fewer than eight times in the Gospel. First, Jesus tells the Pharisees and priests that he will go to the one who sent him, but they cannot come (7:33–6; 8:14–30). The Pharisees and priests are confused by his statement. They speculate that Jesus means he will go to the Jews scattered across the Roman Empire. They don't realise that he is speaking figuratively (16:25). Then Jesus tells his disciples he is going somewhere they cannot come, although Peter (the pronoun 'you' is singular) will come there later (13:33–7). The disciples too are confused and troubled. Next Jesus tells the disciples he is going to his Father's house, a place with many dwelling places, to which he will bring the disciples later (14:2–4). The disciples are still confused (14:5–8). Jesus later makes clear where he is going: to the Father (14:28), to the One who sent him (16:5).

Where Jesus is going, he will not be seen (16:10), but then after a little while he will again be seen (16:16). These statements leave the disciples more confused than ever (16:17–18). Jesus' ensuing explanation (16:28) finally seems to bring everything together: 'I came from the Father and entered the world; now I am leaving the world and going back to the Father.' The disciples reply, in effect, 'Finally you're speaking clearly! Now we believe that you came from God.' Strangely, this response – not that they understand where Jesus is going, but that they believe where he has come from – elicits a powerful affirmation from Jesus: 'You believe at last!' (16:31). These words are especially significant in view of the theme of belief that runs through John's Gospel (see John 1:7, 12, 50; 2:22, 23; 3:12, 15, 16, 18, 36; 4:21, 39, 41, 42, 48, 53, and so on, through to 20:31).

23. This interchange, by the way, perfectly parallels a conversation Jesus had with James and John when their mother asked for seats to Jesus' right and left in his kingdom (Matt. 20:20). There, instead of using the language of 'going where I go', Jesus uses the phrase 'drink the cup I drink'. Like Peter, the Zebedee boys claim great loyalty, and Jesus similarly affirms that someday, indeed, they will suffer for him – but not now.

24. Very few stories are included in all four Gospels, and this is one of the few. But while Matthew, Mark and Luke include it at the end of Jesus' ministry, John places it near the very beginning.

25. Jesus is constantly speaking 'figuratively' and confusing nearly everybody in John's Gospel – along with, we might add, a lot of us since.

26. This reading is strengthened by the fact that both Paul and Peter use the image of the temple of God and the household of God (echoing John's 'in my Father's house') to refer to the Church. For temple, see 1 Cor. 3:16; 6:19; Eph. 2:21; 1 Pet. 2:5. For household, see 1 Tim. 3:15; 1 Pet. 4:17.

27. This, by the way, is the general line of interpretation followed by Lesslie Newbigin in his commentary on John, called *The Light Has Come* (Eerdmans, 1982). It takes seriously the mystical character of the book as few other commentaries seem to do.

28. What Jesus seems to be after – what he wants his disciples to believe and understand – is not so much where he is going, but *where he is from*, meaning the Father. That comes through clearly at the climax of this whole 'I'm going away' theme in John 16:27–31. The ultimate point is that his disciples have confidence in him, believe in him and believe he is from the Father.

29. Most interpreters assume that when Jesus says 'that you also may be where I am', he means 'you will then be where I will then be'. But in the light of 12:26, Jesus may be saying 'you will then be where I am now, at this moment', meaning in full communion and oneness with God. This experience of communion, inter-being, abiding and oneness with God, then, could be the 'place' to which he will bring them (14:3). It is the place of being alive because Jesus is alive (14:19), the place of knowing that 'I am in my Father, and you are in me, and I am in you' (14:20; also 10:38). This place or experience or kingdom would transcend death (11:25–6), since it would be the same experience before and after death.

30. As I read it, this fascinating interchange between Thomas and Jesus mirrors Martha's equally fascinating interaction with Jesus in 11:17ff. Like Thomas and so many others in John's Gospel, she's working on a 'flesh' level, not a 'spirit' level (6:63). She talks about the resurrection that she believes will occur sometime in the future. But Jesus directs her, just as he does with Thomas, away from her line of thinking, so that she will see a reality that is right in front of her face in the present moment. Just as Jesus says to Thomas, 'I am the way and the

truth and the life,' to Martha he says, 'I am the resurrection and the life.' He tries to help her see a 'life' that is in him (1:4) and that he is (11:25), and that all who believe can share, a life that 'never dies' (11:26). The two passages, taken together, have themes that resonate through John (in the image of 'living water', for example – 4:13; 7:38), and they have much to say to our considerations in this book, and the spirit in which they should be pursued.

31. He is falling into the trap that people slip into again and again in John (2:21; 3:4; 4:15, 33; 6:52; 7:39; 8:57; 11:12; 13:8; 21:23) – taking literally what Jesus intends as a figurative statement, forgetting that 'the words I have spoken to you – they are full of the Spirit and life' (6:63).

32. This reading takes seriously the play on the word 'know'. Thomas is saying, 'How can we have intellectual clarity on where you're going or the route or technique to get there?' Jesus replies, 'You don't need intellectual clarity: you need personal knowledge. It's not a matter of "knowing about", but rather, "knowing".' Similarly, when Philip says, 'Lord, show us the Father,' Jesus replies, 'Philip, don't you *know* me?' Remember, this theme of personal knowing as interactive relationship (closely related to friendship) is strong through all of John's Gospel – and in just two chapters, Jesus will say, 'Now this is eternal life: that they know you, the only true God, and Jesus Christ, whom you have sent' (17:3). 'I am the life' in John 14:6, then, has a powerful resonance in John 17:3 with 'eternal life is to know God and to know Jesus Christ, whom he has sent'.

33. By the way, it would also make me want to scream if you misread what I'm saying to mean, 'It doesn't matter what you believe. Anything goes. God doesn't care, as long as you're sincere.' That would be equally ridiculous! By looking at what

Jesus cares about, we see what God cares about, including what displeases God: carelessness towards the poor and vulnerable, putting religious rules over relationships, complacency, a lack of compassion, and so much more. What we believe matters profoundly, as does how we believe it and how we live it out.

34. In this context I recall a footnote, hidden away in *The Divine Conspiracy* (Zondervan, 1998), where Dallas Willard speaks of 'vampire Christians' who want Jesus for his blood and little else.

Chapter 20

1. Jesus himself seemed nervous about hype, frequently telling people who had experienced miracles that they should keep quiet about them. Imagine that!

2. And vice versa.

3. This was a theme of my book *Everything Must Change* (Thomas Nelson, 2007).

4. Here are Luther's famous words: 'Unless I am convinced by Scripture and by plain reason and not by Popes and councils who have so often contradicted themselves, my conscience is captive to the word of God. To go against conscience is neither right nor safe. I cannot and I will not recant. Here I stand. I can do no other. God help me.'

5. Here's how Luther recounted his conversion experience: 'Though I lived as a monk without reproach, I felt that I was a sinner before God with an extremely disturbed conscience . . . I did not love, yes, I hated the righteous God who punishes sinners, and secretly, if not blasphemously, certainly murmuring greatly, I was angry with God . . . Thus I raged with a fierce and troubled conscience . . . At last, by the mercy of God, meditating day and night . . . I began to understand that the righteousness of God is that by which the righteous lives by a gift of God, namely by faith. And this is the meaning: the righteousness of God is revealed by the

gospel, namely, the passive righteousness with which merciful God justifies us by faith, as it is written, "He who through faith is righteous shall live." Here I felt that I was altogether born again and had entered paradise itself through open gates. There a totally other face of the entire Scripture showed itself to me. Thereupon I ran through the Scripture from memory. I also found in other terms an analogy, as, the work of God, that is what God does in us, the power of God, with which he makes us wise, the strength of God, the salvation of God, the glory of God.' See http://homepage.mac.com/shanerosenthal/reformationink/ mlconversion.htm.

6. For scholars who see Church history in this dynamic way, see Diana Butler Bass, *A People's History of Christianity* (HarperOne, 2009); Lamin Sannch, *Whose Religion is Christianity?* and *Translating the Message* (Eerdmans, 2003, and Orbis, 2008); David Bosch, *Transforming Mission* (Orbis, 1991); and Harvey Cox, *The Future of Faith* (HarperOne, 2009). My book *Finding Our Way Again: The Return of the Ancient Practices* (Thomas Nelson, 2008) also explores this theme of continuity with a deep tradition.

7. One of the most stimulating and provocative examples of macro-history, in my opinion, is Ken Wilber's *A Theory of Everything* (Shambhala, 2001). His insights are seeded throughout this chapter. Resonant with Wilber's work, as I understand both, is Huston Smith's, especially as seen in *Beyond the Postmodern Mind* (Quest, 2003). Also see Jared Diamond's work, beginning with *Guns, Germs and Steel* (Norton, 2005), and Karen Armstrong's *A History of God* (Ballantine, 1994). The theme of this chapter clearly echoes her subtitle: *The 4,000-Year Quest of Judaism, Christianity, and Islam.*

8. This schema is a version of another schema called *spiral dynamics*, using different colours for the parallel stages, as follows

(spiral dynamics – this version): beige – red, purple – orange, red – yellow, blue – green, orange – blue, green – indigo, yellow – violet. This ordering of the colours follows the colours of the spectrum, and so I think will be a little easier to remember.

9. By 'emergent conversation', I mean one small node in an expanding global network that spans denominations and generations. For more on the emergent conversation in the US, see www.emergentvillage.com. For three excellent introductions to the emergent conversation, see Tony Jones, *The New Christians* and Doug Pagitt, *A Christianity Worth Believing* (both Jossey-Bass, 2008), and Ryan Bolger and Eddie Gibbs, *Emerging Churches* (Baker, 2005). For windows into the larger network of which the emergent conversation is part, see Phyllis Tickle, *The Great Emergence* (Baker, 2008) and Tom Sine, *The New Conspirators* (IVP, 2008).

10. Albert Einstein is famously quoted for saying that a problem can never be solved at the level of thinking that created it.

11. This difference – between Jesus and the Christian religion in any of its colours or zones – makes all the difference. This distinction explains why as a Christian I do not believe in Christianity the way I believe in Jesus. I am a Christian who does not believe in Christianity as I used to, but who believes in Christ with all my heart, more than ever.

12. Most subcultures, including churches and denominations, have their centre of gravity in one 'colour' or stage, although two or even three stages may live as guests or refugees in their community. Over time, denominations and churches may shift from one colour to another, either moving higher on the spectrum or regressing to a previously transcended stage.

13. Non-dual (or beyond-dual) thinking is a powerful theme of my Franciscan friend Fr Richard Rohr (http://www.cacradical-grace.org/aboutus/founder.html). See especially his upcoming

book, *How to See Like a Mystic* (details to be announced).

14. *Glory to Glory* (St Vladimir's Seminary Press, 1995), pp. 59–60, emphasis mine.

15. Adapted from 1 Cor. 13.

16. We might distinguish between inhabiting a zone and experiencing a zone. I think many of us have extraordinary peak experiences where we enter a higher zone for a few moments or hours. Depending on our tradition, we might call these experiences mystical experiences, being filled with the Holy Spirit, deep contemplation, the beatific vision, and so on. But these experiences are always intense and short-lived, like a wonderful vacation to an exotic country, or like a child's dream of being able to fly. In order to live in that higher zone rather than just visit it occasionally, we need a community to help us learn its practices and ways, which brings us back to the need for traditions, faith communities and generative friendships within them.

17. This might be a good time to find a Bible and read Rev. 21.

Chapter 21

1. Bernard of Clairvaux understood what it means to be a friend to yourself. He spoke of four stages in the spiritual life, beginning with learning to love yourself for your own sake. This is the infant, nursing at his mother's breast, ecstatic in the warmth of being held and filled, but unaware of anyone outside his own skin. Then comes loving God for your own sake. This is the child who learns to appreciate his mother, maybe to draw her a picture or gather her a bouquet of flowers, overflowing with love mixed with gratitude for all she does for him. Then comes loving God for God's own sake. This is the adolescent or young adult who begins to see his mother for who she is, not just for what she does for him, and his love

grows even deeper. One wonders how any love could go deeper than this, but Bernard sees yet another dimension to the journey of life: loving yourself for God's sake. This is the young man who has made a mess of his life and feels knocked down and beaten up, but then thinks of how much his mother loves him, and her love inspires him not to give up, but to get up and give life another go. What would it mean for you to stand with God, to join God, and learn to see yourself with God's eyes, to love yourself with God's great heart? Others might call you a heretic for raising questions like the ten we're raising here; others might call you a dreamer or a martyr or an idiot. But how does God see you? Does God understand your fears, your struggle, your agony of being caught 'between something wrong and something good'? Does God empathise with you? Appreciate you? Cheer you on? Can you dare to join God and do the same as a friend to yourself?

2. For more on being a friend to yourself, see my article at www.brianmclaren.net.

3. From a lecture Kenzo gave in Kampala, Uganda, May 2007, sponsored by amahoro-africa.org.

4. Consider a wise old grandfather who sits quietly in his rocking chair. Over at the dining room table, the 'grown-ups' – his children – fight and argue. He doesn't jump up and tell them all the way it is. He just rocks, watching, listening, understanding, until you, a grandchild, come up and say, 'What do you think about this, Grandpa?' (Thanks to Claudio Oliver for this image.)

5. To self-differentiate means to learn to speak for yourself, to say gently, 'Others may not agree, and I wouldn't expect them to, but here's how I feel . . . here's how I see things . . . here's what I wish for . . . here's what concerns me'. It means having the courage to differ along with the grace not to expect others to be convinced of your viewpoint. It means differentiating your

identity from that of the congregation (and the identity of its leaders). Some groups not only aren't ready for change; they are unwilling to tolerate difference – and you have to allow them to be who and where they are. If you 'lose' and need to leave that congregation, remember to leave (as my wise friend Phyllis Tickle puts it) 'with a kiss, not a kick'. But (as another wise friend, Joan Chittister, puts it) that doesn't mean you have to leave in silence and secrecy. You have four ways to leave a congregation: angry and vocal, angry and silent, kind and silent, or kind and communicative. I recommend the last option whenever possible, meaning that you explain why you feel the need to leave, but you do so with kindness and a goodbye kiss of blessing and thanks. Your kindness increases the possibility that your departure can increase openness to change in the future in a way that neither leaving angry nor leaving silent ever could.

6. To return to the language of the previous chapter, even if indigo-zone followers of Christ can survive in a yellow-zone church, yellow (or green or blue) church members often cannot tolerate them. So, in the absence of any church in a hospitable zone, they may need to form an indigo-zone faith community for their spiritual survival. That will create problems too, but problems go along with survival.

7. In the US, I highly recommend the work of Alan Roxburgh, Patrick Kiefert, Bill Easum, Tom Bandy, Len Sweet, Reggie McNeal, Joe Myers, Sally Morganthaler, Linnea Nilsen Capshaw, Ron Martoia and Denise Van Eck in this regard, all of whom can be found through an online search.

8. I'm especially enthusiastic about the work of consultants associated with www.deepshift.org and www.velocityculture.com.

9. One such parallel structure would be a *missional abbey*, by which I mean a community of people who are primarily bound

not by duty or responsibility or constituency management (like a governing board), but by spiritual practices and mission. Chief among these practices is the use of 'queries', meaning questions that invite people to self-report about way-of-life issues. Queries distract our attention from fruitless arguments and attract our attention to things that matter. For example: 'When have you overflowed in gratitude to God this week? When have you brought grief, sadness, or contrition to God? When has creation made you mindful of the Creator? When have you felt especially close to and distant from God? When have you been able to befriend through presence and attentiveness a person in poverty or pain this week? A child? A person used to being ignored or stigmatised? What did you learn and gain from this encounter? What were you able to give? When have you been able to advocate for an important cause this week? How did you do, and how could you do better next time?' One of the best writers I've found on this subject is Alan Roxburgh, especially in his *Missional Leader* (Jossey-Bass, 2006).

10. Methodism was later ejected by Anglicanism – or broke away from it, depending on whose version of the story you accept.

11. See www.newmonasticism.org and www.emergentvillage.com.

12. Seasoned leaders learn to 'move with the movers', meaning they focus their energy on the people who are willing to move forward rather than exhausting everyone by bothering those who are resistant. But seldom is there enough critical mass inside a stalled or stagnant organisation to move it forward only with insiders (otherwise, it would already be moving). Almost always, a new day will begin with movers on the inside welcoming in new movers from the outside.

13. A tremendous example of this change by addition is happening at this time, as the Belhar Confession (developed to faithfully oppose apartheid in South Africa) is added to existing core documents in

several Reformed denominations. The act of adding something new opens up new space, giving testimony to the fact that the Reformed tradition is alive and still reforming rather than frozen in a past reformation. It simultaneously removes the old documents from their previous status as absolute. Vatican II provides another example, although its full promise has yet to be realised.

14. The writings of Walter Wink and Robert Greenleaf are especially helpful in this regard, as is the work of www.seeingthingswhole.org.

15. When priestly editors and officials included the writings of the prophets in the biblical canon, including those writings that were highly critical of the priestly establishment, they demonstrated the power of institutions and social movements working in creative tension.

16. The song of the Apocalypse is not, 'The kingdom of this world is replaced with the kingdom of God', but rather, 'The kingdom of the world *has become* the kingdom of our Lord and of his Messiah, and he will reign for ever and ever' (Rev. 11:15, emphasis mine).

17. Haidt beautifully explains these lines of moral reasoning in a mere nineteen minutes here: http://www.ted.com/index.php/talks/jonathan_haidt_on_the_moral_mind.html.

18. It also helps explain why liberals often consider conservatives to be regressive: for liberals, justice and compassion are higher values, while purity, in-group loyalty and tradition are seen as regressive.

19. Matt. 15:10–12.

20. The ten questions in this book could be used to facilitate such a listening team. Listeners could ask these questions of dropouts and non-churchgoers, and churchgoers, seeking to understand the tensions between the two groups.

Conclusion

1. An old friend of mine used to say, 'You can't steer a bicycle unless it's moving'. Perhaps, similarly, the Spirit can't guide us unless we're on a quest; or, better said, perhaps we're unguidable unless we're searching for something more, something beyond, something better than we have.

For additional resources to supplement this book, please go to **www.brianmclaren.net**.